Asian Development:
Problems
and Prognosis

John Badgley

The Free Press · New York
Collier-Macmillan Limited · London

The Free Press
A Division of The Macmillan Company
866 Third Avenue, New York, New York 10022

Collier-Macmillan Canada Ltd., Toronto, Ontario

Library of Congress Catalog Card Number: 78–142354

printing number
1 2 3 4 5 6 7 8 9 10

Contents

Deals with the delusion of attempting to command change through American actions. Views Vietnam as the catalyst for common awareness of our impotence. Emphasizes the value of less ambitious objectives with longer time perspectives. Places change within the time frame of the scientific revolution which has only recently become a political force in Southeast Asia. Questions the meaning and applicability of national development.

part one The Future Asian Milieu

Formulates a taxonomy of more and less viable Asian states upon the basis of comparative graphic indicators of rates of change in all Asian states. Their viability is analyzed first by correlating trends in population, productivity, energy, transportation, and education, then through a comparison of nine factors intrinsic to their individual capability.

Rates the states in terms of measurable achievements and subjective evaluation of such factors as morale, cultural homogeneity, and leadership qualities. Essentially an input-output analysis.

Considers the institutional barriers to development. Focuses upon the paucity of authority in the civil sphere: the political, legal, and administrative institutions created by colonial powers. Compares the results of the several colonial policies toward the development of civil institutions. Discusses the discontinuities within new societies attempting to meet the demands of old communities or minorities and new ideological oppositions.

part two Development and Security Policy

Describes types of conflict within Asian states, then discusses the security implications consequent to these problems in Southeast Asia, particularly for the United States in its relations with other great powers in the area.

Discusses the misapprehensions that often follow from applying to conflict, intrinsic to Southeast Asia, terms used in the conduct of the cold war and great power relations. Attention is given especially to the concepts of regional security and development, balance of power, and popular participation.

Relates the innate barriers to development as well as cultural strengths to the policy goal of regional security. Speculates about how priorities in American policy might be modified so as to accommodate the political changes that are forecast in Chapter One. Envisages a declining intensity but persistently wide range of American activities, including economic investment as well as military and technical assistance, largely to maintain connections with new political groupings that will emerge. Also encourages a greater knowledge among Americans of the cultural forms in Southeast Asia which constitute more than barriers to change, but the very foundation of political identity.

Introduction

Who would be serene about man's prospects in the final third of this century? Even though the tumult of our mightiest wars fades, lesser conflicts explode around us, exasperated youth join their weary elders in an appeal for an era of peace, and civilization seems on the brink of destruction. The bomb culture has come of age. Hippies, rock music, drugs, radical theater, mad art, and militant politics mark our anxiety. When have we been so interdependent? Yet those with an inner eye weep at the loneliness seen thereby! Our earth never seemed so fragile as when photographed from the moon, although that very achievement proves the promise in Genesis—that man could be master of the earth.

The paradox wrought by wedding man's freedom to responsibility for his destiny commenced its final epic journey when science and technology were joined in the Occident. Goethe recognized its diabolic fruit.

> Out on the open ocean speeds my dreaming;
> The glassy flood before my feet is gleaming,
> A new day beckons to a newer shore!
> A fiery chariot, borne on buoyant pinions,
> Sweeps near me now! I soon shall ready be
> To pierce the ether's high, unknown dominions,
> To reach new spheres of pure activity!
> This godlike rapture, this supreme existence,
> Do I, but now a worm, deserve to track?
> Yes, resolute to reach some brighter distance,

(Notes for the introduction begin on p. 201.)

On Earth's fair sun I turn my back!
Yes, let me dare those gates to fling asunder,
Which every man would fain go slinking by!
'Tis time, through deeds this word of truth to thunder;
That with the height of gods Man's dignity may vie! [1]

Dostoyevsky reaffirmed this perspective of a self-imposed destiny a half-century later. "The Lord gave you your fair share of intelligence. Think it out yourself; as soon as you have the mental strength to ask the question: 'Am I responsible or not responsible for my acts?' it means for certain that you're responsible." [2]

Today, in consequence of technology's achievement, America boasts the richest citizenry in history, but at what cost? A host of domestic and foreign critics would agree that modern men, and Americans especially, have refused to accept responsibility for freedom to avoid polluting our minds with the half-truths of mass media and our environment with the hideous by-products of technical progress. Western man should have long since learned to live comfortably with the power bequeathed him by science; that he has not confirms the truth in Goethe's Promethean vision.

With the course of time, the fabric of responsibility for mankind's destiny has woven itself around the governments and leaders of non-Western societies as well. In a curious lapse of imagination, those most involved with transferring the technical knowledge of the Occident have labelled it "development." Who gives serious thought to the eschatological question: What is the purpose of development? What was once a paramount answer—the Puritan ethic of dignity in work and pride in ownership—is adrift, its moorings cut by a New Left pleading for "the abolition of money. . . . A society which works toward and actively promotes the concept of 'full unemployment.' A society in which people are free from the drudgery of work. Adoption of the concept 'Let the Machines do it.' " [3]

One of Asia's most distinguished intellectuals, Soedjatmoko, states the problem more eloquently.

. . . When we speak about development we speak about goals, we speak about values, we speak about motivation. And when we speak about development—economic or social development—we cannot escape from speaking about what is even more central than the economic and social processes that are taking place. We are speaking about the modernization of the soul.

We cannot avoid either speaking of the unspoken purposes of society, of the deepest motivation for social action, which are imbedded in our traditional cultures, in the religio-cultural matrix. We cannot avoid speaking of the symbols, the images, the myths, and in a modern sense, the ideology—that is, the accumulative elements that go into the creation of new structures of meaning, which are essential in providing a new sense of direction for social action.

At the same time it is important for us to become more acutely aware of the ways in which these people in . . . Southeast Asia who are involved in this process of development see their present, the wars in which they see their past, their future, and the problems they are facing. I can assure you that in many ways one of the greatest problems they are facing is the apparent lack of relationship between problems presented by the external view of the development process and the way the interior view presents them. Yet it is through a more serious attention given to this interior or internal view that we can develop a perspective on some of the most important determinants for social action, and of social dynamics. . . .

. . . We have to assume the will to development—that is, the will to modernize. That will is a political will. It is a political will because it concerns the problem of power and the uses of power. The power problem is in fact essential to the whole question of social change and economic development. It is central to all underdeveloped countries. One could put it in a slightly different way and say that development is in the first place a political problem. In practically all the new nations the most fundamental immediate question is that of the creation of power, of types of power. Which types of power are conducive to development? Which types are not? As AID works through government, it would seem to me that much greater attention paid to the role of power in this whole process of economic and social development would be in order. Still, practically no work is being done. . . .[4]

This book is a partial response to Soedjatmoko, for it is addressed to Asian as much as to American critics of United States foreign policy. There is an overwhelming need to consider audiences within, as well as without, Asia when discussing problems confronting this half of mankind and to attempt to understand Asian views and priorities.

What follows is an interpretative evaluation of political change in Southeast Asia and its new implications for policy makers in all of Asia as well as the industrial world. Because it is interpretative, it raises questions that generally are obscured in the current writings about development and foreign policy. Recurrent is the query: Is the nation–state a suitable political institution through which to advance Asian civilizations?

Most scholars assume that the best strategy for guided change is to create nation–states in Asia. It is illustrative that both Gunnar Myrdal (*Asian Drama*) and Theodore Geiger (*The Conflicted Relationship*), despite their considerable contributions to our understanding of factors that impede change, by-pass the possibility that nation-building may be itself a barrier to attaining higher goals. Then consider these comments by Lucian Pye, representing the views of the Committee on Comparative Politics within the Social Science Research Council. "Some members . . . have suggested that it may be useful to conceptualize the processes of political development as involving essentially six crises that may be met in different sequences but all of which must be successfully dealt with for a society to become a modern nation–state." [5] The Committee conceives of identity, legitimacy, penetration, participation, integration, and distribution as crises that appear in the development of any country with the "particular pattern of development in any country depend(ing) largely upon the sequence in which these crises arise and the ways in which they are resolved. . . . In most of the new states the crises are all appearing simultaneously, and governments are, for example, striving to use the distribution crisis to resolve the identity problem." [6]

Apart from the usefulness of these terms as partial descriptions of universal social processes, especially in the modern world, they are incomplete conceptualizations of the situation found in most new states, particularly in Southeast Asia. Other processes must be described if the internal view, noted by Soedjatmoko, is to be understood. Often the internal problems are countervailing forces to the centralization viewed as "development" in the Pye interpretation; for example, ethnic and local consciousness, described by Geertz as primordial sentiment, appears to be strengthening, not dissipating; the drive for regional autonomy is stronger than ever in several states; segregation of elite bureaucracies from villagers is more rather than less prevalent; most central governments are increasingly isolated from their constituencies as the forms of governance come under attack from anarchic or revolutionary oppositions.

These trends signify that the process of political change in Asia may be *slower* generally than in the more modern states. One has difficulty grasping the depth of the revolution overtaking the industrial world and the values that will emerge from the current assaults on establishments in Japan, Europe, and the United States; to the contrary, in Southeast Asia one can be certain that most people, at the end of the century, will still be remote from government and lack the amenities of life considered important in the West. Indeed, it is more likely that many will be starving or in prison than that they will have economic and political security. One can predict for Southeast Asia, with some assurance, a number of macroeconomic and social changes—greater urbanization, industrialization, electronic communication, and bureaucratization—but the rate of change in institutions and political processes is going to be predictably slow. The twenty-first century may well belong to Asia, but the remainder of the twentieth will continue to be a severe struggle to thresh out approaches to change that can accommodate advanced technology within human institutions rooted to prescientific cultures in Asia.

Thanks to the enormous work by Myrdal and many other economists, as well as the propaganda efforts by UNCTAD and the UN affiliates, there is a popular awareness of the widening gap in productivity between industrial and nonindustrial societies; however, the widening political gap in rates of political change is largely unappreciated. Karl Deutsch reveals an awareness of the drag effect only in the most recent edition of his important text, *Nation-Building*. Four years separated the first and second editions, yet he made this observation in the foreword of the latter, after noting that the world of developing countries is becoming more rather than less nationalistic:

> Even then, some of the new countries may not stay in one piece. To speak of a single "indivisible" nation, and to speak of "territorial integrity" as of paramount importance in countries where loyalties are fluid and national unity may not in fact exist —this is to let rhetoric obscure reality. If governments increasingly depend on the consent of the governed for most of their powers, just or not, so do nations increasingly depend on that same consent for their cohesion.
>
> Where this consent is lacking, and where there are no con-

ditions for its early development, even a new nation, recently split off from a larger empire, may be likely to split into still further fragments. Finding the size for any state at which it will be cohesive and stable is in part a process of historical trial and error. . . . In recent years, these pressures toward smallness of countries seem to have been somewhat more powerful than the pressures toward greater size.[7]

This cogent observation runs quite contrary to the assumptions found in the text. There Professor Deutsch commences a discussion of "problems in nation-building" that other prestigious authors pursue in their chapters without reference to the implicit assumption that "nations" may be a questionable concept to use for either descriptive or analytic purposes in much of the world.

Even Rupert Emerson, who has offered one of the best analyses of the change from colonial status to independence throughout the Third World, rests his argument upon the concept of nationhood as both a descriptive and analytic term. One can find little to fault Professor Emerson for in his account of the decolonization period; still, he uses "nation" as a rubric to include primary political loyalties and identities. Thus "the plain fact is that the state structure derived from the past only occasionally and accidentally coincided with the *national* make-up of the world. That is, indeed, what all the furor was about. To bring the states into line with man's new-found national aspirations required a major act of political reconstruction." [8] Is that really what all the furor is about? Our contention is that commitment to the concept of nation itself poses a barrier to political change, for it casts up an artificial cultural unit, with political content meaningful to the West and compelling to first-generation leaders of the new states, but increasingly revealed as removed from the reality of daily political life within many states. It fails to account for the plural cultures within most states.

Eventually, after considerable change in the socioeconomic structure of Southeast Asian states, it is likely that there will be a literary, artistic, and historical foundation for national sentiment. But the workings of contemporary politics require the use of less evocative and peculiarly Western terms to describe the polity and upon which to base trends. Since the nation is often misleading, it may be useful for some to create neologisms, such as Fred Riggs's concept of "clect," to describe a metamorphic grouping of leaders within a state. However, this study will eschew such an effort and adhere to ordinary conceptualizations familiar to students of traditional political thought. For the problem is not, we suspect,.the use of value-free terms (which "nation" is not) that accurately portray a new phenomenon; it is more a problem of making proper use of classic political terms to describe processes (which "nationalism" is) that are not so much alien as vaguely comprehended. With the passage of time since independence, indigenous political forces have etched themselves more clearly on the surface of governments; thus political analysis, forecasting, and comparison are somewhat less difficult than they have been up to now.

In addition to analysis of what is happening, of immediate concern to policy makers is the question of great power and, particularly, American interests in Southeast Asia. What is the significance of these clearer trends for that policy? The suitability for these cultures of the nationhood concept obviously relates to American interests, for the oft-stated goal of United States' Asian policy is the stabilization of relations among independent nations so that they might gain more security. However, if many do not have the substance that permits them to retain their sovereignty, or if their strength is enhanced by cultivating nonnational pluralist systems, then such an objective is not sound, at best, and at worst could be disastrous for both Southeast Asians and Americans. For Asian statesmen to support a pluralism that is not nationalistic is almost unthinkable; yet, if the long-term interests of some 2 billion Asians today, and some 4 billion twenty-five years hence, are to be served, surely the question of where sovereignty should rest deserves to be reconsidered. In Southeast Asia we find a superb illustration of the problem.

Forces are afoot that prevent the clear exercise of national sovereignty, not so much the apparent bogies—America, Japan, China, or Russia—but advanced technology and world-wide economic and communications systems that cause ineluctable erosion of both local power and traditional culture. The merit to either side of the argument about neoimperialism is lost if the sovereign state is a white elephant. Considering that suzerain, hegemonic, and tributary best describe the previously independent political systems in Southeast Asia, and that interdependent characterizes most modern states today, is there not something arcane in the term sovereign nations when used to describe Asian peoples, or "nation-building" as the goal of policy and the process of change in which they are engaged? Furthermore, when Indonesia seeks the sanction of the International Monetary Fund in designing its monetary policies, and when it must have the approval of the Indonesia Consortium in planning its import policies, or when Southeast Asian states must depend for their international security upon sophisticated nuclear weapons supplied ultimately by either the Soviet Union or the United States—then it would seem that other processes than that of creating nation–states are under way.

Without military aid, the states of Southeast Asia are impotent; yet the goal of secure independence is, and has been, the most commonplace utterance by their statesmen as well as by those in Washington. This paradox of impotent self-rule is evident in the Vietnam case. The unprecedented amount of outside assistance poured into both North and South Vietnam demonstrated the dependence of both governments upon other powers, and the tenuousness of their capability. Both Hanoi and Saigon served as lightning rods for the cold war, as did Seoul and Phongyang a decade earlier. When active warfare declines, as in Korea, both regimes, if they survive, will probably retain client–state relationships, which suggests something less than sovereignty.

The problem of security is not, fundamentally, in the client relationship of so many governments, but it is intrinsic in their lack of political authority within the states they attempt to govern. How can a body of men be expected to exercise power when the polity they speak for has little or no institutional link with most villagers? The states that most Southeast Asian governments represent are as alien to villagers as are other Western institutions introduced by colonial rulers and indigenous intellectuals. To expect the villager to participate or even understand the concept of statehood is like asking the citizen of Spokane to understand the Chinese tributary system and then submit himself as a loyal subject to some cosmologically sanctioned regime in Washington, D.C.

The nature of the problem being raised is in part conceptual, and that aspect is explored more fully in Chapter Five. Another aspect is perhaps best understood by those trained to be sensitive to culture —the anthropologists and the intellectual historians. The cultures of the Orient are distinct from those of the Occident, their characteristics differing in several fundamental respects that relate to politics. Perceptions of the meaning of governance, of the purpose of rulers, and of the relationship between man and his government vary in a basic fashion which cannot be dismissed merely as the difference between traditional and modern life styles. These perceptions cause attitudinal and institutional differences that weaken the state; indeed it is incomplete as a functioning polity. Yet these same perceptions may contribute to the strengthening of multistate groups. This issue is elaborated upon in Chapter Three.

Popular expression of political views reflects values inculcated by the cultures that are the bedrock of Asian intellectual and artistic life, be they Confucian, Buddhist, Muslim, or Hindu in heritage. The civilizations that prospered adjunct to these religious and philosophic institutions were not swept from the memories of Asians by the colonial occupations or advanced technology. A mature illustration of the survival of classic behavior patterns and institutions is Japan, where a mixture of modernity and tradition flourishes. This characteristic of Japan could be a prelude for other Asian civilizations that survive and absorb modern ways over the coming century. The differences between classic and modern ways have emerged more distinctly in other countries as the years have passed, and one can forecast with a measure of certitude the conflict situations arising from these differences. That forecast is the subject of Chapter Four.

The strengths of major Asian civilizations cannot be dismissed as merely negative influences upon change. Already several new states exhibit characteristics of rapid economic and social change. Homogeneous societies with contiguous cultures enjoy more rapid change. The evidence for this conclusion is offered in Chapter One in discussing factors contributing to, and inhibiting, the survival of Asian states.

Although this book is primarily concerned with impediments to the attainment of those political goals of leaders in Asia as well as those sought by the United States, it is essential to consider the goals themselves. With few exceptions, there is an implicit assumption in the statements of most American leaders that we have a great contribution to make in Southeast Asia. The prospect that policy goals might include a greater humility, or at least a greater willingness to learn from experience, is raised in Chapter Six.

The importance of the traditional cultures to future change is discussed as part of a comment upon the need for a complex design of bilateral and multilateral—governmental and private—relations that will promote a pluralist Orient and Occident. No doubt there will be greater competition, no matter what policy the United States pursues, among other powers in Asia, notably Japan, China, India, and the Soviet Union, and probably there will be a persistent range of both public and private American activities. Despite the flux generated by such competition, a declining intensity of American military involvement is anticipated, and the justification for that decline is discussed in the context of a national interest in a pluralist world.

Stimulation for preparation of this book comes from many quarters. William C. Johnstone is chiefly responsible for formulating the problem originally, while Herbert Dinerstein, Frank Lester, C. B. Marshall, and Robert E. Osgood of the Washington Foreign Policy Research Center spurred me to question its implications for United States policy. Charles Morrison, who gathered the statistics for Chapter One, has been a helpful critic and, with others in my seminar, performed the valuable service of seriously questioning my ideas. I am especially grateful to the Johns Hopkins School of Advanced International Studies and the Washington Foreign Policy Research Center for their generous support. Although I welcome the contributions of these colleagues to my findings and recommendations, any errors of fact and judgment are solely my responsibility.

My wife, as always, has been a friend to the reader through her editorial advice; however, my greatest debt to her arises from her considerable insight into the Japanese and Burmese cultures from which we both have derived a rich sustenance.

part one

The Future
Asian
Milieu

chapter one

Prospects for Survival*

To view critically the prospects of a new corporation, a young actress, or a colt entered in the Derby is conventional, but prognosis of a state's capacity to survive, or prosper, is often considered a vain effort. Who can account for the whim of fortune, or the perverse decision of a political leader? This book, and particularly this chapter, challenges those who despair about the usefulness of present knowledge as a basis of political forecasting and assumes that fortune, though an unaccountable factor, is only one factor. Social-science research has contributed significantly to our capacity to comprehend trends, despite the still low levels of reporting available in Asia. More to the point is that if we avoid judgment about the course of events, we abdicate the essentially human trait that enables us to link action with values. Increasingly, the issue is not whether we humans *can* do things but rather what *should* we do, given our new, if frail, capability to influence our future. Surely the torment of Vietnam is sufficient evidence of the potency of Southeast Asia to disturb our lives because we did not reflect seriously after World War II about the future in that area, and just as surely the enormous power of the United States has demonstrated its capacity to disrupt the lives of Southeast Asians. In the end, this book is a prescription, a suggestion about how to guide the course of change so as to restrict and help reduce what I see as a recurrently high level of violence looming ahead in Southeast Asia.

* Chapters One and Two were written with the collaboration of Charles Morrison and are revisions of a study prepared for the Washington Foreign Policy Research Center, "The Balance of Power in Asia, circa 1980."

(Notes for this chapter begin on p. 201.)

The purpose of this chapter is to present an analysis of salient societal factors within the states of Asia and to forecast the barriers as well as the desirable courses to development that emerge from these trends. Upon the basis of trend lines for the past fifteen years, we forecast the movements over the next two decades. Unfortunately, our fifteen-year base is too narrow to allow for confident prediction. Analysts working on Western states, where the data are much more complete and run back into the nineteenth century, can project growth with much more assurance than can we for Asia where the collection of statistics is a new art and where most states are only two decades old. Despite these severe qualifications imposed by the area being examined, world-wide aggregate analysis (undertaken by Alker, Russett, Ginsberg, Lipset, Halbeson and Myers, Banks and Textor, and Deutsch, to name the more prominent) does enable us to understand regional and country development through careful comparative analysis and discrete isolation of critical factors contributing to the development process. In short, world-wide historical trends suggest parameters for the probable changes to come in Asia.

Differences among these countries are marked and it is that condition which most interests us. The capability of Japan is widely recognized today; yet few realize how great it will be two decades hence, compared to other Asian states. Conversely, our projections underline the grave problems faced by heavily populated states—China, India, Pakistan, and Indonesia—in racing to keep ahead of the population explosion and elite expectations. The failure, particularly of China, India, Indonesia, and Pakistan over the past decade, to develop administrative capability to cope with the disintegrative political demands placed upon the state by provincial or communal oppositions is a serious threat to Asian security.

The dynamics of planning implementation work both negatively and positively: past failures increase the possibility of future regressions, whereas past successes compound the chances of rapid advances in the future. The best examples of the positive phenomenon are the Koreas, Taiwan, and Thailand. All four have made prudent domestic investments in human and material resource development over the past decade, and the key indicators clearly reflect the advances. Conversely, Burma and Indonesia suffered from chronic domestic disturbances and dogmatic ideological commitments that caused both governments to waste time and resources. The Philippines seems to be entering the same course, for a different reason, and the downward cycle of productivity per capita, although not as grave a problem as in Burma and Indonesia, prior to 1966, erodes its future power potential. We can compare, for example, Burma and Thailand. Three decades ago both countries were about equal in population and productivity. By 1985, Thailand will probably have four times the GNP (gross national product) of Burma and a third larger population. Consequently, Thailand's ability to defend itself, or contribute to an alliance, or influence the direction of regional politics, should be greater than Burma's. An even more dramatic example of this dynamic process is exhibited in comparing China's and Japan's development patterns. In the mid-1950s, China's industrial capacity was comparable to that of Japan. By the mid-1980s, Japan will have more than twice China's capacity and a far greater export capability.

We have two fundamentally different types of trends in the states under consideration. The first occurs within the underdeveloped states where the model of an input–output system helps to clarify the capacity of these states. Those states with decisively advancing economics probably will have increasing influence on politics in the region, whereas those with trend lines that illustrate failure to cope with domestic needs are likely to generally decrease in influence.

The second type of trend occurs among the industrially developed states where the issue of reconsidered priorities suggests greater debate about public policy, or at least greater dissent from any one policy advocated by the government. The quality of life is being reexamined, as in the crisis over pollution. This is an era of flux in the values of modern man, perhaps the most severe since the modern period began with the introduction of science. One cannot measure the influence of this trend, but its impact must be taken into account in any study of power relations. The impact of reconsidered values upon policies of advanced states may well be the reduction of financial support for the more traditional instruments of statecraft—foreign aid and military alliances for example—while at the same time increasing private and public support for urban development, the arts, educational television, and other forms of communication and transport that directly enhance the influence of those countries skilled in their production. Urban renewal, pollution and population control, and education crises raise costs that will challenge military budgets. The sources of insecurity become internal rather than foreign. Awarding the M.B.E. (Member of the Order of the British Empire) to the Beatles in the same year the British commenced a final military withdrawal from the Far East was prophetic, and illustrates the possible trend among advanced states.

The ratio of GNP to population, and the trend of that ratio over time, is the critical statistic. Related to that factor is the much closer clustering of indicators among developed countries compared to the developing countries. Thus Japan, Australia, and New Zealand reveal a balanced trend that suggests considerable economic stability. Among those countries with a large but latent natural resource base, particularly Indonesia, note the wide range of possible change. By 1985 their economies could be moving upward at a rapid rate, or these countries could become economically nonviable and disintegrate.

Two of the giant countries, China and India, have little chance for sharp improvements. Note how the probable range of GNP rests only a few notches above the probable population range. The key indicators (food, manufacturing, exports) reveal a greater chance for India, rather than China, to meet the demands upon the state and the economy, but compared to most of the other Asian states the prospects are bleak in either case for major improvements. China's development prospects are especially dim, suggesting continual dissatisfaction with any central government and the possibility of the more productive provinces developing autonomous political systems to protect themselves against the drain of the poorer regions.

The graphs and tables presented in this chapter can be separated into two categories: a country series and a comparative (cross-country) series. The former allows us, in individual countries, to follow trends of certain indicators of development. The latter serves to indicate the comparative differentials in the important indicators of national power—e.g., population, gross national product, educational output, and defense and education expenditures. The country series indicates the vitality of particular countries; the comparative series seeks to illustrate the relative power of contiguous states.

The Comparative Series

The purpose of the comparative series is primarily to measure the strength of various Asian countries vis-à-vis one another. Our most fundamental indicators of national power are population and gross national product, a measure of the total economic performance of a country. Graphs and tables on defense and educational expenditures and educational enrollment also provide important measures of national power.

Population. The chart on population (Figure 1-1) indicates midyear populations provided by the United Nations (except for Pakistan and mainland China). Projections are based on probable assumptions listed with the country graphs. The most significant feature of population trends is the high growth rates in tropical countries and lower growth rates in temperate countries such as China, Korea, Japan, Australia, and New Zealand.

Gross National Product. The chart on gross national product (Figure 1-2) is based upon AID (Agency for International Development) figures converted at official exchange rates, except for estimates for mainland China and Indonesia. Comparative data for gross national product is limited by certain qualifications: exchange rates understate actual purchasing power by different amounts in different countries. Statistical information may be inaccurate, and in underdeveloped countries numerous transactions are of an informal nature and are not included in gross national product accounts.

Defense and Educational Data. Two graphs (Figures 1-3 and 1-4) have been provided showing defense expenditures as a percentage of total central government expenditure. These quantitative measures provide evidence for policy priorities within each country. Again, comparative data is distorted by disparate methods of accounting, hidden expenditures, and the differing scope of the central governments in the public expenditures. In Pakistan, for example, defense expenditures are a much higher proportion of the total central government expenditures than in New Zealand because more functions are covered by central expenditures in the latter than in the former where state governments are important.

The graphs show the changing emphasis of Asian countries on defense. For many, including Japan, Thailand, New Zealand, and the Philippines, defense expenditure as a percentage of total government outlay has steadily declined. For others involved in the Vietnam war, principally Australia and South Korea, there was an upturn after long periods of decline, and then a new decline. India and Malaysia increased expenditures rapidly after threats in 1962 and 1963. South Korea and Taiwan maintain high expenditures because of the threat

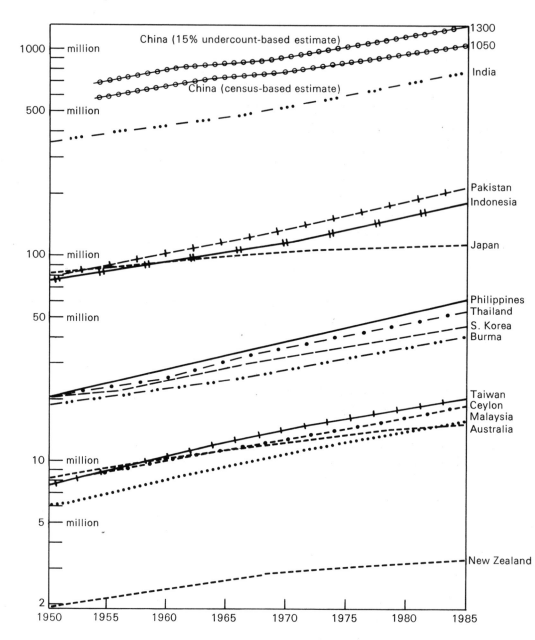

Figure 1-1. Comparative Asian populations, 1950-1985.

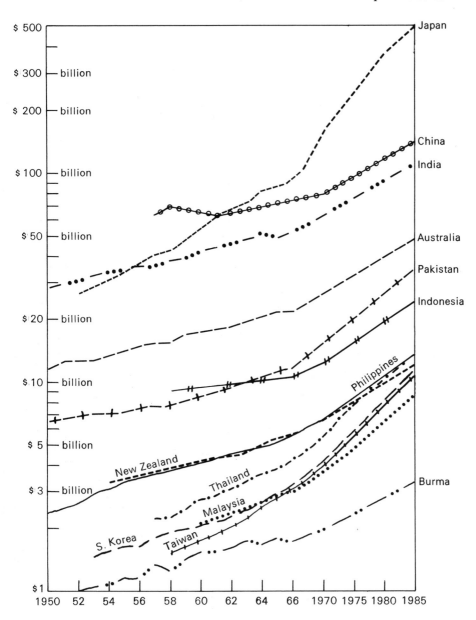

Figure 1-2. Major East Asian and Pacific countries: gross national products ($'s billions). The data for China and Indonesia are very tentative. The projections are based on "probable rates." The lines are steeper after 1966 because the time scale is reduced. GNP figures in billions of 1965 dollars.

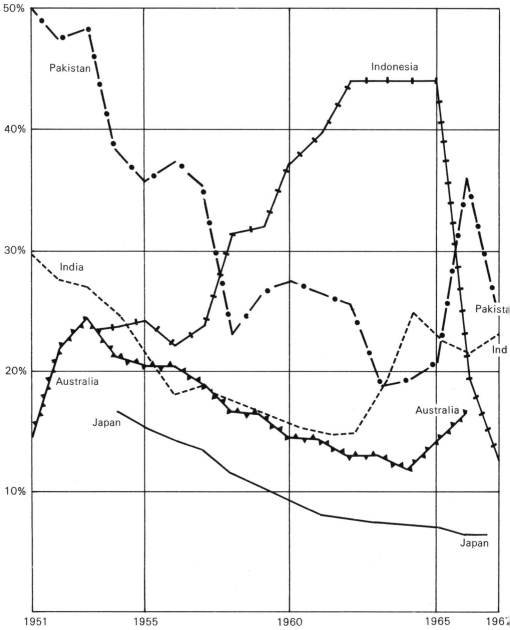

Figure 1-3. Principal East Asian and Pacific powers: defense expenditure as a percentage of total central government expenditure, 1951-1967. *Source:* United Nations, *Statistical Yearbooks* (various issues).

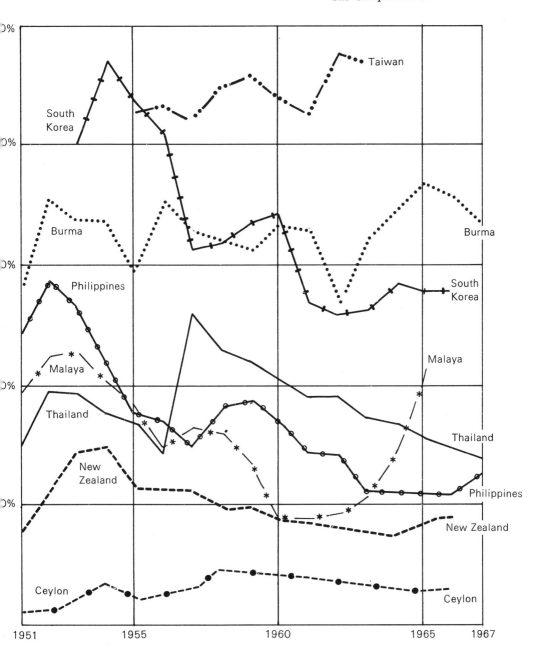

Figure 1-4. Middle-sized East Asian and Pacific countries: defense expenditure as a percentage of total central government expenditure, 1951-1967. For New Zealand and Taiwan, defense expenditure as a percentage of total current central government expenditure. *Sources:* United Nations, *Statistical Yearbooks* (various issues); United Nations, *Yearbook of National Account Statistics,* 1965.

Prospects for Survival

of external invasion; Burma has consistently devoted a third of its budget to defense because of widespread internal insurgency. The high proportion in Malaya in the 1950s was also the result of internal subversion.

Some of the problems of comparison are eliminated if defense expenditures can be expressed as a percentage of gross national product. This is done for both defense expenditures and educational expenditures in a separate table.

The tables on education provide a measure of the educated manpower produced by East Asian and Pacific countries. For three of these—Australia, New Zealand, and Japan—literacy rates and the percentage of primary-aged children attending school approach 100 percent (Table 1-1). All the others will increase their rates. In com-

Table 1-1.—Comparative Enrollments: Primary Education, 1954 and 1964

Country	Total Enrollment (000's)		Enrollment per Thousand Population		Percent of Children Aged 5–14 in Primary School
	1954	1964	1954	1964	1960
Afghanistan	106	358	9	24	5
Australia	1,258	1,630[d]	140	146[d]	78
Burma	1,208	1,887	66	78	29
Cambodia	243	691	60	103	41
Ceylon	N.A.	1,780	N.A.	162	N.A.
China	51,200	90,000[c]	85	130[c]	57
India	20,810[a]	42,300[d]	56[a]	90[d]	32
Indonesia	7,034	9,640[c]	93	94[c]	42
Japan	11,751	10,030	142	104	62
Laos	78[b]	145	49[b]	76	22
Malaysia	813	1,372	120	150	58
New Zealand	355	462	170	178	86
Pakistan	3,970	6,384	45	57	22
Philippines	3,443	5,233[d]	170	167[d]	56
South Korea	2,708	4,730	128	171	60
South Vietnam	490	1,563	49	99	N.A.
Taiwan	1,133	2,189	132	181	67
Thailand	2,938	4,500	133	152	54

Notes: N.A.—not available; [a] 1953; [b] 1956; [c] 1961; [d] 1963. Low level for Japan in 1964 is accounted for by the higher median age.

Sources: United Nations, Statistical Yearbooks, United Nations, Demographic Yearbooks. For last column: United Nations, Statistical Papers: Series K, Number 2, Compendium of Social Statistics, 1963.

paring educational enrollments over a decade, the rate of increase as well as the absolute level of enrollment is shown (Table 1-2). The Philippines, with relatively high proportions of total population attending primary and secondary schools in 1954 and a very high proportion attending college in 1950, has only managed very modest increases in the lower levels while enrollment in college per hundred thousand population has recently declined (Table 1-3).

Enrollments as a percentage of population give some indication of the proportion of educated manpower a country will have, but where the median age of population varies, some anomalies are produced, as in the case of primary enrollment in Japan. Many Asian countries have concentrated on primary enrollments in the past, and now secondary education is expanding rapidly, particularly in those

Table 1-2.—Comparative Enrollments: Secondary Education, 1954 and 1964

Country	Enrollment (000's)		Enrollment per Ten Thousand Population	
	1954	1964	1954	1964
Afghanistan	4	34	3	22
Australia	349	673	395	600
Burma	285	497	142	205
Cambodia	4	82	9	134
Ceylon	N.A.	818	N.A.	745
China	3,587	N.A.	50	N.A.
India	6,410[a]	14,600[c]	169[a]	310[c]
Indonesia	257	754	31	74
Japan	7,653	9,210	870	950
Laos	2[b]	4	13[b]	20
Malaysia	73	305	108	334
New Zealand	80	154	380	595
Pakistan	1,123	2,401	127	215
Philippines	556	823[c]	243	274[c]
South Korea	518	904	226	327
Taiwan	125	483	145	400
Thailand *	252	312	114	105
South Vietnam	45	329	45	209

Notes: N.A.—not available; [a] 1953; [b] 1956; [c] 1963.

Sources: United Nations, *Statistical Yearbooks,* United Nations, *Demographic Yearbooks.*

* The figures for Thailand are probably wrong since enrollment swelled to about 600,000 in 1960, then fell back to 300,000. There was a new definition of "secondary" students.

Table 1-3.—Comparative Enrollments: Higher Education, 1950 and 1964

Country	Enrollment		Enrollment per Hundred Thousand Population	
	1950	1964	1950	1964
Afghanistan	376	3,461	3	23
Australia	36,069	116,550	441	1,044
Burma	3,333	20,515	18	85
Cambodia	87	4,763	2	78
Ceylon	4,276	12,485	57	114
China	138,731	810,000[a]	25	116[a]
India	404,019	1,310,000[c]	112	279
Indonesia	6,183	65,635[a]	8	68[a]
Japan	390,817	985,077	470	1,018
Laos	0	129	0	7
Malaysia	243	8,856	5	87
New Zealand	15,159	47,425	742	1,822
Pakistan	69,898	229,063	93	208
Philippines	290,590[b]	359,465[c]	1,397[b]	1,189[c]
South Korea	36,385	142,629	177	516
South Vietnam	N.A.	23,437	N.A.	149
Taiwan	6,665	64,010	88	531
Thailand	27,676	57,276[c]	138	198[c]

Notes: N.A.—not available; [a] 1961; [b] 1951; [c] 1963.

Sources: for 1950: United Nations, Statistical Papers, Series K, Number 2, *Compendium of Social Statistics,* 1963. For 1964: computed from information in the United Nations *Statistical Yearbooks* and *Demographic Yearbooks.*

countries with a high rate of overall economic growth. In Taiwan, for example, secondary enrollment has increased from 145 per ten thousand population in 1954 to 400 per ten thousand population in 1967, and university enrollment from 88 per hundred thousand to 531.

The data on education and defense expenditures is less meaningful among the less-advanced states than among those at or near modernity (Table 1-4). This is due to the reporting techniques, which frequently obscure or distort the actual content and impact of education. For example, gross expenditures of South Korea and the Philippines on education are roughly equal; yet South Korea has gained much more from its system. Overemphasis on degrees as status indicators and on the wrong type of education in the Philippines is creating a large group of miseducated urbanites who are both ill-trained and nonproductive. Yet the data on education used by the

Table 1-4.—Public Expenditure on Defense and Education as a Percentage of Gross National Product

Country	Period	Expenditures on Defense as Percentage of GNP	Expenditures on Education as Percentage of GNP (all levels)
Afghanistan	1962–64	1.6	N.A.
	1965	1.6	1.2
Australia	1950–59	3.3	1.7
	1960–64	2.7	2.1
	1965	2.9	2.3
Burma	1950–59	5.6	N.A.
	1960–64	5.8	1.7[a]
	1964	5.8	1.8
Ceylon	1950–59	0.6	2.8[b]
	1964	0.9	N.A.
Mainland China	1964	5.4 (minimum)	4.0
India	1950–59	1.9[c]	0.9[d]
	1960–64	2.9	1.4[d]
	1964	3.7	1.4[d]
Japan	1950–59	1.8[e]	1.6[f,g]
	1960–64	1.0	1.6[g]
	1965	1.0	2.0[g]
Malaysia	1955–59	3.0	2.3
	1960–64	2.2	3.2
	1964	3.4	3.8
Mongolia	1964	5.0 (rough)	5.0 (rough)
New Zealand	1950–59	2.4	2.1[g]
	1960–64	1.9	2.5[g]
	1964	2.0	2.4[g]
Pakistan	1950–59	3.0	N.A.
	1960–64	2.9	1.0
	1964	3.0	1.2
Philippines	1950–59	1.8	2.4[h]
	1960–64	1.5	2.8
	1965	1.6	2.9
Thailand	1952–59	2.6	N.A.
	1960–64	2.4	2.6
	1965	2.5	2.6
South Vietnam	1960–64	8.7	N.A.
	1964	10.4	N.A.

Notes: [a] 1962–64; [b] 1950–57; [c] 1955–59; [d] state governments only; [e] 1952–59; [f] 1953–59; [g] central government only; [h] 1954–59.

Source: International Bank for Reconstruction and Development, Economic Department, *World Tables,* Looseleaf, mimeo. Figures at variance with Table 4-2 due to different sources. Probably *Strategic Studies* data are more accurate.

United Nations and UNESCO make the Philippines appear more advanced than it is. Manila, for example, probably has the largest ratio of college students per capita of any city in the world.

Defense expenditures are even more misleading because of the way in which the funds are used. In both Taiwan and South Korea, the very large armies serve to relieve unemployment, to teach skills to rural youth, and to politicize many people previously untouched by the political system. Conversely, Indonesia, with an even larger-sized army, has not been able to fulfill these quasi-military functions effectively.

Because we in the United States are accustomed to regard the socialization and skill training functions as educational tasks, we tend to misread the implications of large defense budgets. They may, or may not, indicate important manpower training programs. Further studies should be made of the social and political significance of military training in these countries so that the data currently available would have more meaning. Generally, the proportion of defense expenditures to total national product has declined since 1950, and the expectation is for a continued slow drop. However, in several countries the military budgets are characterized by great fluctuations, making prediction impossible except to demonstrate how whimsical perspectives of security can be.

The Country Series

Six indicators of development are included on the country graphs: population, gross national product, food production, manufacturing production (where data are available), electrical energy production (both thermal and hydro), and exports. In order to compare such disparate categories as people, dollars, and kilowatt hours, the statistical data have been converted into index numbers with the value for 1958 equal to 100 in every case except Malaysia and South Korea, for which the base year is 1963.[1] The graphs, therefore, show rates of growth rather than absolute values. The steeper the curve, the greater the growth rate.

In order to relate the graphs to each state's political prospects, the indicators may be thought of as representing demands on a country and capabilities of that country to supply those demands. The greater the population, the greater the food, manufacturing, electricity, and foreign exchange requirements will be. When the growth rate in any of these fields is below population growth rate, per capita consumption in that area is declining, and presumably discontent is increasing. Many countries have recurrent difficulties in at least one area—e.g., China, North Korea, the Philippines, India and Pakistan with food distribution and storage, and Ceylon with exports. Other countries—Burma, Indonesia, and mainland China—have experienced per capita declines in more than one sector over fairly substantial periods of time, suggesting greater chances of internal conflict.

Although per capita declines in consumption over long periods are a clear indication of conditions encouraging discontent, this discontent may be deflected from the government for some time. Suitable scapegoats may be found in foreign "imperialists," "capitalists," or "communists"; indigenous "capitalistic" classes or Chinese middlemen and Indian moneylenders; or certain corrupt individuals may be blamed for problems rather than the political system itself. The 1965 coup in Indonesia and Red Guard troubles in China indicate, however, that scapegoats are not likely to be effective over long periods of time.

Obviously, there are many other factors that affect development besides the indicators listed here. Less quantifiable factors such as the strength of national identity, the morale of certain classes or groups in the country, performance and recruitment of civil servants and militia, all affect a country's prosperity. Even if a country shows positive per capita growth rates, it may not necessarily be meeting demands in a satisfactory way. Typically, per capita demands increase with rising incomes, i.e., demands upon a country increase at some rate greater than the population growth [2] From these qualifications, it is clear that these graphs are not enough to arrive at a prognosis for certain countries. They merely represent some of the factors over time. We expect rapid change only where growth rates of these factors are steep and where the less quantifiable forces which sustain political cohesion are also strong.

Projections. We provide projections of the indicators on the country graphs for 1970, 1975, 1980, and 1985. These projections are based primarily on extrapolations from past growth and emphasis in development plans. With each graph we have provided some of these data, some short commentary on special problems, and listed our assumptions for the projections. These are divided into high and low projections, indicating the probable range in the future, and a modal point or "most probable" value. Note that longer ranges imply much greater dependency upon leader decisions for there is great room for choice and mistakes. Short ranges, à la Japan, indicates a strong infrastructure and little chance of serious economic shortcomings. These projections allow great latitude for possible change; however, they do set the limits for change that can be most reasonably expected. Consider now the indicators not already commented upon.

Projected Export Earnings. This indicator tells a great deal about the capacity of each country to purchase essential goods and services. It particularly reveals the state's economic viability, for underdeveloped countries are very dependent upon their exports to secure foreign exchange. None of the Asian states, Japan excluded, earns significant amounts of hard currency from other sources, or is likely to do so in the period considered unless the industrial powers greatly augment their current foreign-aid programs. Note that Burma, China, and Ceylon all have low rates of export increase and that even their maximum increase is much lower than those countries likely to change most quickly—Japan, Australia, South Korea, and Taiwan. If China can develop the industrial sector rapidly, then conceivably the potentially huge size of the domestic market will allow for the efficiencies of mass production and comparative advantage in a wider range of industrial products than will be the case for the smaller countries. This has been the case in Japan. There are discernible signs of a similar development in India which has just begun to export electronic equipment as well as durable manufactures. But the development programs of the smaller countries are in grave trouble if they do not export commodities with a continuing world demand; probably these should be processed commodities which provide more favorable and stable terms of trade than is the case now. Ceylon, Burma, Malaysia, and the Philippines especially suffer from this problem; Indonesia may continue to do so unless the bountiful natural resources are tapped and marketed more rapidly in the 1970s.

Food and Manufacturing Indicators. These trend lines reveal the type of economy in each country. Generally those countries with a substantial or growing industrial sector and changing rural sector are likely in the long run to enjoy somewhat larger rates of increase in food production (e.g., Malaysia and Thailand).

Such states enjoy the advantages of greater modernity, which means a rising efficiency in agricultural production and more financial resources for investment in fertilizers, machinery, and better seeds. Such states normally have improved marketing arrangements with less loss due to poor storage facilities, weak transportation links, or inefficient milling devices. Most basically, a large or growing industrial sector means a better-trained populace with greater capacity to adapt new methods and knowledge about agriculture as well as manufacturing. Australia is the prize example of this phenomenon. Exceptions to this generalization are Japan and North Korea where land is already used intensively, where capital inputs are relatively high, and where topography and fertility are unfavorable. Future growth of food production is likely to be slow despite heavy industrialization and substantial growth in the past.

Electricity Production and Manufacturing. These indicators are most sensitive to the spread of technology and show large gains in most countries. They have been heavily emphasized in planning. Of course most of the states under study started off with a low base in these two areas, which explains why all show increases of ten to sixty times the electrical output of 1958 and four to twenty times the manufacturing output of 1958 in 1985. However, this bold increase does not necessarily mean a general condition of industrial health throughout Asia. Much of the manufacturing is likely to be noncompetitive on the world market and will serve as an import substitute for countries short of foreign exchange. Japan and Australia are major exceptions to this generalization, for both have very bright prospects; yet both start from a high base compared to the mainland Asian and Southeast Asian states. Note that in 1985 Japan will have a GNP of 500 to 550 billion dollars for a population of 125 million, and Australia will have 50 billion dollars for 15 million people—an amazing advancement from their respective power positions in 1950 and as high a per capita income as that enjoyed in the United States today. Both states will be able to achieve this condition because of their enormous capacity to utilize energy for manufacturing, agriculture, and the production of services.

We have not projected other indicators that would reveal more about the achievements and needs of states in the region. Data are available on transport, communications, diet, health and medical conditions, and land usage; however, in our view, these are largely dependent and highly correlated variables which elaborate upon the conditions roughly defined by our key indicators.

Finally, we have not included projections on North or South Vietnam, Cambodia, Laos, or Hongkong and Singapore because of the unusual problems each presents. The war heavily distorts the economies of both Vietnamese states and Laos. Cambodia, like China, has been reticent in revealing statistics to the UN agencies and, unlike China, has not been important enough to have research groups analyzing it to deduce the probable economic and manpower conditions; consequently, we have little information about Cambodia. Hongkong and Singapore are city states with tenuous status. Both are enjoying rapid economic and social development and both have been analyzed by competent authorities using reliable data; yet neither enjoys a power potential that could significantly influence the Asian–Pacific region.

The Sources. For population: United Nations, *Demographic Yearbooks;* for gross national product: AID, *Gross National Product, Growth Rates, and Trend Data by Region and Country* (March, 1967); for food production: ECAFE, *Economic Survey of Asia and the Far East;* for electrical energy production, exportation, and manufacturing production: United Nations, *Statistical Yearbooks* and United Nations, "Monthly Statistical Bulletins" (various issues).

Food production figures are counted for the latter part of the crop year; food poduction for 1952–53, for example, appears on the graph for 1953, although this produces some anomalies in temperate countries.

Development Indicators: **Australia**

1. POPULATION

The current annual rate of population growth is 1.8%. The crude birth rate has declined slightly from 23 per thousand in the early 1950s to about 20 per thousand in 1965. The crude death rate has remained in the 8.5 to 9.0 per thousand range for a decade. Australia's population level will be affected by immigration.

Projection assumptions
Maximum rate: 2.25% annual increase for 1966–85.

Probable rate: 1.75% annual increase from 1966 to 1970, 1.5% annual increase from 1971 to 1985.

Minimum rate: 1.5% average annual increase from 1966 to 1970, 1.25% from 1970 to 1975, 1.0% from 1975 to 1980, 0.75% from 1980 to 1985.

2. GROSS NATIONAL PRODUCT

The average annual growth rate was 4.5% for 1956–66 and 4.2% for 1960–66.

Projection assumptions
Maximum rate: 5.0% annual increase for 1966–80.
Probable rate: 4.25% annual increase for 1966–80.
Minimum rate: 2.5% annual increase for 1966–80.

3. FOOD PRODUCTION

The average annual rate of growth was 4.1% for 1955–65 and 5.5% for 1960–65. Food production will be affected by technological advances and irrigation schemes.

Projection assumptions
Maximum rate: 5.5% annual increase for 1965–85.
Probable rate: 4.25% annual increase for 1965–85.
Minimum rate: 3.0% annual increase for 1965–85.

4. MANUFACTURING PRODUCTION

The average annual rate of growth has been 5.4% for 1957 through 1966. Growth has varied from a 10% increase in 1958–59 to a 1% decrease in production in 1960–61.

Projection assumptions
Maximum rate: 6.0% annual increase for 1966–85.
Probable rate: 5.5% annual increase for 1966–85.
Minimum rate: 3.5% annual increase for 1966–85.

5. ELECTRICAL ENERGY PRODUCTION

The average annual increase in the output of electrical energy has been 9% over the period 1955–65.

Projection assumptions
Maximum rate: 10.0% annual increase for 1965–85.
Probable rate: 9.0% from 1965 to 1975, 8.0% for 1976–85.
Minimum rate: 5.0% annual increase for 1965–85.

6. EXPORTS

The average annual growth rate of the value of exports was 5% for 1956–66 and close to 6% from 1961 to 1966. Principal exports have been

AUSTRALIA

Population and Gross National Product: average values for 1951-54, 1957-60, 1963-66, and projections for 1970, 1975, 1980, and 1985.
1958 = 100.

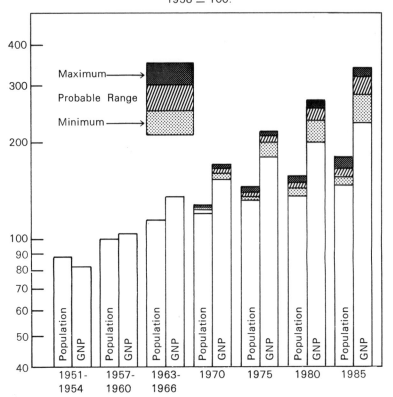

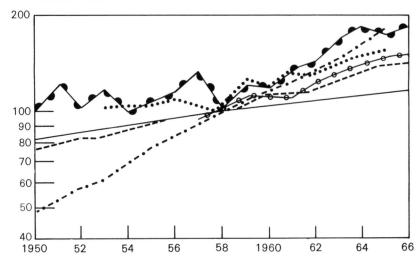

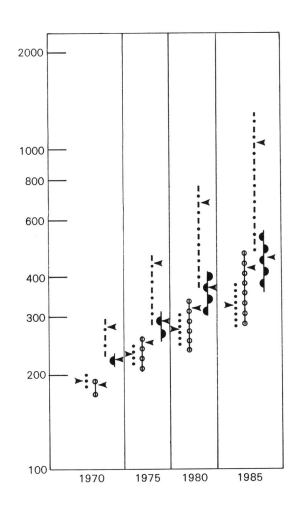

Figure 1-5

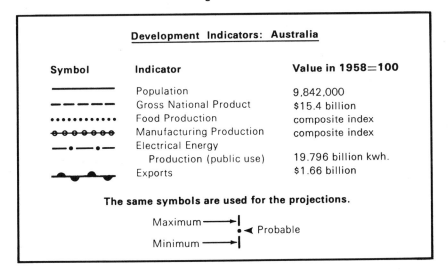

Development Indicators: Australia

Symbol	Indicator	Value in 1958=100
———	Population	9,842,000
– – – –	Gross National Product	$15.4 billion
••••••••••••	Food Production	composite index
⊖⊖⊖⊖⊖⊖⊖	Manufacturing Production	composite index
—•—•—	Electrical Energy Production (public use)	19.796 billion kwh.
●▬●▬●	Exports	$1.66 billion

The same symbols are used for the projections.

Maximum ———▶ |
• ◀ Probable
Minimum ———▶ |

wool, foods, and base metals and manufactures. Great Britain's share of the Australian export trade has fallen in recent years to less than 18%, indicating that the effects of a possible British entry into the Common Market are not likely to be serious.

Projection assumptions
Maximum rate: 6.0% average annual increase for 1965–85.
Probable rate: 5.0% average annual increase for 1965–85.
Minimum rate: 3.5% average annual increase for 1965–85.

Development Indicators: **Burma**

1. POPULATION

The current annual rate of increase is about 2.1%. Burma has a high birth rate of between 40 and 50 per thousand, but the mortality rate is also very high—about 20 per thousand, twice that of mortality rates in Thailand and the Philippines. Since mortality rates will decrease faster than fertility rates, the rate of population increase will rise.

Projection assumptions
Maximum rate: 2.25% annual growth for 1967–70, 2.75% for 1971–75, 3.0% for 1976–80, and 3.25% for 1981–85.
Probable rate: 2.0% annual growth for 1967–70, 2.5% for 1971–80, 3.0% for 1981–85.
Minimum rate: 1.75% annual growth for 1967–85.

2. GROSS NATIONAL PRODUCT

The annual growth rate for 1956–66 was 3.9%, but more recently this has leveled off. The rate for 1960–66 was 2.0%, causing a slight decline in per capita income due to population growth. The growth rate fluctuated from a 3.8% drop in 1958 to a 13% rise in 1959.

Projection assumptions
Maximum rate: 7.0% annual growth for 1967–85 (cf. Thailand, 1959–66).
Probable rate: 3.5% annual growth for 1967–85.
Minimum rate: 1.75% annual growth for 1967–85.

3. FOOD PRODUCTION

The average annual increase was 3.3% for 1955–65, but was less than 3% in the 1960–65 period.

Projection assumptions
Maximum rate: 4.0% annual growth for 1966–75, 6.0% for 1976–85.

Probable rate: 3.0% annual growth for 1966–85.
Minimum rate: 2.0% annual growth for 1966–85.

4. MANUFACTURING PRODUCTION

There is no UN index for manufacturing in Burma. A comparison of the early Pyidawtha Plan (1952–56) with later two 4-year plans shows that public investment in industry was to increase from 9.3% of total developmental public investment in 1952–56, to 9.7% in 1956–60 and 10.6% for 1961–65. Private investment in industry declined sharply after 1957.

5. ELECTRICAL ENERGY PRODUCTION

The average annual increase in production was 10.6% for 1957–64. Expenditure on power development was to be only 7.8% of development funds in 1961–65 as compared to 15.6% for the previous four years.

Projection assumptions
Maximum rate: 10.0% annual growth for 1965–85.
Probable rate: 8.0% annual growth for 1965–85.
Minimum rate: 5.0% annual growth for 1965–85.

6. EXPORTS

The value of exports show no long term trend of increasing or decreasing. From 1952 to 1958 the value of exports declined from $264 million to $193 million. By 1963 it had increased to $270 million, but dropped sharply afterwards, reaching $193 million again in 1966. The price of rice and teak has been gradually rising during the 1960s. In quantity terms, rice exports have declined, but teak exports have increased. Burma has also allowed the quality of its rice exports to decline. Pre-World War II exports were largely 15% brokens or better; in the past decade most rice exports were 15–30% brokens. Export markets appear good if the country can produce larger exportable surpluses. Thailand, for example, has pushed up the quantity of its rice exports by 60% in the 1960s. Like Thailand, Burma can also develop other agricultural exports, e.g., corn, peanuts, or sisal.

Projection assumptions
Maximum rate: Annual growth rate of 5.0% for 1967–75, 8.0% for 1976–85.
Probable rate: 2.0% annual growth for 1967–85.
Minimum rate: A decline of 2.0% annually for 1967–75, a 2.0% annual increase from 1976 to 1985.

BURMA

Population and Gross National Product average values for 1951-54, 1957-60, 1963-66, and projections for 1970, 1975, 1980, and 1985.

1958=100

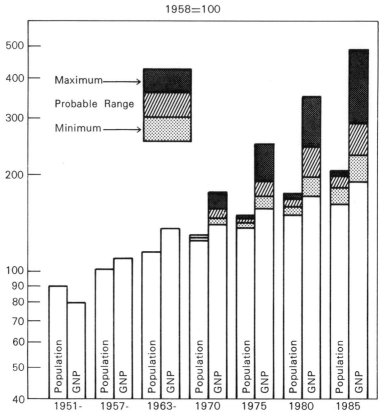

Trends: 1950-66

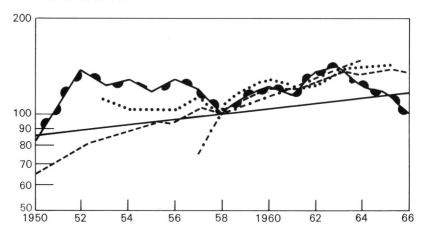

Forecast:

1970-85

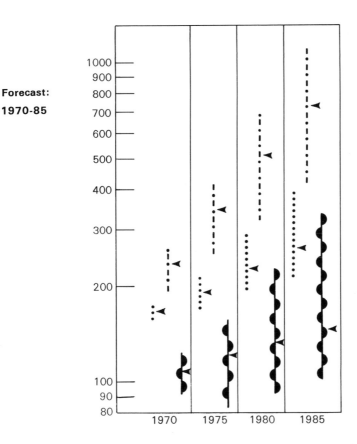

Figure 1-6

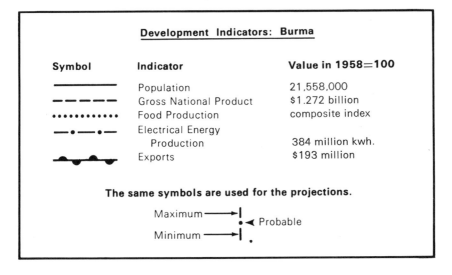

CEYLON

Population and Gross National Product; average values for 1958-59, 1962-63, 1965-66. and projections for 1970, 1975, 1980, and 1985.
1958=100

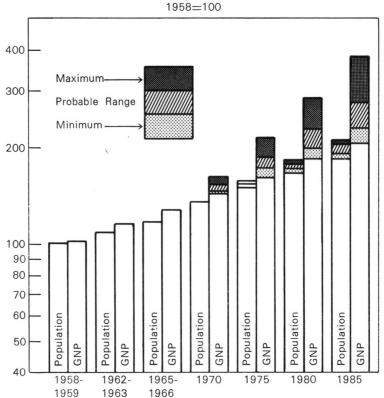

Trends: 1950-66

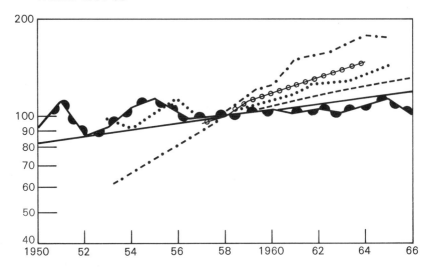

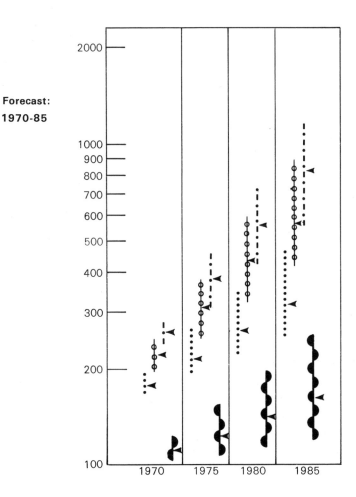

Figure 1-7

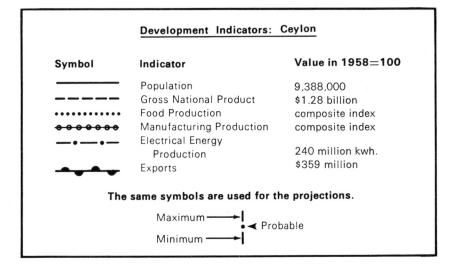

Development Indicators: Ceylon

Symbol	Indicator	Value in 1958=100
	Population	9,388,000
	Gross National Product	$1.28 billion
	Food Production	composite index
	Manufacturing Production	composite index
	Electrical Energy Production	240 million kwh.
	Exports	$359 million

The same symbols are used for the projections.

Maximum

Probable

Minimum

Development Indicators: **Ceylon**

1. POPULATION

The current annual rate of population growth is 2.9%. The crude birth rate has been decreasing slightly during the past 15 years. The crude mortality rate is low and further decreases should be slight. Ceylon appears to have passed the apex of its population explosion.

Projection assumptions

Maximum rate: 3.0% average annual increase for 1967–85.

Probable rate: 2.85% annual growth for 1967–72, 2.5% annual growth for 1973–85.

Minimum rate: 2.75% average annual increase for 1967–70, 2.5% for 1971–75, 2.0% for 1976–85.

2. GROSS NATIONAL PRODUCT

The average annual growth rate for 1960–66 was 3.0%. Growth has been relatively steady during this period, varying from 4% in 1964 to 2% in 1965. The development plan forecasts a 5.5% growth rate for 1965–71.

Projection assumptions

Maximum rate: 5.5% annual growth for 1967–72, 6.0% for 1973–85.

Probable rate: 3.5% annual growth for 1967–85.

Minimum rate: 2.5% annual growth for 1967–85.

3. FOOD PRODUCTION

The annual rate of growth for 1955–65 was 3.7%, but it was higher in the later part of this period and averaged 5.5% from 1960 to 1965. The government has stimulated padi production through subsidies and agricultural development schemes.

Projection assumptions

Maximum rate: 6.0% annual growth for 1966–85.

Probable rate: 4.0% annual growth for 1966–85.

Minimum rate: 3.0% annual growth for 1966–85.

4. MANUFACTURING PRODUCTION

The average annual rate for growth for 1957–64 was 7.4%.

Projection assumptions

Maximum rate: 9.0% annual growth for 1965–85.

Probable rate: 7.0% annual growth for 1965–85.
Minimum rate: 5.0% annual growth for 1965–85.

5. ELECTRICAL ENERGY PRODUCTION

The average annual rate of growth for 1955 to 1965 was 8.9%. Generating capacity increased substantially over this period.

Projection assumptions
Maximum rate: 10.0% annual growth for 1966–85.
Probable rate: 8.0% annual growth for 1966–85.
Minimum rate: 6.0% annual growth for 1966–85.

6. EXPORTS

The value of Ceylon's exports in 1966 was below the 1956 figure as the result of a sharp fall in 1966. During the 1957–65 period the value of exports rose on the average 1½% per annum. Although in quantum terms exports have risen more sharply, Ceylon's commodity terms of trade have declined 12% since 1958. Exports are mainly plantation products: tea, rubber, and coconut products. The market outlook for these products is poor, and Ceylon has not yet made significant efforts to diversify its exports.

Projection assumptions
Maximum rate: 5.0% annual growth for 1967–85.
Probable rate: 2.5% annual growth for 1967–85.
Minimum rate: 1.0% annual growth for 1967–85.

Development Indicators: **Mainland China**

The statistical data for Mainland China came from *An Economic Profile of Mainland China,* Studies prepared for the Joint Economic Committee, Congress of the United States (Government Printing Office, Washington, 1967). Scholars and studies mentioned below refer to contributions to this collection. Statistical data for China are very tentative, and the margins of error are wide.

1. POPULATION

Dr. John Aird of the Bureau of Census has constructed several population models. The average annual rates in these models work out to approximately the following:

MAINLAND CHINA

Population and Net Domestic Product: average values for 1952-54, 1957-60,
1963-65, and projections for 1970, 1975, 1980, and 1985.

1958=100

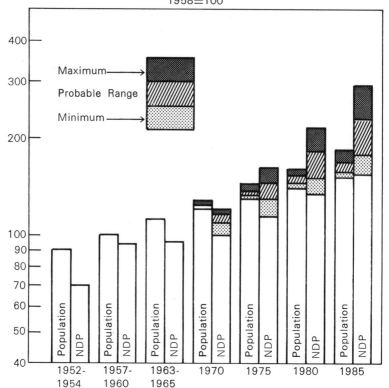

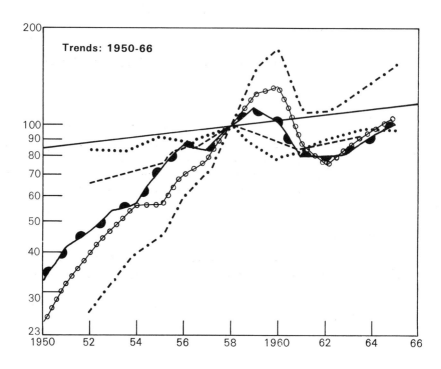

Trends: 1950-66

Forecast: 1970-85

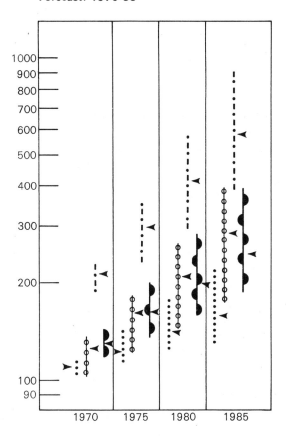

Figure 1-8

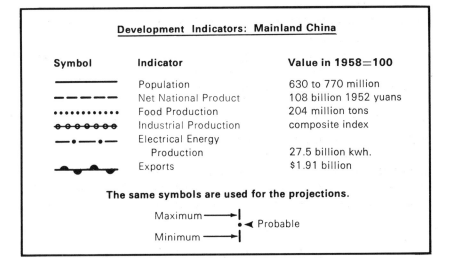

Development Indicators: Mainland China

Symbol	Indicator	Value in 1958=100
————	Population	630 to 770 million
– – – –	Net National Product	108 billion 1952 yuans
••••••••••	Food Production	204 million tons
⊕⊕⊕⊕⊕⊕	Industrial Production	composite index
—•—•—	Electrical Energy Production	27.5 billion kwh.
⬤⌢⬤⌢⬤	Exports	$1.91 billion

The same symbols are used for the projections.

Maximum ———▶ │
  •◀ Probable
Minimum ———▶ │

	Highest	Lowest	
1965–70	1.9%	1.6%	
1970–75	2.2	−2.4	(due to gross mortality)
1975–80	2.1	1.9	
1980–85	2.3	1.7	

Our estimates are more crude and therefore show a broader range.

Projection assumptions

Maximum rate: 2.5% annual growth for 1966–85.

Probable rate: 1.75% annual growth for 1966–70, 2.1% for 1971–75, and 2.0% for 1976–85.

Minimum rate: 1.5% annual growth for 1966–85.

2. NATIONAL INCOME

Ta-chung Liu has estimated the average annual growth of net national product at 6.0–6.2% from 1952–57, 3.2% for 1952–65 (with no net increase between 1958 and 1965), and 4.3% for 1961–65.

Projection assumptions

Maximum rate: 5.0% annual growth for 1966–70, 6.0% for 1971–85.

Probable rate: 3.0% annual growth for 1966–70, 4.0% for 1971–85.

Minimum rate: no growth between 1965 and 1970, 3.0% annual growth for 1971–85.

3. FOOD PRODUCTION

According to the estimates of O. L. Dawson, former U.S. agricultural attache in China (given in the study by Edwin F. Jones) the average annual rate of increase in food production was approximately 1.3% annually from 1952 to 1965, 3.1% annually from 1952 to 1958, and 4.5% annually from 1960 to 1965. China's Third Plan anticipated a 4% annual growth in food production between 1966 and 1970. The Joint Economic Committee estimated that growth would be about 2% for this same period.

Projection assumptions

Maximum rate: 3.0% annual growth for 1966–70, 4.5% for 1971–85.

Probable rate: 2.5% annual growth for 1966–85.

Minimum rate: 1.5% annual growth for 1966–85.

4. INDUSTRIAL PRODUCTION

Michael Field estimates the average annual growth rate at 6.5% for 1955–65. The level of industrial production in 1965 was only slightly above that of 1958 (due to the setback during the "Great Leap Forward"). The Third Plan projected a 5–7% annual increase for 1965–70, and the Joint Economic Committee estimates 5% for the same period. Participation by workers in the Great Proletarian Cultural Revolution may mean that these estimates are on the high side.

Projection assumptions

Maximum rate: 6.0% annual growth for 1966–75, 8.0% for 1976–85.

Probable rate: 4.0% annual growth for 1966–70, 5.0% for 1971–80, and 7.0% for 1981–85.

Minimum rate: no growth to 1970, 3.5% annual growth between 1971 and 1985.

5. ELECTRICAL ENERGY PRODUCTION

John Ashton estimates the average annual gain at 10.3% for 1956–65 and 7.5% for 1962–65. China began from a very low base. Its production now is about a fifth Japan's and slightly larger than India's.

Projection assumptions

Maximum rate: 8.0% annual growth for 1966–70, 10.0% for 1971–85.

Probable rate: 7.0% annual growth for 1966–85.

Minimum rate: 4.5% annual growth for 1966–85.

6. EXPORTS

According to Robert Price's estimates, the value of exports grew at an average annual rate of 7.9% for 1950–65 and 3.5% for 1955–65. Since 1960 China has been shifting its exports from bloc markets to free world markets. Exports to free world markets grew at an average annual rate of almost 12% between 1955 and 1965. Dr. Price links further growth in exportation to the growth of China's agricultural sector, but hazards no guesses on the future.

Projection assumptions

Maximum rate: 7.0% annual growth for 1966–85.

Probable rate: 4.5% annual growth for 1966–85.

Minimum rate: 3.0% annual growth for 1966–85.

Development Indicators: **India**

1. POPULATION

The current rate of annual growth is 2.4%. Both birth and death rates seem to be decreasing, and there is no clear trend to the net. According to the UN *Demographic Yearbook,* death rates are comparable with those

INDIA

Population and Gross National Product: average values for 1951-54, 1957-60, 1963-66, and projections for 1970, 1975, 1980, and 1985.

1958=100

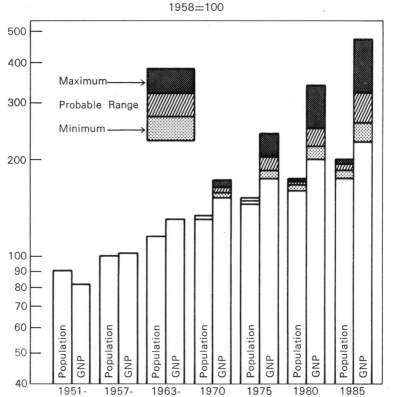

Trends: 1950-66

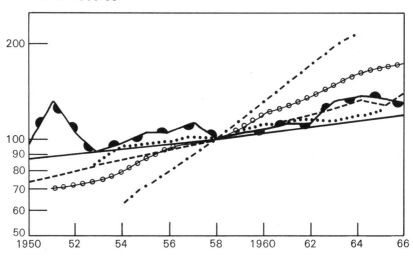

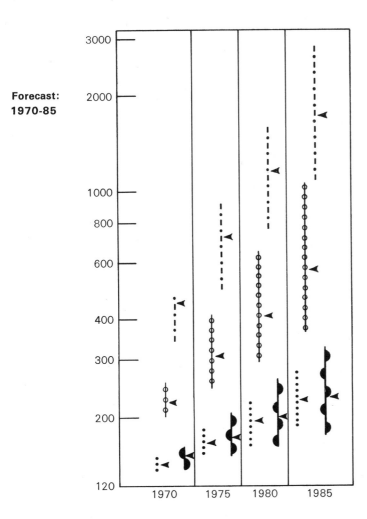

Forecast:
1970-85

Figure 1-9

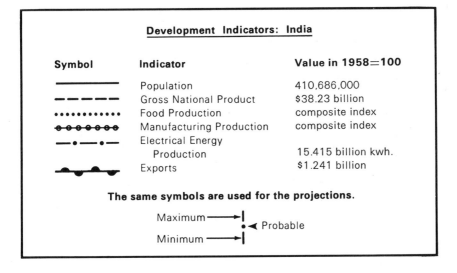

Development Indicators: India

Symbol	Indicator	Value in 1958=100
————————	Population	410,686,000
– – – – – –	Gross National Product	$38.23 billion
••••••••••••	Food Production	composite index
●—●—●—●—●	Manufacturing Production	composite index
—•—•—	Electrical Energy Production	15.415 billion kwh.
●━━●━━●	Exports	$1.241 billion

The same symbols are used for the projections.

Maximum ——→
•◄ Probable
Minimum ——→

Prospects for Survival

in the United States (a result of a lower age median), and therefore will not decline much further. The major question is whether birth rates will increase with rising per capita income.

Projection assumptions
Maximum rate: 2.75% annual growth for 1967–85.
Probable rate: 2.5% annual growth for 1967–85.
Minimum rate: 2.25% annual growth for 1967–75, 2.0% for 1976–85.

2. GROSS NATIONAL PRODUCT

The average annual rate of increase was 3.9% for 1950–55, 4.4% for 1955–60, 3.5% for 1960–66, and 3.8% for 1956–66. The planned rate of growth is 5.5% for 1965–71 and 6.6% for 1960–76.

Projection assumptions
Maximum rate: 6.0% annual growth for 1967–70, 7.0% for 1971–85.
Probable rate: 4.0% for 1967–85.
Minimum rate: 2.75% for 1967–85.

3. FOOD PRODUCTION

The average annual rate of increase for 1954–55 to 1964–65 was 2.5% and for 1959–60 to 1964–65 was 2.0%. The UN index does not extend past 1964–65 (a bumper year), and the last two years, when total food-grain production was considerably lower (due to poor monsoons), are believed abnormal. Agriculture was given "highest priority" in the 1966–67 emergency plan. India hopes for a 3.9% annual growth in agricultural product between 1960 and 1976.

Projection assumptions
Maximum rate: 4.5% annual growth for 1966–85.
Probable rate: 3.5% annual growth for 1966–85.
Minimum rate: 2.0% annual growth for 1966–85.

4. MANUFACTURING PRODUCTION

The average annual increase was 6.8% for 1956–66 and 6.2% for 1961–66. Since 1964 there has been a significant slowdown in the growth rate. The threat of famine and mass civil disorder could disrupt investment over the next decade. The country's planners hope a 10% annual growth rate for 1960–75 can be achieved.

Projection assumptions
Maximum rate: 10.0% annual growth for 1967–85.
Probable rate: 6.5% annual growth for 1967–85.
Minimum rate: 4.0% annual growth for 1967–85.

5. ELECTRICAL POWER PRODUCTION

The average annual growth rate was 13.1% for 1954–64 and 13.2% for 1959–64. During the past decade greatest growth occurred in 1963 with a 15.5% increase and least growth the following year with a 9.3% increase. India plans to increase production 13.3% annually during the 1961–81 period. In readjusting priorities for the 1966–67 emergency plan, some emphasis was taken off power production in favor of agriculture.

Projection assumptions
Maximum rate: 14.0% annual growth for 1965–75, 12.0% for 1976–85.
Probable rate: 13.0% annual growth for 1965–70, 10.0% for 1971–80, and 8.0% for 1981–85.
Minimum rate: 10% annual growth for 1965–85.

6. EXPORTS

The average annual increase in the value of exports was 2.1% for 1956–66, 3.0% for 1961–66, 5.4% for 1958–64, and −2.4% for 1964–66. In 1964 specialized manufactured products began to appear as exports. The market outlook for jute, India's principal export and approximately 20% of the total, is not considered good because of substitutes.

Projection assumptions
Maximum rate 5.0% annual increase for 1967–85.
Probable rate: 3.0% annual increase for 1967–85.
Minimum rate: 1.5% annual increase for 1967–85.

Development Indicators: **Indonesia**

The statistics for Indonesia are the least reliable and most dated of any we have used. Nevertheless, they suggest general trends that cannot be rapidly modified.

1. POPULATION

The current annual rate of population increase is between 2.1 and 2.4%. The birth rate may be decreasing, but the mortality rate is still very high and is likely to decrease. As a result the net will probably increase.

Projection assumptions
Maximum rate: Average annual growth of 2.75% for 1967–72, 3.25% for 1973–80, and 3.0% for 1981–85.
Probable rate: Annual growth for 2.5% for 1967–70 and 3.0% for 1971–85.

INDONESIA

Population and Gross National Product: average values for 1952-54, 1957-60, 1963-66, and projections for 1970, 1975, 1980, and 1985.
1958=100

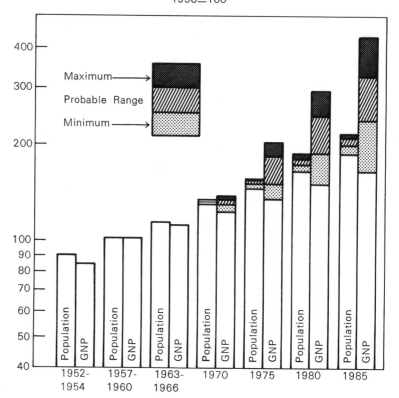

Trends: 1950-66

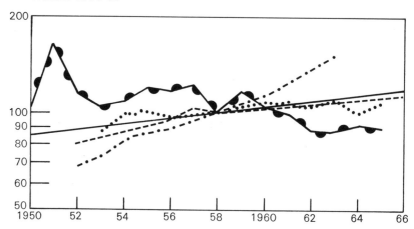

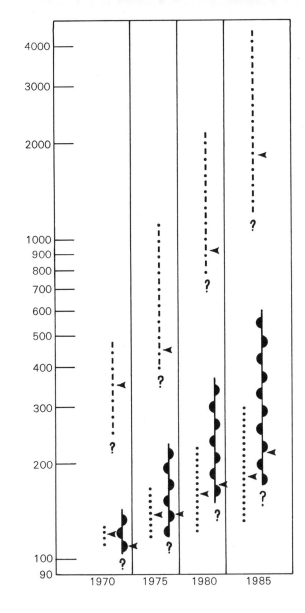

Forecast:
1970-85

Figure 1-10

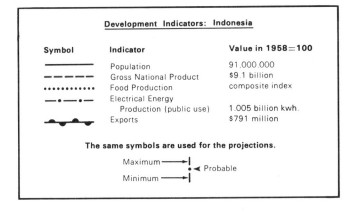

Prospects for Survival

Minimum rate: Annual growth of 2.25% for 1967–70 and 2.5% for 1971–85. There is a grim possibility of a reduction in the rate of increase as the result of civil strife or famine, a trend that characterized China in the 1930s.

2. GROSS NATIONAL PRODUCT

ECAFE estimated a 3.6% average annual growth rate for Indonesia during the 1950s, but most growth was achieved before 1955. On the graph, GNP is projected from 1959 to 1966 at a 2.0% annual rate.

Projection assumptions

Maximum rate: Annual growth of 5.0% for 1967–70, 8.0% for 1971–85 (cf. Thailand, 1959–66).

Probable rate: Annual growth of 4.0% for 1967–70, 4.5% for 1971–75, and 5.0% for 1976–85 (based on gradual stabilization).

Minimum rate: Annual growth of 2.0% for 1967–85. Presumably this could be so low as to not sustain viability.

3. FOOD PRODUCTION

Average annual growth rate for 1955–65 was about 1¼% and for 1960–65, it was about ½%.

Projection assumptions

Maximum rate: Annual growth rate of 3.0% for 1966–70 and 6.0% for 1971–85. There is the slender possibility of high rates in Indonesia because so many improvements could be made in utilizing its rich natural resource base.

Probable rate: Annual growth rate of 2.0% for 1966–70, 2.5% for 1971–75, and 3.0% for 1976–85.

Minimum rate: Annual growth rate of 1.0% due to failure to reform the land use system.

4. MANUFACTURING PRODUCTION

There is no UN index. Existing industrial enterprises are only utilized to a third their capacity because of a lack of spare parts and raw materials. As with food production, the potential for major increase is high if new investment and resource utilization patterns are developed.

5. ELECTRICAL ENERGY PRODUCTION

The average annual rate of increase was 8.0% for 1953–63 and 9.3% for 1959–63. Production in Indonesia is less than that in Malaysia, a country with a tenth its population. The potential for rapid increase is high during the next two decades.

Projection assumptions

Maximum rate: 18.0% average annual growth for 1964–75, 15.0% for 1976–85.

Probable rate: 8.0% annual growth for 1964–70, 12.0% for 1971–75, and 15.0% for 1976–85.

Minimum rate: indeterminate.

6. EXPORTS

The value of exports has decreased an average of 2.9% annually from 1956 to 1965. Petroleum has provided some stability to the otherwise dismal export picture and could spark a rapid rise in the future if Indonesia pursues pragmatic export promotion policies.

Projection assumptions

Maximum rate: 10.0% average annual increase for 1966–85.

Probable rate: 4.5% average annual increase for 1966–85.

Minimum rate: indeterminate.

Development Indicators: **Japan**

1. POPULATION

The current annual rate of population growth is 1.0%. The 1964–68 Middle-Term Plan projected an annual rate of 0.9%. The birth rate decreased from 30.2 per thousand in 1945–49 to 19.4 per thousand in 1958 and 10.9 per thousand in 1961. Since then it has increased to 18.6 per thousand in 1965. The mortality rate is steady and below the level of that of the United States and most Western European countries.

Projection assumptions

Maximum rate: 1.0% annual growth for 1967–70, 1.5% for 1971–85 (rate increase due to new affluence).

Probable rate: 1.0% annual growth for 1967–70, 0.75% for 1971–85.

Minimum rate: 0.8% annual growth for 1967–70, 0.6% for 1970–80, almost constant population from 1980 to 1985.

2. GROSS NATIONAL PRODUCT

The annual growth rate for 1956–66 was 9.9% and for 1960–66 was 9.3%. During the past decade the growth rate varied from 3.7% in 1958 to 13.3% in 1964. The Middle-Term Plan assumed an 8.1% growth rate. The higher rate was, in part, a consequence of U.S. war procurement. A slower rate of increase in the working age population, higher expenditures on social

JAPAN

Population and Gross National Product: average values for 1952-54, 1957-60, 1963-66, and projections for 1970, 1975, 1980, and 1985.
1958=100

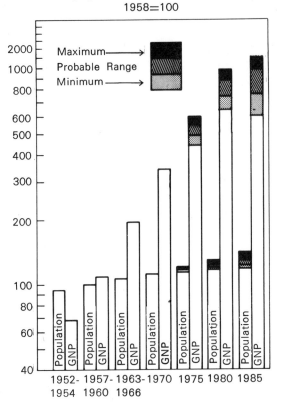

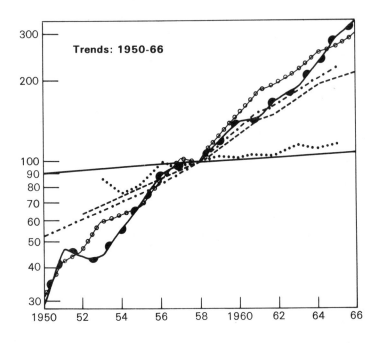

Trends: 1950-66

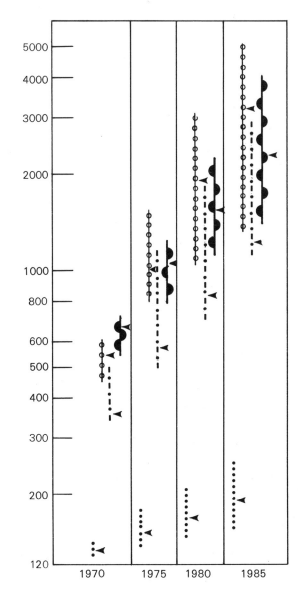

Forecast:
1970-85

Figure 1-11

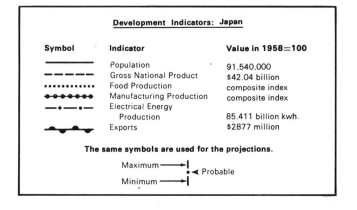

Development Indicators: Japan

Symbol	Indicator	Value in 1958=100
─────	Population	91,540,000
─ ─ ─ ─	Gross National Product	$42.04 billion
··········	Food Production	composite index
◆●◆●◆●	Manufacturing Production	composite index
─●─●─	Electrical Energy Production	85.411 billion kwh.
⬤⬤⬤⬤	Exports	$2877 million

The same symbols are used for the projections.

Maximum ⟶ ▮
⟍ ◄ Probable
Minimum ⟶ ▮

overhead capital, and reduced scope for adapting already discovered techniques to industry (as Japan moves to the forefront in technology) militate against maintaining the 9–10% growth rate after the mid-1970s.

Projection assumptions
Maximum rate: 12.0% annual growth for 1967–75, 10.0% for 1976–85.
Probable rate: 12.0% annual growth for 1967–70, 10.0% for 1971–75, 8.0% for 1976–80, and 7.0% for 1981–85.
Minimum rate: 12.0% annual growth for 1967–70, 6.0% for 1971–80, and 4.0% for 1981–85.

3. FOOD PRODUCTION

The average annual increase was 3.5% for 1955–65, and 2.5% for 1960–65. The land is already used intensively and the youth are rapidly leaving the farm causing a rural labor shortage.

Projection assumptions
Maximum rate: 4.0% annual increase for 1966–85.
Probable rate: 2.5% annual increase for 1966–85.
Minimum rate: 1.5% annual increase for 1966–85.

4. MANUFACTURING PRODUCTION

The average annual increase was 13.6% for 1956–66 and 10.9% for 1961–66. During the past decade the yearly growth rate varied from −2% in 1958 to 26% in 1959.

Projection assumptions
Maximum rate: 20.0% annual growth for 1967–75, 15.0% for 1976–85.
Probable rate: 17.0% annual growth for 1967–70, 13.0% for 1971–80, and 11.0% for 1981–85.
Minimum rate: 12.0% annual growth for 1967–75, 6.0% for 1976–85.

5. ELECTRICAL ENERGY PRODUCTION

The average annual rate of increase for 1955–65 was 11.4%.

Projection assumptions
Maximum rate: 18.0% annual growth for 1966–75, 10.0% for 1976–85.
Probable rate: 10.0% annual growth for 1966–75, 8.0% for 1976–85.
Minimum rate: 8.0% annual growth for 1966–85.

6. EXPORTS

The value of exports increased at an average annual rate of 14.6% from 1956–1966. Since 1963 the growth rate has been 22.5% annually; this is partially attributable to the Vietnam war.

Projection assumptions
Maximum rate: 22.0% annual growth for 1967–70, 12.0% for 1971–85.
Probable rate: 19.0% annual growth for 1967–70, 10.0% for 1971–75,
8.0% for 1976–85.
Minimum rate: 15.0% annual growth for 1967–70, 7.0% for 1971–80,
5.0% for 1981–85.

Development Indicators: **North Korea**

Most of the statistical data for North Korea has been taken from a recent book edited by Joseph S. Chung, *Korea: Patterns of Economic Development* (Korea Research and Publication, Inc., 1966). The data are based on communist sources.

1. POPULATION

The average annual rate of increase for 1958–64 was 3.0%. According to a Soviet source, the birth rate is probably declining.

Projection assumptions
Maximum rate: 3.0% average annual increase for 1967–85.
Probable rate: 3.0% average annual increase for 1967–70, 2.75% for
1971–75, 2.5% for 1976–80, and 2.0% for 1981–85.
Minimum rate: 2.75% average annual growth for 1967–70, 2.5% for
1971–75, 2.0% for 1976–80, and 1.75% for 1981–85.

2. NATIONAL INCOME

Average annual increase claimed for 1954–62 was 20%, but growth was much slower in the latter half of this period. For 1958–62, national income grew 8.6% annually.

Projection assumptions
Maximum rate: 8.5% annual growth for 1963–75, 7.0% for 1976–85.
Probable rate: 6.0% annual growth for 1963–85.
Minimum rate: 4.0% annual growth for 1963–85.

3. FOOD PRODUCTION

Average annual growth for 1954–65 was 7.6%. From 1962–65, however, growth was only about 1% per annum. North Korea's 1961–67 Seven Year Plan projected an average increase in grain production, but heavy fertilization and improved seeds are essential to further improvements. One authority, Yoon T. Kuark, writing in the Chung book, concludes that "it

NORTH KOREA

Population and Gross National Product: average values for 1953-54, 1957-58, 1961-62, and projections for 1970, 1975, 1980, and 1985.

1958=100

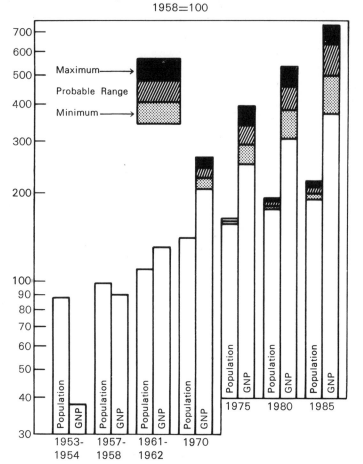

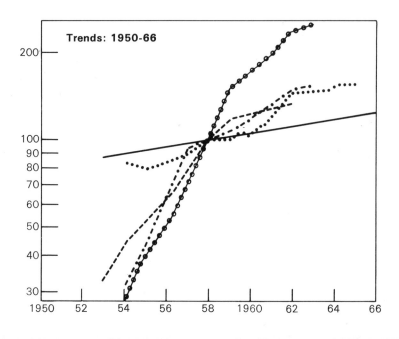

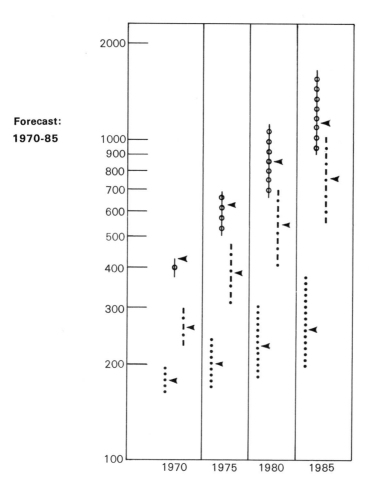

Forecast:
1970-85

Figure 1-12

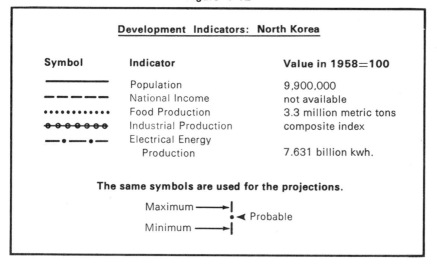

Development Indicators: North Korea

Symbol	Indicator	Value in 1958=100
————————	Population	9,900,000
– – – – – –	National Income	not available
••••••••••••	Food Production	3.3 million metric tons
⊕⊕⊕⊕⊕⊕⊕	Industrial Production	composite index
—•——•—	Electrical Energy Production	7.631 billion kwh.

The same symbols are used for the projections.

Maximum ——→ |
• ◄ Probable
Minimum ——→ |

appears that, despite all the impressive mechanization and continued irrigation works by the collective farmers, North Korea's agriculture may have reached the point of diminishing returns."

Projection assumptions
Maximum rate: 4.5% annual growth for 1966–85.
Probable rate: 2.5% annual growth for 1966–85.
Minimum rate: 1.0% annual growth for 1966–85.

4. MANUFACTURING PRODUCTION

Average annual growth from 1958 to 1962 was claimed to be about 25%. In 1963 and 1964, the growth rate apparently fell to about 8%, but in 1965 the government claimed a 14% increase. As the industrial base becomes broader and as problems arise in supplying managerial expertise and manpower, the accelerated rates of increase of earlier years cannot be sustained.

Projection assumptions
Maximum rate: 8.0% annual growth for 1964–70, 10.0% for 1971–80, and 8.0% for 1981–85.
Probable rate: 8.0% annual growth for 1964–75, 6.0% for 1976–85.
Minimum rate: 6.0% annual growth for 1964–85.

5. ELECTRICAL ENERGY PRODUCTION

The average annual rate of increase for 1955–65 was 15.5%. The high rate is partially explained by rebuilding after the war and the low initial base.

Projection assumptions
Maximum rate: 10.0% annual growth for 1965–75, 8.0% for 1976–85.
Probable rate: 8.0% annual growth for 1965–75, 7.0% for 1976–85.
Minimum rate: 6.0% annual growth for 1965–85.

Development Indicators: **South Korea**

1. POPULATION

The current annual rate of population growth is 2.8% and may be slightly decreasing. The Second Five Year Economic Development Plan (1967–71) predicts that the population growth rate will be "kept below 2%" for the 1967 to 1981 period.

Projection assumptions
Maximum rate: 3.0% average annual increase for 1967–85.

Probable rate: 2.75% annual increase for 1967–70, 2.5% for 1971–75, 2.25% for 1976–80, and 2.0% for 1981–85.

Minimum rate: 2.5% annual increase for 1967–75, 1.75% for 1976–80, and 1.5% for 1981–85.

2. GROSS NATIONAL PRODUCT

The average annual growth rate was 6.8% for 1956–66, and 7.5% for 1960–66. During the past decade growth has varied from 2½% in 1959–60 to 10% in 1965–66. The development plan foresees a yearly 7% rise to 1981.

Projection assumptions
Maximum rate: 8.5% average annual increase for 1967–85.
Probable rate: 7.0% average annual increase for 1967–85.
Minimum rate: 4.0% average annual increase for 1967–85.

3. FOOD PRODUCTION

The average annual growth rate was 3.5% for 1955–65 and 5% for 1960–65. The development plan anticipates an average annual increase in metric tons of grains, bean, and potato production of about 6½% for 1965–71, and for rice and barley (the bulk of South Korean food production) of 4½% for 1965–81. The country hopes to achieve self-sufficiency in food by 1972.

Projection assumptions
Maximum rate: 6.5% average annual increase for 1966–72, 5.0% for 1973–85.
Probable rate: 4.0% average annual growth for 1966–85.
Minimum rate: 2.5% average annual growth for 1966–85.

4. MANUFACTURING PRODUCTION

The average annual growth rate was almost 11% for 1956–66, and 13.4% for 1961–66. In value added terms, mining and manufacturing is expected to grow 10.7% annually from 1967–71. The development plan allocates 29% of investment funds to manufacturing.

Projection assumptions
Maximum rate: 15.0% average annual growth for 1967–75, 10.0% for 1976–85.
Probable rate: 10.0% average annual growth for 1967–85.
Minimum rate: 8.0% average annual growth for 1967–85.

5. ELECTRICAL ENERGY PRODUCTION

The average annual rate of increase for 1955–65 was 14%. Planned growth for the 1965–71 period averages 15.7% annually.

SOUTH KOREA

Population and Gross National Product: average values for 1953-54, 1957-60,
1963-66, and projections for 1970, 1975, 1980, and 1985.
1963=100

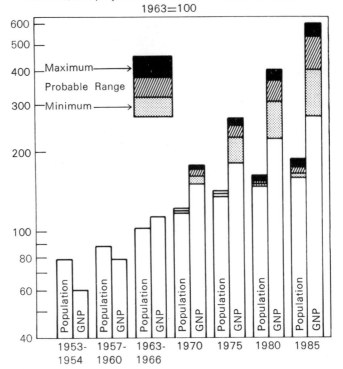

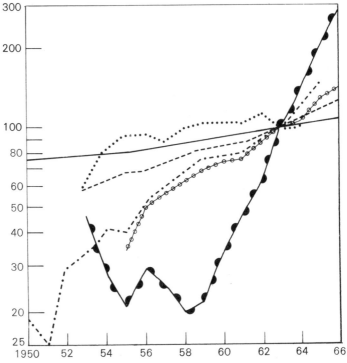

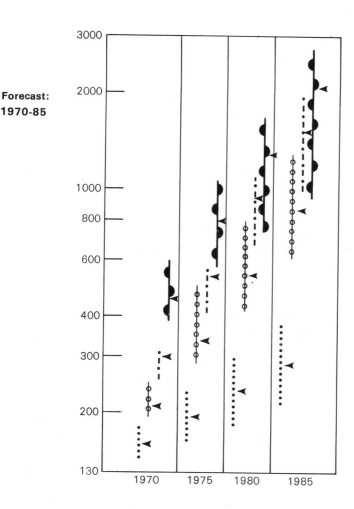

Forecast:
1970-85

Figure 1-13

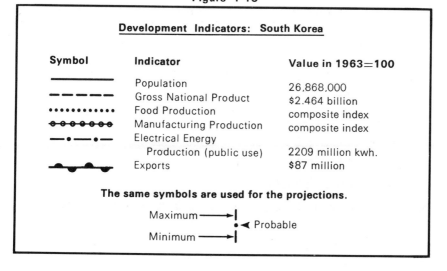

Development Indicators: South Korea

Symbol	Indicator	Value in 1963=100
———	Population	26,868,000
— — —	Gross National Product	$2.464 billion
••••••••••	Food Production	composite index
●-●-●-●-●	Manufacturing Production	composite index
—•—•—	Electrical Energy	
	Production (public use)	2209 million kwh.
●—●—●	Exports	$87 million

The same symbols are used for the projections.

Maximum ——→ ▌
• ◀ Probable
Minimum ——→ ▌

Projection assumptions

Maximum rate: 16.0% annual growth for 1966–71, 13.0% for 1972–85.

Probable rate: 15.0% annual growth for 1966–71, 12.0% for 1972–80, and 10.0% for 1981–85.

Minimum rate: 12.0% annual growth for 1966–70, 10.0% for 1971–80, and 8.0% for 1981–85.

6. EXPORTS

The average annual rate of increase for the decade 1956–66 was almost 26%. The value of exports declined from $40 million in 1953 to $17 million in 1958. From this very low level, exports have shot up almost fifteen times to $250 million in 1966. As higher levels are achieved, the growth rate will decrease.

Projection assumptions

Maximum rate: 20.0% average annual increase for 1967–70, 12.0% for 1971–75, and 10.0% for 1976–85.

Probable rate: 12.0% average annual increase for 1967–75, 8.0% for 1976–85.

Minimum rate: 8.0% average annual increase for 1967–75, 5.0% for 1976–85.

Development Indicators: **Malaysia**

1. POPULATION

Current annual population growth is about 3%, down from the 3½% annual growth rate of the mid–1950s. The crude birth rate decreased from 46.7 per 1000 in 1956 to 39.1 in 1964. Mortality rates are now around 9 per 1000 and will henceforth decrease slowly. The development plan anticipates a growth rate of 2.7% in 1970, 2.4% in 1975, 2.2% in 1980, and 2.0% in 1985.

Projection assumptions

Maximum rate: 3.0% annual increase for 1966–70, 2.75% annual increase from 1971 to 1985.

Probable rate: 3.0% annual increase for 1966–70, 2.75% for 1971–75, and 2.5% for 1976–85.

Minimum rate: 2.75% annual increase for 1966–70, 2.25% for 1971–75, and 2.0% for 1976–85.

2. GROSS NATIONAL PRODUCT

The growth rate for Malaysia was 6.1% annually from 1960 to 1966. For

Western Malaysia (Malaya) the average annual growth rate for 1955–64 was 4.6%. Malaysia's Perspective Plan projects the following growth rates for gross national product: 4.9% annually for 1965–70, 5.5% for 1970–75, 6.0% for 1975–80, and 6.5% for 1980–95.

Projection assumptions
Maximum rate: 7.0% annual growth for 1967–85.
Probable rate: rates given in the Perspective Plan.
Minimum rate: 4.0% annual growth for 1967–85.

3. FOOD PRODUCTION

For Western Malaysia only, the average annual increase was 6.0% for 1955–65 and 7.3% for 1960–65. Development plans have concentrated on increasing agricultural production as it has been the government's policy to equalize incomes through improving the economic condition of the rural, predominantly Malay peasantry.

Projection assumptions
Maximum rate: 6.5% annual growth for 1966–70, 6.0% for 1971–75, and 5.5% for 1976–85.
Probable rate: 5.0% annual growth for 1966–75, 4.0% for 1976–85.
Minimum rate: 2.0% annual growth for 1966–85.

4. MANUFACTURING PRODUCTION

There is no UN index. Because manufacturing accounts for only about 11% of gross domestic product, there is scope for rapid growth. The First Malaysia Plan (1966–70) expects the value of manufacturing production (at constant prices) to increase 10.0% annually over the plan period.

5. ELECTRICAL ENERGY PRODUCTION

The average annual growth rate was 9.1% for 1955–65 and 12.8% for 1960–65. Demand is expected to rise 8.5% per year from 1965 to 1980.

Projection assumptions
Maximum rate: 12.0% annual growth for 1966–75, 9.0% for 1976–85.
Probable rate: 10.0% annual growth for 1966–72, 8.0% for 1973–85.
Minimum rate: 7.0% annual growth for 1966–85.

6. EXPORTS

Export statistics include trade between constituent parts of the Federation. The average annual increase for 1956–65 was 3.5%, although specific years have deviated widely from the trend line. During this period fluctuations varied from a 11% drop in 1958 to 28½% rise in 1959.

MALAYSIA

Population and Gross National Product: average values for 1960-62, 1964-66, and projections for 1970, 1975, 1980, and 1985.
1963=100

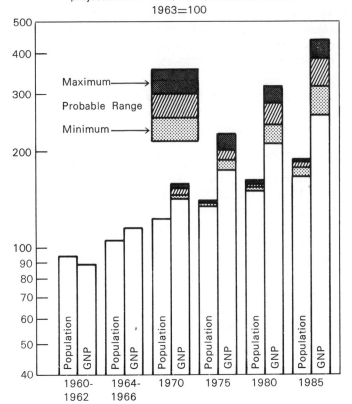

Trends: 1950-66

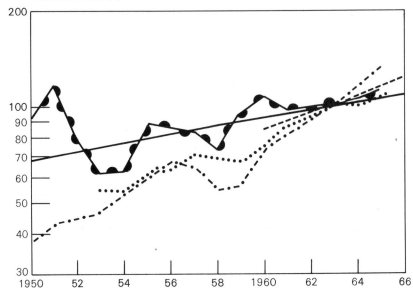

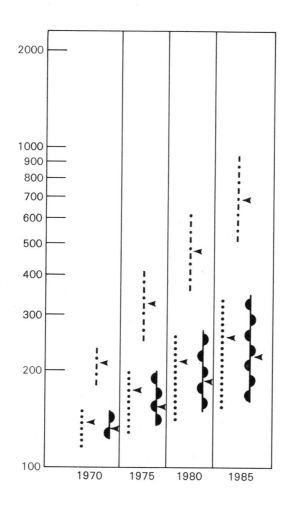

Forecast:
1970-85

Figure 1-14

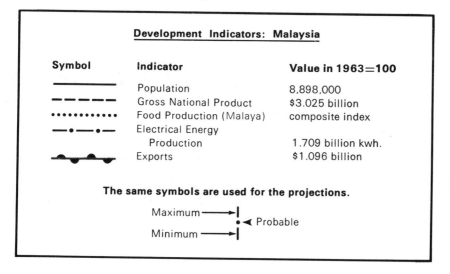

Development Indicators: Malaysia

Symbol	Indicator	Value in 1963=100
————	Population	8,898,000
– – – –	Gross National Product	$3.025 billion
••••••••••	Food Production (Malaya)	composite index
—•—•—	Electrical Energy Production	1.709 billion kwh.
⌣⌣⌣	Exports	$1.096 billion

The same symbols are used for the projections.

Maximum ——► |
                    • ◄ Probable
Minimum ——► |

NEW ZEALAND

Population and Gross National Product: average values for 1954-56, 1959-61,
1964-66, and projections for 1970, 1975, 1980, and 1985.
1958=100

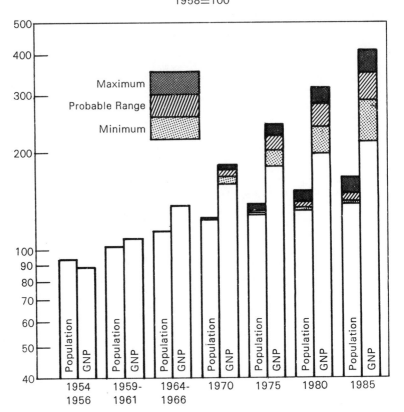

Trends: 1950-66

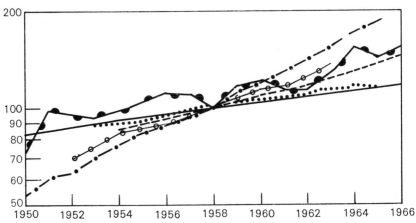

Forecast: 1970-85

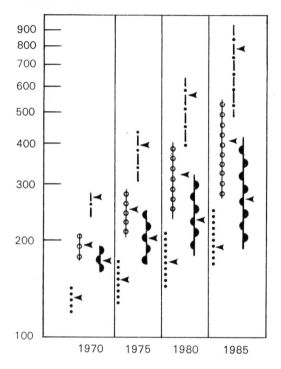

Figure 1-15

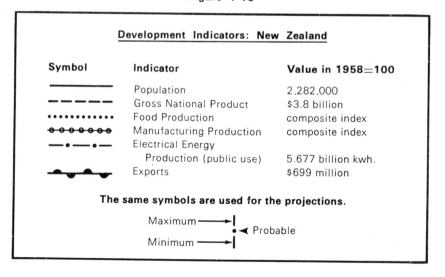

Development Indicators: New Zealand

Symbol	Indicator	Value in 1958=100
————	Population	2,282,000
– – – –	Gross National Product	$3.8 billion
··············	Food Production	composite index
⊕–⊕–⊕–⊕–⊕	Manufacturing Production	composite index
—·—·—	Electrical Energy Production (public use)	5.677 billion kwh.
⬤–⬤–⬤–	Exports	$699 million

The same symbols are used for the projections.

Maximum ⟶ ▮
               •◄ Probable
Minimum ⟶ ▮

Development Indicators: **New Zealand**

1. POPULATION

Current average annual population growth is 1.4%. The crude birth rate was 22.8 per thousand in 1965, a slight decline from 26 per thousand in the mid-1950s.

Projection assumptions

Maximum rate: 1.5% annual increase for 1967–70, 2.0% for 1971–85 (due to immigration).

Probable rate: 1.25% average annual increase for 1967–73, 1.0% for 1974–85.

Minimum rate: 1.25% average annual increase for 1967–70, 0.8% for 1971–75, 0.7% for 1976–85.

2. GROSS NATIONAL PRODUCT

The average annual growth rate for 1956–66 was 4.7%. Growth has varied during this decade from 3% in 1962 to 6.2% in 1957.

Projection assumptions (downward because of probable lower population growth)

Maximum rate: 6.0% annual growth for 1967–75, 5.5% for 1976–85.

Probable rate: 4.5% annual growth for 1967–75, 4.0% for 1976–85.

Minimum rate: 2.5% annual growth for 1967–75, 1.75% for 1976–85.

3. FOOD PRODUCTION

The average annual growth rate for 1955–65 was 2.5%. This varied from no increase in 1957 to a 5.8% increase in 1959.

Projection assumptions

Maximum rate: 4.0% annual growth for 1966–85.

Probable rate: 2.5% annual growth for 1966–85.

Minimum rate: 1.5% annual growth for 1966–85.

4. MANUFACTURING PRODUCTION

The latest UN figure is 1963. The average annual growth rate for 1953–63 was 6.1%.

Projection assumptions

Maximum rate: 6.5% annual growth for 1964–85.

Probable rate: 5.0% annual growth for 1964–85.

Minimum rate: 3.5% annual growth for 1964–85.

5. ELECTRICAL ENERGY PRODUCTION

The average annual growth rate for 1955–65 was 8.3% and for 1960–65 was 9.2%. New Zealand expects production to increase 8% annually between 1965 and 1970 and 7.5% annually between 1970 and 1975. (Cf. New Zealand Department of Statistics, "Monthly Abstract of Statistics," February, 1967).

Projection assumptions
Maximum rate: 9.0% annual growth for 1966–75, 8.0% for 1976–85.
Probable rate: 8.0% annual growth for 1966–70, 7.5% for 1971–80, 7.0% for 1981–85.
Minimum rate: 5.0% annual growth for 1966–85.

6. EXPORTS

The average annual increase in the value of exports was 3.3% for 1956–66 and 6.4% for 1961–66. The main exports are wool and dairy products. The commodity terms of trade have improved 25% since 1958. A major problem in the future may arise if Great Britain, the major market, should join the EEC and New Zealand lose its preferences in the British market.

Projection assumptions
Maximum rate: 5.5% annual growth for 1967–85.
Probable rate: 3.0% annual growth for 1967–85.
Minimum rate: 1.0% annual growth for 1967–85.

Development Indicators: **Pakistan**

1. POPULATION

The current annual population growth rate is about 3.2% and has been rising.

Projection assumptions
Maximum rate: 3.5% annual growth for 1967–85.
Probable rate: 3.25% annual growth for 1967–75, 3.0% for 1976–85.
Minimum rate: 3.0% annual growth for 1967–70, 2.75% for 1971–80, 2.5% for 1981–85.

2. GROSS NATIONAL PRODUCT

The average annual growth rate for 1956–66 was 4.6% and for 1960–66, it was 5.5%. Before 1960, the rate of increase of GNP did not exceed the rate of population increase. The development plan projects an average annual growth rate of 7.2% from 1965 to 1985, broken down as follows: 6.5% for 1965–70, 7.3% for 1970–75, 7.5% for 1975–85.

PAKISTAN

Population and Gross National Product: average values for 1951-54, 1957-60, 1963-66, and projections for 1970, 1975, 1980, and 1985.

1958=100

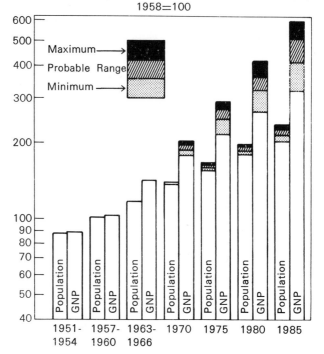

Trends: 1950-66

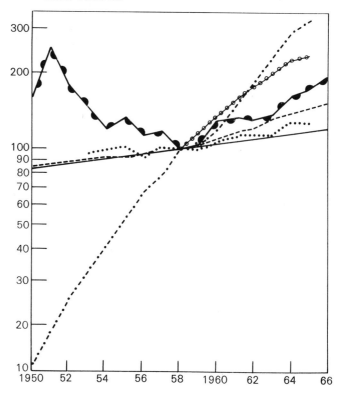

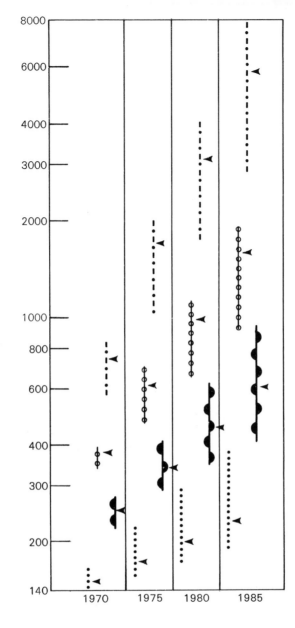

Forecast:

1970-85

Figure 1-16

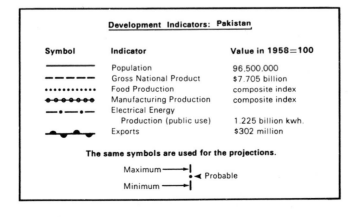

Projection assumptions
Maximum rate: 7.5% annual growth for 1967–85.
Probable rate: 6.0% annual growth for 1967–85.
Minimum rate: 4.0% annual growth for 1967–85.

3. FOOD PRODUCTION

The average annual growth rate was 2.5% for 1955–65 and 3.0% for 1960–65. The development plan estimates that annual increase in agricultural production will average 5.6% over the 1965–85 period.

Projection assumptions
Maximum rate: 5.5% annual growth for 1966–85.
Probable rate: 3.0% annual growth for 1966–85.
Minimum rate: 2.0% annual growth for 1966–85.

4. MANUFACTURING PRODUCTION

The average annual growth rate was 13.1% for 1958–65. The development plan expected an average growth rate of 10.2% over the 1965–85 period in industrial product.

Projection assumptions
Maximum rate: 11.0% annual increase for 1966–85.
Probable rate: 10.0% annual increase for 1966–85.
Minimum rate: 7.0% annual increase for 1966–85.

5. ELECTRICAL ENERGY PRODUCTION

The average growth rate for 1955–65 was 20.2%. Pakistan began from a very low base and, despite this growth, still produces only a little more than half what Taiwan produces.

Projection assumptions
Maximum rate: 20.0% annual growth for 1966–75, 15.0% for 1976–85.
Probable rate: 18.0% annual growth for 1966–75, 13.0% for 1976–85.
Minimum rate: 12.0% annual growth for 1966–80, 10.0% for 1981–85.

6. EXPORTS

The average annual growth rate was 5.8% for 1956–66 and 8.5% for 1961–66. Pakistan experienced a very sharp decline in the value of its exports between 1951 and 1958. The development plan expects an average annual growth rate of 7.9% for 1965–85.

Projection assumptions
Maximum rate: 8.5% annual growth for 1967–85.
Probable rate: 6.0% annual growth for 1967–85.
Minimum rate: 4.0% annual growth for 1967–85.

Development Indicators: **the Philippines**

1. POPULATION

The current annual rate of population growth is 3.4%, one of the highest in the world. Death rates have decreased sharply and now stand at 6 per thousand (due to a young population). Birth rates have declined from 31.2 per thousand in 1956 to 26 per thousand in 1963–64. A Catholic country, the Philippines will probably follow the Latin American pattern in maintaining a high rate of population growth.

Projection assumptions
Maximum rate: 3.5% annual growth for 1967–85.
Probable rate: 3.4% annual growth for 1967–70, 3.25% for 1971–80, and 2.9% for 1981–85.
Minimum rate: 3.25% annual growth for 1967–70, 2.75% for 1971–75, 2.5% for 1976–85.

2. GROSS NATIONAL PRODUCT

The average rate of increase was 4.6% for 1956–66 and 4.8% for 1960–66. The Philippines has shown the most steady growth of any Southeast Asian country since World War II, but in recent years its gains have not been so spectacular as those of Thailand and Malaysia. The development plan calls for a 5.5% annual increase in GNP between 1965 and 1970.

Projection assumptions
Maximum rate: 6.5% annual growth for 1967–85.
Probable rate: 5.0% annual growth for 1967–85.
Minimum rate: 3.5% annual growth for 1967–85.

3. FOOD PRODUCTION

The average annual rate of increase for 1955–65 was 2.7% and for 1960–65 was 2.8%. The development plan anticipates a 3.5% annual rate of growth in agricultural product and newly developed rice strains could improve the field significantly.

Projection assumptions
Maximum rate: 4.0% annual growth for 1966–74, 6.0% for 1975–85.
Probable rate: 3.0% annual growth for 1966–85.
Minimum rate: 1.75% annual growth for 1966–85.

REPUBLIC OF THE PHILIPPINES

Population and Gross National Product: average values for 1951-54, 1957-60, 1963-66, and projections for 1970, 1975, 1980, and 1985.

1958=100

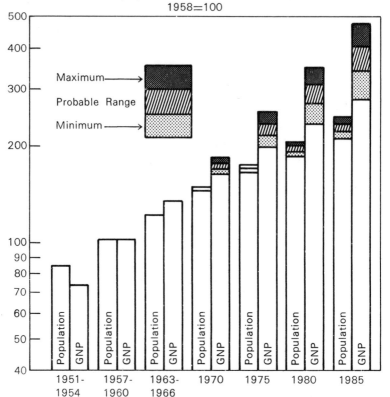

Trends: 1950-66

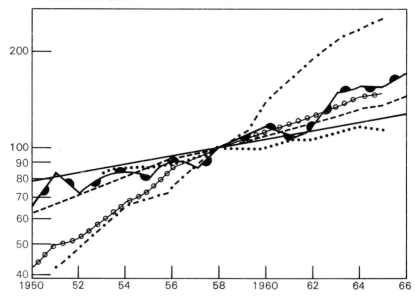

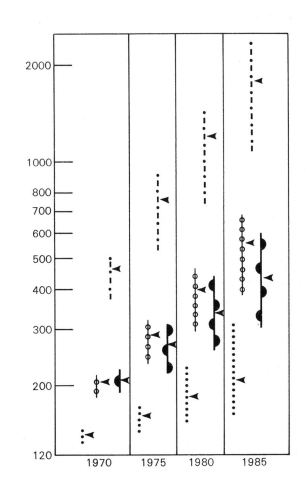

Forecast:
1970-85

Figure 1-17

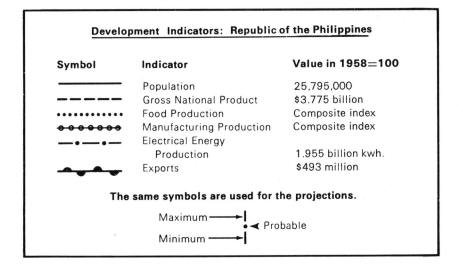

Development Indicators: Republic of the Philippines

Symbol	Indicator	Value in 1958=100
————	Population	25,795,000
– – – –	Gross National Product	$3.775 billion
••••••••••••	Food Production	Composite index
⊙⊙⊙⊙⊙⊙⊙	Manufacturing Production	Composite index
–•–•–	Electrical Energy Production	1.955 billion kwh.
⬤⬤⬤	Exports	$493 million

The same symbols are used for the projections.

Maximum ——▶
Probable
Minimum ——▶

4. MANUFACTURING PRODUCTION

The average annual rate of increase was 6.3% for 1955–65 and 6.0% for 1960–65. The development plan emphasizes private investment in manufacturing (the role of the public sector is to provide a favorable investment environment) and calls for a rate of increase of 7% through 1970.

Projection assumptions
Maximum rate: 7.5% annual growth for 1966–85.
Probable rate: 6.5% annual growth for 1966–85.
Minimum rate: 4.5% annual growth for 1966–85.

5. ELECTRICAL ENERGY PRODUCTION

The average annual rate of increase for 1955–65 was 14.2% and for 1960–65 was 12.4%. Installed capacity is being increased at a rate fast enough to sustain the high growth rate of the past.

Projection assumptions
Maximum rate: 13.0% annual growth for 1966–75, 10.0% for 1976–85.
Probable rate: 12.0% annual growth for 1966–70, 10.0% for 1971–80, and 8.0% for 1981–85.
Minimum rate: 7.0% annual growth for 1966–85.

6. EXPORTS

The average annual rate of growth was 6.3% for 1956–66 and 9.6% for 1961–66 in the value of exports. The sharp increase since 1961 is, in part, the result of the gradual devaluation of the peso. The commodity terms of trade have tended to move unfavorably and by the beginning of 1966 were estimated at 12% below their 1958 value.

Projection assumptions
Maximum rate: 7.0% annual growth for 1967–85.
Probable rate: 5.0% annual growth for 1967–85.
Minimum rate: 3.0% annual growth for 1967–85.

Development Indicators: Taiwan

1. POPULATION

The current annual rate of population growth is 2.75%. The birth rate has dropped 30% since 1952, and mortality rates are among the world's lowest because of the low age median. The development plan assumes a sharp decrease to a 2.26% annual growth rate in 1968.

Projection assumptions

Maximum rate: 3.0% annual increase for 1967–85.

Probable rate: 2.75% annual increase for 1967–70, and 2.25% for 1971–85.

Minimum rate: 2.5% average annual growth for 1967–70, 2.25% for 1971–75, 2.0% for 1976–85.

2. GROSS NATIONAL PRODUCT

The average annual growth rate for 1956–66 was 8.7% and for 1960–66 was 9.7%. During the last decade the yearly increase varied from 4.8% in 1956 to 13.4% in 1964. The 1965–68 development plan forecast an average 7.0% increase.

Projection assumptions

Maximum rate: 10.0% annual increase for 1967–75, 9.0% for 1976–85.

Probable rate: 7.0% annual increase for 1967–85.

Minimum rate: 5.0% average annual increase for 1967–85.

3. FOOD PRODUCTION

The average annual growth rate from 1955 to 1965 was 4.5%. The development plan projected a 4.5% annual increase in the value of agricultural production for 1965–68 and a 4.0% annual increase for 1965–74.

Projection assumptions

Maximum rate: 5.0% annual growth for 1966–85.

Probable rate: 4.5% annual growth for 1966–70, 4.0% for 1971–85.

Minimum rate: 2.5% annual growth for 1966–85.

4. MANUFACTURING PRODUCTION

The average annual increase was 14.3% for 1956–66 and 16.3% for 1961–66. The 1965–68 development plan expected a 10.8% annual increase in the value of manufacturing production during the plan period.

Projection assumptions

Maximum rate 15.0% annual growth for 1967–70, 10.0% for 1971–75, 8.0% for 1976–85.

Probable rate: 12% annual growth for 1967–75, 7% for 1976–85.

Minimum rate: 10.0% annual growth for 1967–70, 7.5% for 1971–75, and 5.0% for 1976–85.

5. ELECTRICAL ENERGY PRODUCTION

The average annual increase was 12.4% for 1955–65, and the yearly growth during this decade varied from 6.8% in 1963 to 17% in 1965. Taiwan expected to treble installed capacity by 1975.

TAIWAN

Population and Gross National Product: average values for 1953-54, 1957-60, 1963-66, and projections for 1970, 1975, 1980, and 1985.

1958=100

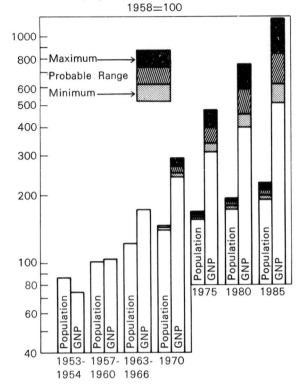

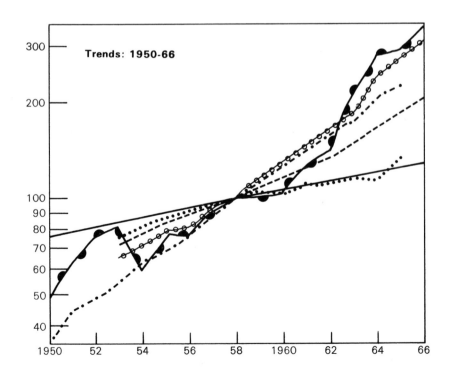

Trends: 1950-66

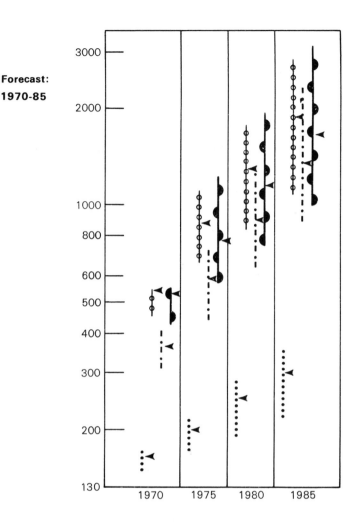

Forecast:
1970-85

Figure 1-18

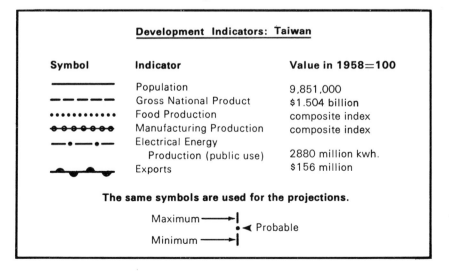

THAILAND

Population and Gross National Product: average values for 1953-54, 1957-60, 1963-66, and projections for 1970, 1975, 1980, and 1985.
1958=100

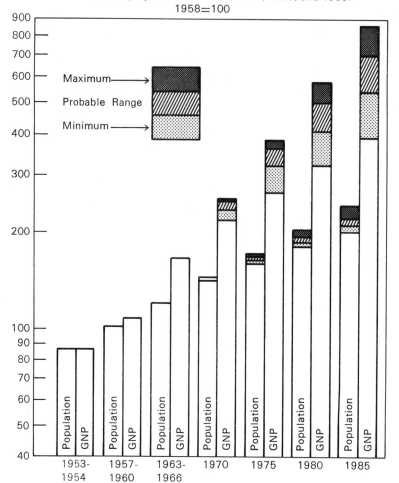

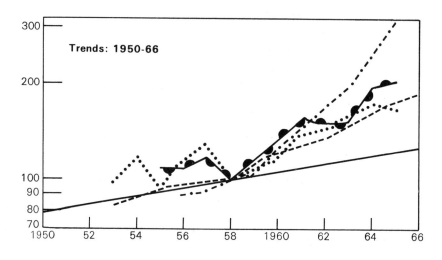

Trends: 1950-66

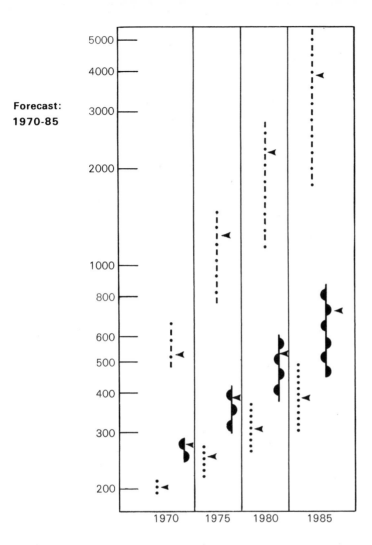

**Forecast:
1970-85**

Figure 1-19

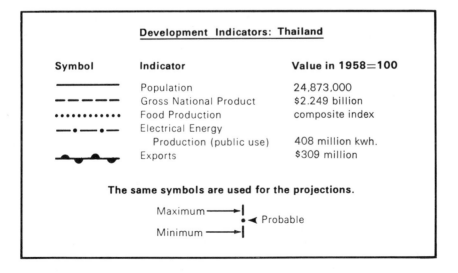

Development Indicators: Thailand

Symbol	Indicator	Value in 1958=100
————	Population	24,873,000
– – – –	Gross National Product	$2.249 billion
••••••••••	Food Production	composite index
–•–•–	Electrical Energy Production (public use)	408 million kwh.
⬤⬤⬤	Exports	$309 million

The same symbols are used for the projections.

Maximum ——➤
• ◄ Probable
Minimum ——➤

Projection assumptions
Maximum rate: 13.0% annual growth for 1966–85.
Probable rate: 10.0% annual growth for 1966–75, 9.0% for 1976–85.
Minimum rate: 7.0% annual growth for 1966–85.

6. EXPORTS

The value of exports increased on the average 13.8% per year for 1955–65 and 22.7% for 1960–65. Sugar and fruit exports have increased remarkably. The commodity terms of trade have fluctuated.

Projection assumptions
Maximum rate: 12.0% annual growth for 1967–75, 10.0% for 1976–85.
Probable rate: 11.0% for 1969–70, 8.0% for 1971–85.
Minimum rate: 6.0% for 1967–85.

Development Indicators: **Thailand**

1. POPULATION

The present annual rate of increase is 3.1%. The birth rate has been increasing, and the mortality rate is already at comparatively low levels. The current development plan allows for a 3.3% annual increase.

Projection assumptions
Maximum rate: 3.5% annual increase for 1967–85.
Probable rate: 3.0% annual increase for 1967–75, 2.75% for 1976–85.
Minimum rate: 3.0% annual increase for 1967–70, 2.5% for 1971–80,
  and 2.0% for 1981–85.

2. GROSS NATIONAL PRODUCT

The average annual growth rate was 6.8% between 1956 and 1966. Since 1960 the growth rate has averaged 7.2% annually. The development plan forecasts an 8.5% average annual growth rate (in Gross Domestic Product) for the five-year 1966–71 period.

Projection assumptions
Maximum rate: 8.5% annual growth for 1967–85.
Probable rate: 7.0% annual growth for 1967–75, 6.0% for 1976–85.
Minimum rate: 4.0% annual growth for 1967–85.

3. FOOD PRODUCTION

The average annual growth rate between 1954 and 1964 was 3.9%. Food production has been subject to wide fluctuations. The development plan projects a 4.3% growth rate in agricultural product for 1966–71. During the First Plan period (1961–66), 14% of development funds were allocated directly to stimulating agricultural production; during the Second Plan (1966–71), 20% was allocated.

Projection assumptions
Maximum rate: 5.5% annual growth for 1966–75, 6.0% for 1976–85.
Probable rate: 4.25% annual growth for 1966–75, 4.0% for 1976–85.
Minimum rate: 3.0% annual growth for 1966–85.

4. MANUFACTURING PRODUCTION

There is no UN index for manufacturing activity in Thailand. Planned growth for 1966–71 is 10.8% per annum.

5. ELECTRICAL ENERGY PRODUCTION

The average annual rate of increase was 16.4% annual growth for 1955–65. The rate of increase has been fairly consistent over this period. A smaller proportion of development funds are allocated to power development under the Second Plan than under the First Plan, because Thailand plans to expand the use of existing facilities rather than construct new ones.

Projection assumptions
Maximum rate: 16.5% annual growth for 1966–75, 14.0% for 1976–85.
Probable rate: 15.0% annual growth for 1966–75, 12.0% for 1976–85.
Minimum rate: 9.0% annual growth for 1966–85.

6. EXPORTS

The average annual rate of increase in the value of exports was 6.5% for 1955–65. Principal exports are rice, rubber, corn, and tin. The commodity terms of trade have improved by 11% since 1958.

Projection assumptions
Maximum rate: 7.5% annual growth for 1966–85.
Probable rate: 6.5% annual growth for 1966–85.
Minimum rate: 4.0% annual growth for 1966–85.

A Prognosis of State Viability
in Southeast Asia, Korea,
and Taiwan

The foregoing charts offer insight into the social and economic change within Southeast Asia over the past two decades, and also a comparison with change in surrounding states. The political consequences of these trends are not assured, but the insights do suggest probable directions. For example, irrespective of the antipathy that may divide Communist and non-Communist states in Asia, our evidence reveals substance to the argument that Communist aggressiveness is successful only in the most favorable circumstances. China, the major Communist power, faces such enormous drains from domestic demands that there is no reasonable expectation of external military ventures over the next decade. Therefore, it follows that Southeast Asian states are not prudent in gambling their skimpy resource bases upon military expenditures for the purpose of repelling Chinese invasions; however, domestic insurgency is another matter and may well merit greater attention than it has yet received from local governments, particularly the homeopathic remedies that can reduce tension between ethnic groups. Indeed, most Southeast Asian states share with China a future in which enormous demands for welfare and educational investment will threaten the very existence of states, and will certainly encourage the overthrow of politically inept regimes.

In this chapter we focus on the future viability of Southeast Asian states, with comparison to the Koreas and Taiwan. Integration of political and economic analysis permits assessment of their viability, a prognosis that builds upon the foundation of data contained in Chapter One. Both chapters are forecasts of situations that seem likely to evolve and permit us to proceed from the givens, or pa-

(Notes for this chapter begin on p. 201.)

rameters, to a subsequent discussion in Part Two of conflicts and policies that the United States should adopt.

The factors contributing to the viability of any state are many and deeply interrelated. By viability we mean a condition in which a state maintains sovereignty, sustains political and economic processes that advance the condition of civility and mutual trust among the populace, and is able to pursue courses in domestic and foreign affairs that serve its interests. How can we measure viability? Because of the vague boundaries and fusion between functions in any society, it serves little purpose to isolate the x factor, such as GNP, without also analyzing the relationship between it and other key variables. For example, a highly productive economy connotes many related social conditions but does not alone denote a viable state, e.g., Singapore; conversely, an inability to satisfy a key function, e.g., defense against a potential enemy, does not necessarily denote a nonviable state. Thus, if we are to say something intelligent about future viability we must engage in two types of analysis: one which isolates elements of power in each state and a second which weighs the relationships among the power elements that affect viability and evaluates the importance of inhibitors to development in each country. These country estimates provide a perspective appropriate for the time span under consideration.

Before entering into the details of the analysis, however, and in order to save the time of those concerned primarily with our conclusions, we state them at the outset, much as one presents the odds on a horse race. Indeed, we share the same problem as the bettor who knows many details about the participants (thirteen states), and the distance to be covered (two decades), but who can never know the outcome at the time of making the bet. Rather, he makes odds, a method we follow in an adjectival sense by assigning three categories of viability—high, moderate, and low—plus a fourth category for those states that are in our view unpredictable. Probably some of these estimates will be changed within a few years due to the vagaries of politics in this region, but at this point in time we believe the evidence best sustains these "odds."

Power Elements

To assign a power configuration for the 1980s, four basic questions will be asked about each state. What will be its resource base?

A Prognosis of State Viability in Southeast Asia, Korea, and Taiwan

What level of integration will it attain? What is likely to be the condition of morale in terms of the expectations of elites and the public compared to the reward distribution? And what will be the relative capability of each state compared to its enemies? Eleven elements of power will be evaluated in answering these questions:

The resource base will be assessed in terms of (1) population size, (2) manpower, (3) facilities for transport and communications, (4) energy and productivity, and (5) materials.

The level of integration likely to be attained will be assessed in terms of probable consolidation of competing (6) cultural, (7) political, (8) economic, and (9) military institutions. Less-integrated states suffer severe challenges to the center institutions by authoritative traditions among minorities or groups at the periphery.

The elements of (10) morale and (11) relative capability constitute the least reliable portion of our estimates, but are essential factors to consider in the overall process of power development.

The latitude for inaccuracy in these evaluations is large in view of the unstable conditions in these countries. Nevertheless, the effort proves fruitful, since it reveals the conditions of ignorance and enlightenment in which we operate when dealing with the dynamics of power. Bold assertions about the potential of countries, without knowledge of the constituent parts of that potential, are misleading if not useless. The overall relationship between the power elements and the specific inhibitors to development vary greatly between countries, which makes an overview for each country a vital concluding statement.

In presenting the analysis we will answer each of our four basic questions by grouping the states on the basis of their relative viability, the "A" Group being those with the brightest prospects, the "B" Group those with moderate prospects, the "C" Group those with questionable viability, and the "D" Group the unpredictables.

Viability, c. 1980

A. High	B. Moderate	C. Low	D. Unpredictable
South Korea	Malaysia	Burma	Singapore
Taiwan	North Korea	Cambodia	South Vietnam
Thailand	North Vietnam	Indonesia	
	Philippines	Laos	

This grouping of Asian states is characterized by both vulnerability, for it includes many of the small Asian powers, and by cores of military strength, for it also includes six states which maintain armies in excess of 300,000 men: Indonesia, North and South Korea, Taiwan, and North and South Vietnam. Southeast Asia as a region is weak compared to the three cores of power in Northeast and South Asia: Japan, China, and India. Only Indonesia can be compared with these major Asian powers, although with an economic consortium or alliance arrangement the smaller Asian powers might jointly compete with their huge neighbors. The latter prospect is dim and outside our consideration now because this chapter is at once more limited and elemental. Ours is a comparative analysis of the ability of these thirteen individual states to retain their own viability.

Resource Bases

Group A: POPULATION. The populations of South Korea, Taiwan, and Thailand are expanding rapidly, somewhat under 3% annually, but they are quite unlike one another. Thailand and South Korea have comparable numbers, about thirty million in 1965, and growth rates which will push each past the forty-five million mark between 1980 and 1985. Taiwan is smaller, with about thirteen million people in 1966, and will have considerably less than half the people in Thailand or South Korea by 1980 because population control is more advanced, thus lowering fertility.

MANPOWER. Educational statistics offer a key to future manpower resources. Sustained economic growth is associated with the following enrollments as a percentage of total population: primary 10%, secondary 2%, and higher education above 0.3%.[1] The exact ratio is not as important as the balance among these three if we are to use the developed states as a criterion for a desirable educational model. Based on this kind of measure, South Korea appears to be the strongest of the three Group A states by 1980. Its student population is nearly triple Taiwan's and Thailand's at the secondary and higher education levels, although the Taiwan–South Korean rates are similar. The percentage of total population enrolled at each level in South Korea as of 1966 was 14.2, 3.0, and 0.47, which is above the recommended minimum levels in each category. In Taiwan it was 16.7, 3.2, and 0.31; and in Thailand the ratios were 14, 0.99, and 0.16. The rate of expenditure on education in all three countries is not rising, but Korea has established a higher base for the critical secondary level. Vocational training programs in South Korea and Taiwan are relatively advanced, and the military in both countries seems exceptionally adept in training youths to become skilled and motivated workers during their two-to-four years of military duty. Both the manufacturing and agricultural sectors are rapidly absorbing modern techniques which create more skilled labor.

Thailand is not well-off in terms of manpower resources; in fact, its educational ratios are comparable to the Group C states. The military also has less of an impact on manpower training as it is considerably smaller than in either South Korea or Taiwan. Trade unions are very weak so there is little apprentice training. For these several reasons we must sharply qualify Thailand's potential compared to the other Group A states. Indeed, the only reason for including it in this category is its recent economic success, largely because of reasons other than skilled manpower.

TRANSPORTATION AND COMMUNICATION. Facilities for transport and communications are considerably more advanced in South Korea and Taiwan than in Thailand or in any of the other states, Singapore excepted. This hastens mobility, increases the breakdown of localism, and advances nationalization of the society, the economy, and the political system in these two states. For example, Taiwan has double the number of cinemas of South Korea or Thailand, even more than the Philippines which has the largest film industry of the thirteen states.[2] Radio communication is also better developed in Taiwan, although the revolution imposed by the low-cost transistor has struck all countries. Thailand, by way of example, had a twentyfold increase in receiver sets between 1960 and 1964.[3] Television use is expanding rapidly in all three Group A states with perhaps a million sets already in Korea and Thailand, although on a per capita basis Taiwan is ahead. Newspaper circulation further confirms the generalization that in communications Taiwan and South Korea are developing most rapidly. Both have double the circulation of the most advanced Group B states and, in 1961, had a circulation of 70 per 1,000 compared to 15 per 1,000 in Thailand.[4] Given the greater proportion of student population in Taiwan and South Korea, their circulation rates are likely to continue the rapid advance over the next two decades until they are comparable to Japan's rate today—over 300 per 1,000.

In transportation, Taiwan is again the most advanced. The road and rail network is twenty times as intensive as Thailand's (1 km per 0.6 sq mi) and about 20% more intensive than South Korea's (1 km per 0.8 sq mi versus 1 km per 0.6 sq mi).[5] Thailand utilizes extensive water transport to supplement the road and rail links in the Chao Phraya basin, but has poor transport and communication links in the Korat plateau and frontier hill regions to the north, west, and in the peninsula.

PRODUCTIVITY. The productivity of these three Group A countries is likely to increase at about the same 4–5% net rate. Whereas Thailand had a GNP of about four billion dollars in 1966 while Taiwan and South Korea had about three billion each, by 1980 Thailand's GNP will reach ten billion and that of the other two countries should be around eight billion. All three should enjoy a rapid expansion of the export sector and of manufacturing and construction through consumption of spectacular increases in electrical energy output.

MATERIALS. The raw-material resource base in Thailand and South Korea is strong. Both countries have a relatively high proportion of arable land. Thailand particularly will profit from irrigation and land clearance programs which enhance its agricultural capacity. Both have significant mineral reserves (coal in Korea, nonferrous metals in Thailand) which assure each of diversity in their economic development. Taiwan, like Japan, must depend largely on human resources for economic advances as its arable land is already utilized and its mining potential is small. The agricultural, food-processing, industrial, and social-service sectors will provide almost all the growth in the economy because of this small raw-material base. South Korea and Taiwan have unusually well-balanced economies for states at their stage of development.

Group B: POPULATION. The populations of the four states predicted to be moderately viable will range from 14 million (Malaysia) to 51 million (the Philippines) in 1980. North Vietnam will have about 24 million and North Korea about 18 million people. The Philippines has fertility characteristics similar to those of Mexico, both being Catholic states, and will probably experience grave difficulty in population control; consequently, by the ninth decade of this century the Philippines is likely to have the largest proportion of nonproductive inhabitants of any state analyzed in this study. Both

North Korea and Malaysia have commenced some population-control programs and are likely to have under a 2.5% growth rate by 1980. North Vietnam is probably above 3%, and there is little likelihood of a near downturn.

MANPOWER. Manpower development in North Korea will be more advanced than in the other three states. Like all Communist countries except North Vietnam, it places heavy emphasis on education and has over 16% of the total population enrolled at the primary level, 3% at the secondary level, and 2% in higher education.[6] These are ratios like South Korea's, the best of the Group A countries. North Vietnam is much lower: 12.8%, 0.28%, and 0.09%; and Malaysia is 15%, 3.0%, and 0.11%.

The Philippines is somewhat better off at the higher level than is Malaysia, but does less well in the lower levels: 12.7%, 1.7%, and 0.83%. Also it should be noted that the Philippines awards almost half its degrees in the social sciences with little emphasis on vocational skills and technology.[7] At this stage of its development, unfortunately, there is no employment for such a large body of social science graduates. Thus, there will continue to be sizable numbers of educated unemployed in the Philippines until such time as the economy is prosperous enough to utilize their skills.

Malaysia experiences a unique problem in manpower development because of the four language educational systems—Malay, Chinese, English, and Tamil. For example, in 1965 there were 622,000 Malay language students, 506,000 English, 377,000 Chinese, and 73,000 Tamil Indian.[8] The training in each of the languages in related school systems, (except for English) limits the prospects for successful competition at the university level. Those village or town students with no access to English, the language of the university, business, and top political communities, are cut off from higher achievements. Bilingual students with either Chinese–English, Malay–English, or Tamil–English are in the strongest position for future contributions in nearly any field; consequently, bilingualism has become a key goal for educators. Today, however, the vast majority of people are less productive because of the language barrier, and the leaders of the three communities are not likely to give the educators a free hand in resolving the problem.

North Vietnam has experienced rapid social and political mobilization because of the war. The low educational enrollments are therefore misleading in terms of the potential manpower available for productive purposes by the 1980s. The motivation for patriotic service has been markedly heightened by the war and this will influence the country's productivity once the fighting lessens. Although only 10 percent of the populace was urban in 1963, the impact of the war hastens urbanization and industrialization as significant numbers of village youth, because of wartime travel, seek urban opportunities. The urban–rural gap will be reduced by the urbanization trend, a behavior pattern common to modern postwar situations.

TRANSPORTATION AND COMMUNICATION. Transportation facilities in the Philippines and Malaysia are as advanced as among the Group A countries, indeed more developed than in Thailand. In 1963 the Philippines had over a half-million cars and trucks, Malaysia over a third of a million. Both utilize extensive coastal shipping for passenger and freight transport. North Korea depends upon a relatively short rail net (0.8 km per 100 sq km compared to South Korea's 3.2 km per 100 sq km) to make up for a very poor road system, and is second only to the U.S.S.R. in the world for intensity of rail use.[9] North Vietnam, of course, must use water transport to substitute for a road and rail system disrupted by bombing, and may not advance rapidly in this area, because of the high costs of road and rail construction. For example, North Korea still has not recovered from the 1950–53 conflict in transport reconstruction.

Communications in Malaysia and the Philippines are also more advanced than in the two Communist states, largely because of the heavy investment, respectively, of British and American companies in radio, television, and telephone systems. The general availability of television and telephone in urban areas and towns hastens the communications process which has positive political and economic benefits. By 1980 this present response to new technology is likely to be compounded, enabling the pluralist states to integrate more rapidly than would otherwise be possible. Both North Korea and North Vietnam make extensive use of speaker systems in villages and hamlets, as well as radios in urban areas, but telephone communication is much more primitive and television does not exist.

The free press in Malaysia and the Philippines probably contributes to political integration but its relatively low degree of distribution, about 50 per 1,000, suggests that most rural people are outside the influence of newspapers. In both Communist states the press is essentially a propaganda vehicle and tends to reenforce the coercive power of the regimes.

The cinema is extremely important in the Philippines, which has the highest density of seats per capita, outside of Singapore and Taiwan, of the states under consideration. Over a dozen film companies are serious financial enterprises and several hundred films are produced a year.[10] The film industry may be the most active integrating agent in the Philippines in terms of creating national symbols and heroes and crossing language barriers. In Malaysia there is also extensive use of moving pictures, particularly among the Chinese and Indian population, and its entertainment value is no more important than its value as a modernizing agent. Although Malaysians become more modern by watching films, because Malaysia makes few of its own films, the nationalizing effect is not great as in the Philippines. In the two Communist countries, films are primarily propaganda and again North Korea is much advanced over North Vietnam in the development of this communications form. All of the Group B countries place greater emphasis upon communications than do the Group C states.

PRODUCTIVITY. Despite the prospects for moderate political integration in the pluralist states, their integration will remain lower than in the Communist states and consequently their rates of production increases are not likely to be as high as among the Communist states. North Korea's real GNP will rise at nearly double the rate (7%) of Malaysia's and the Philippines', largely because of less political disturbance, a higher rate of saving, a lower base from which to start, and general emphasis on capital rather than on consumer production. North Vietnam is an enigma at this point because of the lack of reliable statistics and the disturbance of the war, but its high degree of political integration will probably enable it to advance rapidly and regain its GNP levels of the early sixties; thereafter the rate of increase is not predictable.

MATERIALS. The raw-material base of Malaysia is excellent in nonferrous metals and fairly good in iron ore and petroleum. Its rubber industry has been modernized, but future terms of trade will continue to work against it. The Philippines is rich in minerals, forest products, sugar, and other agricultural products. If the political problems can be worked out, this raw-material base will be a major contribution to greater viability. Both business and labor are relatively well-organized in urban areas, as is also true in Malaysia, but in neither country is there effective linkage with the vast majority of the population in rural areas, a link that will be essential if the raw-material potential is to be fully exploited by developing an integrated economic system.

North Korea has good reserves of iron ore and coal as well as a responsive agrarian sector. North Vietnam has abundant coal, phosphate, and chromite and, like North Korea, a substantial manufacturing sector, considering the GNP and skill level of the population. Each produces most of the consumer goods for its domestic population enabling both states to use most of their foreign earnings for capital goods purchases to develop the raw-material sector or for military purchases. Again, North Vietnam's economy is presently so disturbed that prediction is less reliable, but the raw-material base is sufficiently diverse (in agriculture as well as mining) and developed to allow for steady improvement once the war conditions recede.

Group C: POPULATION. Burma, Cambodia, Indonesia, and Laos all share high fertility and declining mortality rates. By 1980 Indonesia's population will exceed 160 million, Burma's—36 million, Cambodia's—10 million, and Laos's—5 million. The median ages will be under 20 and the growth rates will probably remain at or above 3%. Thus, these countries will have nearly a maximum possible number of nonproductive inhabitants pressing serious demands on the economy.

MANPOWER. The manpower base in all these states was very weak at independence, with only a few hundred university graduates at most. By 1963, the last reporting date, the ratios of enrollment to population were (primary, secondary, higher): Burma—8.4%, 1.1%, 0.08%; Cambodia—9.8%, 0.82%, and university insignificant; Indonesia—9%, 0.70%, 0.06%; Laos—6.1%, 0.2%, 0.01%.[11] These low percentages illustrate the long distance each of these states must travel before their manpower base will be on a par with the Group B or Group A countries (but for Thailand). Although their primary enrollments are rising, except for Cambodia, all the Group C countries have very weak secondary systems and greater education lags behind the other countries. The military of Indonesia has been a catalyst for modernization, as in the other "large army" countries, but, given the very large population, this impact is not likely to be great. Armies in the three other states may be too small and weak to have significant impact on mass attitudes. Again, none of the Group C states has had labor movements or business communities that create skills on a large scale. Indonesia has, in raw numbers, a large core of educated and experienced people compared to the other three states, but, in proportion to the population, the ratio is comparable to Burma's and Cambodia's. Laos, of course, is exceedingly weak in manpower and has no prospect of becoming viable without major outside support throughout the period under consideration.

TRANSPORTATION AND COMMUNICATION. Transportation and communication in all of the Group C countries is less well-developed than in the poorest of the Group B states. Laos is worst off with no rail system at all and, as of 1965, only 1.1 km of road per 100 sq km of territory, the lowest density of any state under consideration. Burma had 2.5, Cambodia 3.7, and Indonesia 1.6 km of road per 100 sq km and, in the same order for rail development, 0.45, 0.23, 0.01.[12] Thus, Indonesia is badly off in transportation generally, nearly as much so as Laos, but for the use of coastal shipping. Burma and Cambodia are in a slightly better position with Burma having a better rail system and Cambodia having more roads per sq km.

In communications Burma is the most developed of this group, although it is less well off than any of the Group A or B states. As of 1960 Burma had a newspaper circulation of 12 per 1,000 people, Indonesia had 11 per 1,000, Cambodia had 6 per 1,000, and Laos had 0.6 per 1,000.[13] Small increases since then have been at about the same rate in each country. None of the Group C countries has television. All four of these states had less than 10 radios per 1,000 population in 1960 and, although the rise has been significant since then (perhaps now the rate would be 15 per 1,000), they still are considerably behind states in Groups A and B. Laos and Indonesia are both near the bottom of the world distribution chart, only slightly ahead of the black African states in terms of radio communication.

The implication of this generally primitive condition of transport and communication in the Group C countries is clear; they will not be able to develop their economies or political systems rapidly until an infrastructure is built that will accommodate the demands of a modern society. Indonesia is desperately in need of port facilities for its two dozen cities, many of which are near the coast. Burma likewise has great need for port and transport systems which will bring the bulk of the population into a national economy, although at the present rate of production new ports would be uneconomical. Cambodia's one port is still underused due to the low level of exports and, of course, Laos has to depend upon river transport for much of its traffic, because of the embryonic road system.

PRODUCTIVITY. Productivity per capita is highest in Cambodia, somewhat above $100, and has declined in Indonesia to a rate probably not much higher than Burma's, which is under $60. Laos is near $50, the world's minimum.[14] These rates are somewhat deceptive as much of the population in these four states lives on a subsistence, barter economy, outside national income reporting. Nonetheless, they are all poor countries, even by Asian standards, with economic growth rates (but for Cambodia) that have been stagnating for five to ten years. Projected growth rates for Cambodia before the 1970 war were relatively firm, around 2% net, and Indonesia, with good fortune and relative peace, may have an even higher rate of growth. Burma and Laos face a bleak future, although with skillful leadership Burma could regain a significant growth rate (from 1955–58 it was net 3.8% annually).

MATERIALS. The raw-material base of Indonesia is unexcelled in the 13 countries under consideration. Petroleum, ferrous and non-ferrous metals, plantation crops, rice, and timber are the key resources. With proper economic organization the potential for exploitation of natural resources in Indonesia is very high. Much of the territory is still unexplored, geologically, and recent surveys have uncovered a large copper deposit on West Irian. The International Monetary Fund (IMF) is quite optimistic about Indonesia's future because of the resource base and has urged the Indonesia consortium and private investors to accelerate their commitments. Current government policy is considered economically prudent; therefore, the prospects for increasing exploitation are good.

Burma and Cambodia are both primarily riverine states with rich rice cultivation areas and considerable arable land still uncultivated because of the low level of mechanization. Burma also has metals and forest products, as well as exportable cereals which could be developed with proper management and successful recruitment of investors. Since independence, their neutralist foreign policies have worked against large-scale investment from either socialist or "free world" states. Most "free world" aid, except for Japanese reparations, has been multilateral and not committed to exploitation of the raw-material bases which are considerably less than Indonesia's. Cambodia has small amounts of iron ore, extensive fisheries, and potentially valuable forestry reserves, but in both countries the prime area of development must come in agriculture. Political instability caused by minority problems and ideological strife will tend to retard agricultural development.

Group D—Unpredictable: POPULATION. Singapore and South Vietnam have nothing in common except their propinquity and uncertain futures. Singapore split from Malaysia, partially as a consequence of the Indonesia crisis; therefore, the nature of their split may be a transient thing. Lee Kuan Yew has spoken candidly of the value in reunification, but within the next twenty years federation is not likely thanks to communal distrust. In any event, the population will remain the same, ethnically, and the rate of development is not likely to change. The population of 2.1 million in 1970 is about 77% Chinese, the rest being Malays, Indians, and various racial mixtures. The very high growth rate of the 1950s is slowly declining, but is likely to remain above 2.5% for the period of this study, suggesting a predominantly young population with heavy demands for education and services.

South Vietnam had about 16 million people in 1966 and, despite the war, a substantial growth rate, above 2.8%. These are a people caught in a volatile political crisis which makes their future unpredictable. In the event of reunion with the northern zone of Vietnam, the population of Vietnam would be large enough to make it competitive in number of people with Burma, Thailand, Korea, and the Philippines as intermediary powers in Asia.

MANPOWER. South Vietnam is somewhat better off than the northern zone in terms of manpower, the primary, secondary, and higher education enrollment ratios being 9.2%, 1.7%, and 0.11%.[15] The motivation to use skills in the interests of the state, however, has been considerably higher in the northern zone. Efficient assassination of potential leaders and organizers by the Vietcong in the south contributes to lower morale, and the mass mobilization of society on a wartime basis is more effective in the north and among the National Liberation Front (NLF) in the south. Future use of skills learned through this mobilization in both zones will contribute to Vietnam's development once the fighting recedes, but the major variable affecting the motivation of those with skills is the public's acceptance of the government that attempts to lead them. In this regard the Hanoi leaders, after twenty-five years of conflict, may have the edge; however, continued challenge to their legitimacy as nationalist leaders, by Saigon, is earning the challengers greater acceptance. Continuance of the war makes efficient manpower utilization impossible. Yet because the future of the war is unpredictable, a rating of the manpower element is impossible.

Singapore has an extremely potent manpower base because of the organization of its society as well as the educational program. The ratios are: primary—16.6%, secondary—3.6%, and higher—0.38%.[16] The private association structure (strong unions, expanding businesses, a powerful political party, and substantial family organizations) also contributes to the rapid development of manpower. Singapore has more skilled human resources than any of the Group A countries and in the event of reunion with Malaysia would add a considerable increment to its less-advanced society.

TRANSPORTATION AND COMMUNICATION. Transportation and communication in South Vietnam is heavily disturbed by the war. In 1964 there were over 20,000 kilometers of roads and a short rail line, but insurgency prevents utilization of all but the major routes. Coastal, canal, and river traffic accounts for much of the shipping, but again it is interdicted by the fighting, and future development rests entirely on the outcome of the war. A massive television program was introduced in 1965, but its impact in contested areas of the country appears small. Radio communication has developed very rapidly, thanks to American aid and, although data are missing, the use of radio is probably as advanced as in Group A countries. Newspaper circulation is 28 per 1,000—relatively high for the 13 states considered. The cinema has recently become as significant as in Group B states.

Singapore, confined to an island 26 by 14 miles, has the most intensive transport and communications network of any of the states considered. The ratio of vehicles to population is higher than in any other Asian state, possibly excepting Japan, or about one per ten inhabitants, and the public transport is comparable to that of most European cities. Cinema attendance is higher than in any other Asian state, television was recently introduced and usage is rising rapidly, and newspaper circulation is second only to Japan among Asian states (Hongkong is higher in many of these categories, but, of course, is not a state).[17]

PRODUCTIVITY. Productivity in South Vietnam is low—under $80 per capita—and is so disturbed in both agricultural and manufacturing sectors that prediction is difficult. In the late 1950s the savings and capital formation rate was high, with manufacturing and cottage industry moving up sharply. Should that impetus be regained, the state could attain a 3% net growth rate with little difficulty as the arable land is extensive and particularly rich in the Mekong delta. Also, the urban population seems unusually adept in commercial affairs.

Singapore has the highest per capita income of the 13 states considered—nearly $400—and a steady growth rate over the past decade. Most of its employment is in processing and services—employment which feeds on itself by creating more human skills and managerial training. If trade barriers are not erected with Singapore's major trade partners, the prospects for continued rises in productivity are excellent.

MATERIALS. The raw-material bases in both these states are not potentially as significant as in many other Asian states. Singapore, of course, has none; the southern zone in Vietnam has only agriculture and fishing with a few coal beds. Electric power capacity is rising sharply in both states through thermal uses, but how thoroughly it will be exploited in South Vietnam remains uncertain.

Integration

Group A: CULTURAL. The normal criteria for cultural integration are common language, shared historical experience, mutually predictable value patterns, and, usually, a common ecological habitat which encourages development of similar mores and institutions within the geographic boundaries. Because the terrain in Southeast Asia is complex, it has not encouraged widespread integration; rather there has been evolution of diverse customs and languages. Successive migrations further complicated the demographic and linguistic patterns, so that many of the cultural groups today are very small. In the broad riverine valleys (like the Chao Phraya and Irrawaddy), and on those land areas outside of Southeast Asia isolated from the pressure of constant migration (like Japan, Korea, and Taiwan), larger populations and more elaborate cultures evolved as political and social institutions that flourished over extended periods without the destructive impact of incipient warfare characteristic of small cultural groups.

All of the states in the A group enjoy the advantage of such integration, which is high compared to most states in the B and C groups. Religious differences are of no political importance in any of these A states. Ethnically, South Korea has no minority, except for a few thousand Chinese. Taiwan is constituted almost entirely of Chinese although the Kuomintang (KMT) mainland governing faction remains distinct from the Formosans who migrated from Fukein over the past three centuries, and who constitute an 80% majority of the total population. Among people under 25 there is considerable assimilation due to a common education and life experience. The aborigines, the only really indigenous Formosans, live in the eastern mountains and are of no greater social or political significance than are the Ainus of Japan.

Thailand has the only distinct ethnic minorities of the A group. These minority communities include about four million Chinese who are highly influential in Thai economic life and who live largely in urban areas: the hill tribes along the frontier, the Muslim Malays in the south, and the Vietnamese and the Khmer in the east. Assimilation is quite rapid for the Chinese as there is much intermarriage, widespread respect for their business and intellectual acumen, and anxious concern on the part of the Chinese and Thai leaderships that the Chinese be absorbed. No Chinese public schools are permitted; Chinese children adopt Thai names and can learn only Thai in the public schools. The extensive private school system is closely supervised to ensure that no Chinese nationalist sentiment is inculcated. There is ready acceptance among the Thai elite for those Chinese who attain significant wealth, education, or political status within the Chinese community. The several million Lao-speaking peoples along the Mekong are sometimes viewed as a minority ethnic community in Thailand, but the lowland Lao and the Thai are very closely related. Actually, the Thai shade into four cultural subdivisions: the Northern Thai centered around Chiengmai, the Northeastern Phu Thai on the plateau, the Central Thai on the Chao Phraya plain, and the Southern Thai on the peninsula. Vietnamese and Khmer minorities in eastern Thailand have not proved to be assimilative, but are so small in number, under half a million, that they should pose no serious challenge to the political or economic systems.

POLITICAL. Political integration is not well-advanced within any states of the A group as all the governments are dominated by the military, with relatively high degrees of police and military repression of opposition factions. South Korea has made some effort to advance a pluralist political system, and the civil service, business, and academic communities play significant roles in policy making. Yet students, farmers, trade union members, and the lesser educated, who constitute a large majority, today have little voice in the system. The press enjoys greater freedom than in the 1950s but cannot be considered to be free of censorship. Political parties have a weak tradition and perform poorly in the tasks of creating legislation and articulating public interests in a responsible fashion. The potential for political disruption is rather high because of a factionalist tradition within civil as well as military political groups.

In Taiwan the oligarchical dominance of top KMT families, who retain control two decades after moving from the mainland, has provided stability in the past. For the future, the oligarchy could be a destabilizing factor if it fails to broaden the base of participation in decision making. The expanding number of affluent families with well-educated members will demand greater participation. Furthermore, the possibility of reconciliation between a mainland government or faction and a Taiwan opposition group will always be a threat to the Taiwan government if it retains strict control. Greater pluralism may relieve this growing pressure but could also threaten to destroy the political system if change comes too rapidly. Finally, Taiwan is most sensitive to changes in mainland China, making political prediction unusually dangerous.

Thailand has evolved a unique political system which offers considerable rewards to ambitious military officers and entrepreneurs. As long as the economy grows rapidly and the benefits are distributed to both the civil and military elites, the polity will remain stable. But the potential for severe disruptions is ever present as substantial numbers of teachers, rural leaders, and lower-level civil servants will remain dissatisfied wtih military oligarchic rule. Their following will expand rapidly if the economy slows its current expansion. Because substantial numbers of the educated populace do not play a political role, they experience chronic frustration in their relationship with the government. Although a constitutionally based parliament was recreated in 1969, this source of alienation has not disappeared and alienation may increase should the control of government pass into the hands of partisan leaders of more dogmatic vision than the military oligarchy which has dominated for most of the past three decades. Development of a national party organization may allow Thailand to pass through the crisis of more widespread literacy and affluence without grave civil disorder, although past experience with political parties was discouraging because of their severe factionalism. Meanwhile the process of political integration is being disrupted by the terrorist-oriented Thai Patriotic Front. The Front is likely to persist as a subversive movement as long as the political alienation of peasant leaders and rural teachers continues.

ECONOMIC. Economic integration is advancing rapidly in all three states of Group A. Introduction of commercial crops and processing industries over the past decade has enabled export earnings to climb precipitously and bodes well for the future. Among the urbanizing populations there are bound to be economic dislocations which will continually place great demands on the economies; however, booming national markets are appearing in each country and are sustained by an expanding infrastructure and experienced economic leadership. South Korea currently enjoys the most rapid growth, at a rate comparable to Japan's in the early 1950s (9–10% annually). If investment continues to remain as profitable, and if consumer purchasing power continues to expand as rapidly as in the past five years, the expansion of the economy is certain to include most of the population. Taiwan's growth, while not quite so spectacular, is at a very high rate (over 6% annually) and has been sustained long enough to make quite certain the prediction of a widening consumer market and production base. Thailand has latent difficulties due to the cleavage between the Chinese entrepreneurs and those Thai aspiring to enter business. To resolve the problem enterprises with Chinese backing tend to invite Thai senior military to serve on their boards (and gain a share of profits). Tension between these communities is not as severe as in many of the Group B and C states. Thailand's major problem is the failure to include large sections of the rural populace in the economic system.

MILITARY. The military in two of the three Group A countries have been highly effective integrative agents. Rural youth have been assimilated in the larger society through their military experience, and the high turnover of participants in each system—20–30% annually—contributes to its function as an integrator. Taiwan and South Korea have quite consciously used their military to advance national assimilation. In Taiwan, where the problem of Formosan versus mainland identity was severe, the government gradually developed the army around a base of Formosan youth rather than limiting it to the second generation of mainlanders as it might have done. Military service has undoubtedly relieved the sense of alienation characteristic among Formosans in the 1950s, although the higher ranks and honors within the military still seem reserved for mainland Chinese. In South Korea the 1950–53 war provided the military with a solid base of acceptability as a national service institution. There has been little resentment expressed about military service on the part of high school graduates or university students. Establishment of this tradition of military service, popularly viewed as a legitimate demand by the state in Taiwan and South Korea, greatly enhances the nationalization process among peoples who previously had primary identity with provincial or district communities.

In Thailand, where the military is only a fifth the size of the organizations in Taiwan and South Korea, the integrative role is much less significant. Because there has been neither major internal war nor, until 1970, imminent outside threat, the government has not marshalled masses of men in the name of national defense, and the military remains highly traditional. A significant division between officers and the ranks has remained from the premodern period when to gain an officer's rank was to gain social status, rather than to earn graver responsibilities for national service. As long as the Thai officer corps remains essentially a group committed to earning emoluments, thus failing to introduce nationally oriented goals and values to younger officers and enlisted men, the function of the military as an integrative intuition will not be successfully served.

Group B: CULTURAL. Cultural integration in North Korea and North Vietnam is high, particularly in the former country. Language, dress, diet, and world outlook among the populations is ethnically based. In North Korea cultural boundaries are congruent with state boundaries, except of course in the south. North Vietnam, with a montagnard minority of about 15%, a small Catholic minority, and an even smaller Chinese community with the traditional Confucian–Buddhist and a modern Communist mélange, has less unity than either of the Koreas or Taiwan, but more than the other Group B countries.

Malaysia has a unique situation with only a slight ethnic majority (Malay Muslim), as well as territorial loyalties that divide the Malay islanders of Sarawak and Sabah from Malays on the peninsula. The large Chinese minority (about 37%) is much less assimilated than in Thailand on account of religious, marital, employment, and language differences. This problem will certainly continue, for it has long roots going back to the late nineteenth century when immigration of Chinese also increased in Thailand. However, although assimilation is rapid in Thailand, there has been none in Malaysia. Chinese in Malaysia maintain their family names and do not intermarry with Malays; they continue to control commercial business, mining, and manufacturing; they continue to sustain their own private schools and to teach in Chinese; and they continue to be viewed as a serious threat by more conservative Malay leaders. Greater opportunities are offered to Malays for university education, for entry into the civil service and military, and for success in government-promoted business. The more recent mobilization of Malays into modern life (most Malays still are villagers; most Chinese live in urban areas) accounts for this policy which, the government insists, is only a transitional step until Malays can compete successfully with Chinese. The antagonism was deepened by the May 13, 1969 riots which pitted Malay police and military against Chinese civilians.

The Philippines is an overlay of two Western cultures upon a host of linguistic communities, most of which are of Malay extraction. Although Tagalog is the official national language and is understood by 45% of the population, it is only one of nine with major importance. An estimated ten million, or one-third the population, speak English—a remaining American influence. American culture was an overlay on the Spanish influence evidenced by Catholicism and the barrio land-tenure system, which affects over four-fifths of the population today. The tensions and the peculiar blend of cultures that result from this jumble of traditional influences, combined with the complexity of indigenous cultures caused by the island environment, make national consolidation difficult in the Philippines. Like Malaysia, the Philippines suffers from cultural chasms that impede development and harm viability.

POLITICAL. Political integration among the Group B states is clearly a derivative of cultural integration. In North Korea and North Vietnam, where one language and culture predominate, the Communist parties have developed structural organizations that are unchallenged by opposition groups. There have been revolts and attempted coups, but no lasting mass-based opposition that would prevent the centrist regimes from retaining a solid apparatus. Without an ethnic or class base for political opposition, future disintegration is unlikely.

Malaysia and the Philippines, conversely, do not have the political unity of the two Communist states because of their cultural schisms. In Malaysia, if the Malayan Chinese Association is an element of the multiethnic United Malay National Organization, it has little strength within the Chinese community since the May 13 riots. Muslim Malay, Chinese, and Indian associations provide a social structure for each community which reinforces political self-identity. Each state has a political structure which is internally financed and further factionalizes the political process, although in elections there is still crossover voting. In the Philippines, the Liberal and Nationalist parties are confederations of pressure groups without major differences in program or support. Each is financed by the business community, and patronage serves as the major organizing link for each party throughout the barrios. The bulk of the public is politicized, but few believe the existing political system will resolve the chronic tensions within society. Corruption is a way of life for politicians; the public knows it, and Philippine democracy consequently faces an uncertain future. The narrowly partisan views prevalent among most political leaders prevent further political integration and raise the possibility of continuing disintegration of the system. "The Philippine political system has integrated individuals, not groups, and it has integrated them into the political system by highly personal bargaining mechanisms." [18]

ECONOMIC. Economic integration is thorough in the command systems of the two Communist states. Resources are allocated by the planning ministries in both instances, with defense ministries exercising considerable influence. There is little evidence of lost capital due to tax evasion or smuggling, or even partisan use of foreign exchange by cliques, a common problem in the open societies under consideration.

The Philippines is a pluralist system with most economic activity outside direct government control. The disparate centers of economic power—American corporations, Chinese commercial families, Japanese investors, Philippine landholders and commodity enterprises—all pull in different directions. Frequently legislative activity is immobilized (e.g., the Japanese Trade and Investment Act) by these countervailing economic interests. Although the system experienced rapid growth in the 1950s, over the past decade it has suffered from inflation, declining rates of investment and terms of trade, and exceptionally high tax evasion. Associated with the tax problem is smuggling, which was so severe for many years that upward of half of Philippine trade was being conducted illegally. Clearly these divergent personal interests of the business community have outweighed the national interests and worked against central direction to the economy which might enhance long-range equilibrium.

Malaysia's case is almost the reverse of the Philippines. Careful planning, close cooperation with the business community, and enforceable legislation enabled the economy to flourish until 1969. There were real inducements for outside investors as well as for domestic capital until the civil disturbances began. Still, British, Chinese, Malay, and other foreign capital enjoys protection against nationalization or discriminatory practices which threaten elsewhere in Asia. However, the tension between domestic ethnic communities which once tended to be resolved in the economic sector through careful distribution of amenities and a traditional division of labor continues to rise. The Chinese control most commerce and some mining and plantations; British capital is largely in the plantations and utilities; Indian financing and employment tend to be in plantations and small trade; and the Malays own most of the land in small holdings around their villages. There is conflict when Malays try to push into areas traditionally under Chinese or Indian control, and government assistance has not prevented it from becoming politically significant. Future integration into the national economy of the many village Malays could come rapidly as the need for an industrial labor force increases and as agriculture becomes more commercial, but the heavy threat of renewed communal violence slows development.

MILITARY. Military integration into the two Communist states is far advanced. The Korean and Vietnamese wars tended to unify the populace in both Communist states, and military service is an accepted obligation by their youth. Their large armies, as in Taiwan and South Korea, help to transmit skills to rural youth, politicize them, and establish their national identity.

The situation in Malaysia and the Philippines is quite different. Malays dominate the small (eleven battalions) Malaysian armed force and police, with very few Chinese or Indians willing to serve despite inducements by the government. The tradition of military service which has been established, therefore, tends to exacerbate rather than advance national integration except in bridging the gap between urban and village Malays. In the Philippines, as in Thailand, the army is of moderate size (about 120,000 in 1966) with an air force of several hundred jet fighters. Although patriotism has been a popular value since the guerrilla war days against the Japanese, there is little public support for a larger defense budget. Chronic outbreaks of insurgency (Huks of 1948–50, 1966–69) suggest that the military does not have the entire loyalty of villagers, particularly in central Luzon or in Mindanao. The future integrative capability of the military is therefore small unless remarkable leadership can modify its limited role as a modernizing agent within the society.

Group C: CULTURE. Among the four Group C states, only Cambodia has a single dominating culture. The Khmer constitute about 90% of the population; Vietnamese and Chinese make up most of the remainder. Khmer language and Theravada Buddhist customs are the strongest unifying elements in the country with the traditional relationship between Theravada religious leaders and the aristocracy still a powerful unifying link. Khmer is the official language and the only medium of instruction in the schools, but for a French language program sustained by the French government at the secondary level.

Indonesia, Burma, and Laos share a similar set of cultural problems. One language community and one religion in each country (respectively, the Javanese—Muslim, Burmans—Theravada Buddhist, and Laotians—Theravada Buddhist) dominate the nationalization process and most institutions at the national level. Thus, in each of these countries there are important minority communities which find themselves cut off from influence in politics, religion, the military, the universities, and in the economic process. Generally, these are minority groups whose native districts are removed from the capital, often with less-complex cultures and without a literary tradition. In such instances where the minority's cultural forms (religion, music, literature) are competitive with those of the dominant group, there is sharp friction and often continuing violence. Thus, the Burmans face Karen, Shan, and Kachin insurgencies; the Laotians (who inhabit the Mekong plain) are opposed by hill peoples who are traditional enemies; and the Javanese have generally found the Outer Islanders in opposition to their policies because they believe themselves to be deprived of advantages granted to the Javanese. Difficulties of this nature will continue until such time as the political and economic systems of these three states distribute rewards fairly, or until separate states are established.

POLITICAL. Each of the four states suffers from both communal and ideological insurgencies. Cambodia has the Khmer Serai movement which operates out of Vietnam and Thailand, as well as Sihanouk sponsored insurgency encouraged by Vietnamese and Chinese Communist groups. Burma has the White and Red Flag Communist parties, the former with several thousand insurgent members; the Karen National Defense Organization, a loose confederation of Shan and Burman dissidents led from abroad; and a Kachin Independence Army which developed after the 1962 coup. Laos's integrity is sustained by the neutralization agreement of 1962, but there is a strong Communist Pathet Lao group under Prince Souphanouvong with North Vietnamese dominance. There are also right-wing factions within the aristocracy and military which profit from Thai and American largesse and devote very few resources to national development. The hill tribes, particularly the Meo-Yao groups, are not politically unified but have traditional enmity toward both Vietnamese and Lao. As the Pathet Lao have been the more aggressive in their territory since independence, the hostility of the hill tribes has largely been directed toward these forces of Prince Souphanouvong, which are sustained with Soviet supplies and Vietnamese forces. The past failures of Burma, Cambodia, and Laos to reconcile communal antagonisms suggest continued hostility for years to come. Key leaders will pass from the scene and new organizations will be formed, but the foundation of resentment by minorities will certainly remain anchored in their cultural and provincial antagonisms until the economies are advanced to support widespread development.

The minority political problem in Indonesia has not erupted in communal parties as much as it has taken the form of Javanese dominance in all political organizations. The Communist Party of Indonesia (PKI) was controlled by Javanese, as were the Nationalist (PNI) and Masjumi parties. Leaders from the Outer Islands in military and political life have been accepted, but within the ethos of Javanese elites. The most significant violence, however, has been directed by the Javanese, not only against the Chinese minorities but against one another in the startling massacres of 1965–66. Like the Huk rebellion in the Philippines, the anti-PKI slaughter was largely localized within the dominant ethnic community. Minorities on the Outer Islands tend to be divided from one another by the sea, which helps to account for the lower level of hostility between them and the dominant communities as compared to the mainland Southeast Asia states.

ECONOMIC. Economic integration in Cambodia and Burma has been advanced by the heavy intervention of government into private commerce and manufacturing. Yet, in both instances, the primary impact has been to disrupt the economy, for the experienced foreign entrepreneurs have been removed while less-experienced Khmers and Burmans are being placed in managerial positions. In Burma, the new elite is drawn from the military; in Cambodia, leaders in the Sangkum Reastre Niyum (the mass movement created by Sihanouk) provide most of the new economic managers. In both states, antiforeign sentiment is occasionally fostered by the governments which encourage an exodus of the Chinese (and Indian in the case of Burma) businessmen. Thus, economic integration is resolved by chasing out aliens who have developed the economy. This policy has been expensive in terms of the loss of skills and capital. Neither country is likely to recover sufficiently from this loss to engage in rapid economic development within the span of this study. The monetary economy of Laos is largely confined to the towns and is supported by outside aid. Most Laotians and the hill tribes subsist on locally produced foods and materials, are not active in business, and leave commerce to foreign Vietnamese, Chinese, and Thai.

Indonesia has the most complex economic system of the states under consideration. Sumatra alone exports a greater value in primary products than do any of the sovereign states we have examined. Oil, rubber, and tin are its key commodities, although prospects are good for development of other mineral and food products. Most of Indonesia's foreign exchange comes from these exports; thus, Sumatra pays for much of the economic development elsewhere.

The Chinese have been the traditional middlemen, here as elsewhere in Southeast Asia. Although many are fourth- and fifth-generation residents in Indonesia, the antagonisms based on race are high and have a deleterious effect on economic integration. Most villagers buy from the Chinese in towns, although their function is gradually being filled by local rural migrants.

Management of the Indonesian economy since the military seized power after the 1965 *gestapu* affair has been assigned to professional economists, most of them trained in the West. The IMF and IGGI (Inter-Governmental Group on Indonesia) have provided critical talent which has helped to bring under control the rampant inflation characteristic of the late fifties and early sixties. If the corruption which accompanied inflation can be reduced as well, the prospects are bright for a rapidly improving, integrated economy. Nonetheless, distribution of goods remains a serious problem, and famine may threaten again because of the poor transport situation. This impairs economic integration of the more backward regions of Indonesia, particularly the heavily populated rural areas of eastern Java and the eastern islands.

MILITARY. The armies of all four countries are controlled by men from the dominant ethnic communities. In recent years, Indonesia has consciously recruited from the Outer Islands, but most higher-level officers are drawn from the Javanese community. In Burma, minority community officers tend to be placed in technical or specialized duty, away from command positions which are dominated by Burmans. The small Laotian and Cambodian armies have also reinforced ethnic divisions. In these four states, the past failure of the military to assimilate minorities is a critical weakness which contributes to the lower level of state viability. Rather than being the order-maintaining arm of the state, the military has tended to reinforce the interests of the dominant communities.

Group D: CULTURE. Provincial (regional) subcultures are well-developed in South Vietnam. In addition, strong religious identification among minorities—Catholic and Mahayana Buddhist Chinese and Vietnamese, Theravada Buddhist Khmer, Cao Dai and Hao Hoa sects, and animist hill tribes—accentuate the differences among Vietnamese. Finally, tribal groups, although numbering less than a tenth of the total population, occupy over half the territory and further divide the country. The prospects for integration of this mélange of peoples within the next twenty years into one national culture are exceedingly dim. Whatever government controls the countryside, the multifarious identities of the population in South Vietnam will make the process of governing exceedingly difficult.

Singapore has none of the particularist problems that characterize South Vietnam. The populace is more urban, wealthier, and more highly educated than any other of the thirteen states under consideration. Although over five-sixths of the people are ethnically Chinese, most from Fukein and Kwangtung provinces originally, their culture is a unique mixture of English–Chinese urban institutions (business, education, law, policy, religion, and entertainment). Loyalty to the political system is high; therefore, taxes tend to be paid, laws obeyed, and trust engendered in the youth. Responsiveness by the government to public needs is rapid and resourceful. The modern, integrated culture accounts for most of this behavior.

POLITICAL. Singapore has one major political party, the People's Action Party, and a number of small clique groups—the Barisen Socialists and the Communists being the most vociferous among them. The relationship between the leading party and the government has always been close and exceedingly responsive to the demands of the more powerful pressure groups. Labor and teacher unions, business, and students have been the more important of such groups, and their ties within the society are intimate. Singapore probably has the most integrated political system of any state under consideration.

South Vietnam is at the other end of the spectrum. Political parties have a much longer tradition than in Singapore, the nationalist Viet Nam Quoc Dan Dang (VNQDD) and the Indo-Chinese Communist Party (ICP) being the polar parties of the 1920s and 30s. Party activity reemerged after the Japanese occupation, again with Communist and anti-Communist foci, in the Vietminh and the VNQDD. Yet, throughout, the leadership of the parties has been urban, and the gap has been great between the political attitudes of policy makers and the rank-and-file rural cadre men. French colonial suppression hastened the development of the Vietminh as a rural-based organization, but not the VNQDD. The Cao Dai and Hao Hoa sects function as parties in their provinces, but they have had no appeal in other rural areas or in urbane Saigon. Generally, the Vietminh excepted, South Vietnam's parties have functioned as did Thailand's before the Sarit coup, as cliques of like-minded intellectuals and businessmen pursuing partisan interests, similar to pressure groups. Thus, the prospects for political integration are poor.

ECONOMIC. Little more needs to be said about Singapore's economy. It is well-managed because of cooperation and perceived self-interest of business leaders, the government, and the unions. Communication, following the strikes of the late 1950s, has markedly improved between economic interest groups, and Sinapore's recovery from *konfrontasia* has been rapid. Capacity for growth is excellent, assuming that trade partners remain available.

South Vietnam's economy is so disrupted as to be unpredictable. As suggested in the discussion of its resource base, considerable arable land is available for intensive cultivation, and a vital urban population is available to develop the manufacturing sector. Again, however, Chinese control of most commerce impedes native Vietnamese development of commercial and managerial skills. Finally, as long as the bulk of the population remains distrustful of any government's capacity to pacify the country, further economic integration is unlikely.

MILITARY. The Singapore military establishment is small—six battalions—and the state must always depend upon diplomacy and/or alliances for protection. As an integrative factor, therefore, the military is of no relevance. Since 1954 South Vietnam, on the other hand, has recruited hundreds of thousands of rural youth for military service. No Vietnamese institution has done as much to create national consciousness and work toward an integrated society. Yet even in the army, social divisions persist. Common failings by a conspicuous minority of military leaders, such as distrust of minorities, cultural arrogance by the educated officers toward their village recruits, and personal exploitation of rank to gain financial advantage prevent the institution from consolidating the society. These behavior patterns reflect practices of the larger society, however, and the military will not function as a significant integrator until the basic political conflict is reduced.

Morale as an Element of Power

What people expect of their society and government, compared to the actual distribution of rewards, provides a measure of morale within any state. In most of the states under consideration, the bulk of the populations have traditionally expected little from their government. Indeed, their highest hope has often been to be left alone within their village communities. Colonial governments reinforced this traditional attitude toward monarchical governments by providing few amenities for villagers, but still asking for taxes or corvée, and enforcing laws that tended to serve the interests of central governments.

The gravest problem facing Asian states generally, and certainly this is true for all the states under consideration, has been the establishment of the state itself as a legitimate political institution. Government remains unpopular among villagers, and the idea of order maintenance by police and the army is also unpopular, except where personal ties are established between commanders and local leaders. When military leaders or police have created a political base for themselves in a district or province, they can accomplish a great deal if they have modern ideas and a loyalty to the national enterprise. Conversely, they can threaten the government's control if their interests are anticentrist.

Educators, civil servants, health and agricultural officials, and other technicians also serve as arms of the state in the eyes of most people; yet, because they usually have small budgets, except for their own staffs, and little coercive power, they can offer neither a carrot nor a stick to their public. Their ability to induce social change or improve morale is small unless special funds are provided to give opportunities to village leaders comparable to those of the urban elites.

One can accept as general principles the notions that a majority of the rural people in the countries under consideration will continue to expect very little from their governments; that they will assume officials to be corrupt; and, consequently, that most of the populace will not generally be willing to serve the state. Either coercion or rewards are the levers used to modify these traditional attitudes, except in those rare cases where villagers feel that a clear and present outside danger threatens. Assuming the goal of government to be to serve the people so as to earn their loyalty and thus preserve the state, it follows that considerable social change must be introduced if the governments are to become politically resilient enough to survive the pressures from their more powerful neighbors. Although states can endure a lot of stress, they cannot survive indefinitely in the face of dissident political movements, internal and external, which seek their demise or alteration. Improvement of socioeconomic conditions for the politically potent dissidents within the political system is essential to viability.

Among the Group A states, both South Korea and Taiwan have rewarded potential indigenous opposition groups with economic, educational, and social opportunities. If the practices of the recent past prevail, prospects are bright for higher national morale in the future and widespread acceptance of the state, if not always the government in power. Thailand has not been as effective in distributing advantages to potential oppositions, particularly to inhabitants in the provinces distant from Bangkok, and widespread public support for any Bangkok regime remains unlikely. The political significance of the problem is not yet fully grasped by the military elite, suggesting that considerable effort still must be expended by those aware of the importance of national morale to create a viable political system. Generous loyalty to the monarchy, which is widespread, has tended to be mistaken for high national morale, which it is not, as evidenced by rising insurgency in the destitute regions of the northeast and separatist Muslim minority along the Malaysian border.

Within the Group B states it is difficult to assess the quality of national morale in the closed Communist systems. Probably both governments in North Korea and North Vietnam face little organized indigenous opposition to their systems. The sense of constant danger due to the Chinese, American and Japanese presence will continue to provide a focus for political unity in the foreseeable future. More basically, the cultural integration in both states and the high politicization of the rural population sustains loyalty to the state.

On the other hand the two pluralist states, Malaysia and the Philippines, have opinion polls, social science surveys, and party opposition to clearly state the condition of the public morale. The problems of national consolidation and of gaps in trust between communal groups, between urban and rural constituencies, and between the high-status educated and low-status uneducated have not lessened since independence. Although disintegration of either system is unlikely, in neither country is the national morale likely to improve without significant economic gains. Each system is sufficiently sophisticated to be politically affected by unemployment, inflation, or other economic downturns, a problem more severe than in the Group C states with their more primitive political systems. For the period under study, it is unlikely that either the Philippines or Malaysia will enjoy sufficient economic prosperity or political consolidation to create a condition of high national morale, unless they are seriously threatened by an external power.

Within the Group C states the condition of national morale, because of communal frictions and low levels of development, is unlikely to become a significant power factor. Lack of a sense of nationhood and antagonism toward the central government will normally neutralize the positive efforts of even the more successful administrations to raise consciousness of citizenship among peasants and dissidents. Development of successful economies, combined with serious efforts to distribute the rewards of modernization, may occur in Burma, Indonesia, and Cambodia, and perhaps eventually in Laos, but the two decades we are concerned with are not sufficient time to achieve a "national" morale. Sukarno's frantic effort to create one so as to "crush Malaysia" is a useful case study of the energy that must be expended, politically, before central regimes in these states can expect the populace to sustain them in measures aimed at any foreign involvement.

The problem of low national morale is probably the most critical issue facing South Vietnam. Without political consolidation there is no foundation upon which to build a political system, and, thus, no means but coercion is available to sustain the state internally. No factor more challenges the viability of any Saigon regime than the need for a national morale in the southern zone.

Of all the states, Singapore probably has the highest efficiency in the distribution of economic rewards and political honors to the leaders of interest groups. Undoubtedly, its tiny size and intensively urban nature contribute to this capacity; nevertheless, it enables the system to produce leaders who act effectively in the international arena with the support of the domestic population. Although utterly atypical, Singapore fully demonstrates the positive contribution that national morale makes to overall international influence or power.

Perceived Relative Capability

We have no measurement of the perception of capability held in the minds of peoples or elites within Southeast Asia, Taiwan, and the Koreas; yet this factor has affected, and will continue to affect, the viability of many states. The phenomenon is unusually volatile because of its impact upon leaders' personalities. Those states that are clearly weak relative to neighbors with whom they share boundaries (notably Laos, Malaysia, Singapore, Cambodia, and Burma) have all pursued very discrete foreign policies seeking either to reassure neighbors that are potential enemies or to balance the weight of their perceived enemies' alliances with their own alliances. These policies have been cautiously constructed, except by Cambodia which is understandably xenophobic, given its traditional neighbors, Thailand and both Vietnams, and its embryonic international political system dominated by a single figure until recently. In the unstable states, as leaders change, the capacity of each to operate abroad will be especially affected by the abilities of the key leaders.

The geographic position of states contributes a great deal to the leader's perception of relative power and the impact of this view upon the actual policies of the state. Thus, both South and North Korea operate externally with a constant eye on Japan, China, and the Soviet Union, their traditional enemies and occasional allies. Taiwan views China and Japan with the same concern, and both Vietnams must gauge every foreign relationship in terms of its impact upon China. The archipelago states, Indonesia and the Philippines, are sufficiently removed from any major power to conduct foreign policy with considerable freedom of action, if they choose. The Philippines has had a habit of accepting American preponderance in power issues, but that tradition is likely to erode significantly within the period considered. By the mid-1980s both states, assuming Indonesia still exists in its present form, are quite likely to be most concerned with one another and with Japan thanks to their propinquity and to their potentially conflicting and mutual interests as they develop and seek closer ties with Japan.

The confidence of leaders in their own system is another dimension in the perception of relative power. Generally those premiers or military autarks, with a consolidated nation or with self-assurance that they speak for the peasantry, operate vigorously in the international scene, whereas those with a partisan base tend to act abroad with considerable caution. In the first category we find Sukarno, U Nu, Sihanouk, Park, Lee Kwan Yew, and Chiang Kai-shek; and in the latter, Ne Win, Macapagal, Marcos, Rahman, Kim Il-song, and Diem. Although personality plays a role in each case, the domestic political structure appears to have been even more important.

SUMMARY EVALUATIONS OF EACH STATE'S VIABILITY AND INHIBITORS TO DEVELOPMENT

South Korea

None of the states under consideration has as long a history of cultural consolidation as does Korea with its 500 years of Yi dynastic control. After a half-century of occupation and 200 years of earlier isolated stagnation, the Korean society has at last found itself prepared to develop anew. The Japanese occupation policies and the terrible shock of the 1950–53 war probably account for much of this attitudinal change. After a decade of political consolidation the new elite of civilian and military leaders, skilled in the uses of modern technology, has secured authoritative influence over both public and private sectors. Of the eleven elements of power we have analyzed, South Korea rates near the top in all the critical areas. Particularly important is the high level of integration, the rapidly expanding human resource base, and the high capability of the society compared to its major enemy, North Korea. Assuming a continued amity in its relations with the United States and Japan, South Korea will face no unmanageable threat from its traditional great power neighbors, China and Russia. The most severe inhibitors to higher levels of viability is the unstable political system which remains dominated by one interest group, the military, and has not yet evolved into a more sophisticated process that allows for peaceful succession. Riots, mass demonstrations, and some terror still accompany elections. Compared to most Asian states, however, South Korea is well along in political as well as economic development.

Taiwan

The rapid integration of Taiwan's economy over the past decade and the capacity of its manufacturing sector to produce goods in high demand provide the country with excellent prospects for continued economic growth. The capacity of the educational system too is unexcelled among the thirteen states considered, Singapore excepted, and the recently developed pattern of intensive communication hastens the cultural consolidation of diverse groups migrating from the mainland. The army, through conscription, has also advanced the elemental assimilation initiated by the schools so that overall integration, although not as advanced as in Korea, is well along. Forces for both politicization and socialization are strong and affect all but the aboriginal minority in the mountains. A major inhibitor to development is the alienation of well-educated youth from the government and the goals of the refugee generation. The migration of young people to the United States has relieved the pressure for political reform and detracts from the human resource base which will be essential for movement into the higher levels of modernity. Resolution of the conflicts between Chiang Kai-shek's oligarchy and the opposition groups among Formosans as well as former KMT members is a critical problem. Undoubtedly, the fundamental inhibitor to Taiwan's viability is its dependence upon China and the United States for its sovereignty. Japan will play an increasingly significant role in Taiwan's future, particularly during the last of the two decades under consideration. These dependencies are likely to prevent any Taiwan government from playing a significant international role, no matter how rapidly it develops.

Thailand

The relationship among three power elements accounts for Thailand's relatively high rating among these thirteen states, that is the relationship of its size to productivity and material bases. In all other respects Thailand will continue to have difficulty in sustaining viability. Although more culturally homogeneous than most of the Southeast Asian states, it has barriers to further political and social development caused by the distrust of subcultures in different sections of the country, but particularly the northeast. It is probably correct to say that Thailand has a national morale, but it is not rising and political integration is not far advanced from the premodern period. Nevertheless, compared to all of its immediate neighbors, Thailand is a strong state, and this relative position of power is well-understood by its elite. Therefore, despite the many problems that face the country over the next two decades, it will probably remain the most viable of the Southeast Asian states.

Malaysia

The resource base and the condition of morale are very positive power elements in Malaysia. Were it not for the communal cleavage, the country would continue to develop more rapidly than Thailand and may even continue to do so despite the disadvantage of a small population and low levels of cultural, political, and military integration. Malaysia's weakness, the Chinese–Malay communal division, is also the source of its greatest strength, its economic development, for most of the savings and pressure for modernization come from the Chinese. Malaysia has little capacity to defend itself and little inclination within an economically secure elite to become the site of a war; therefore, it is likely to be a major force for regionalism and the peaceful resolution of conflicts. Past policies aimed toward this end have structural reasons behind them and, thus, will continue to be basic to foreign policy. Malaysia's capability in diplomacy is a compensating factor for its military weakness. Consequently, although one of the lesser states, Malaysia may retain its past vitality and, irrespective of economic vicissitudes caused by its rubber exports, may be a continuing stabilizing presence throughout the period under consideration.

The Philippines

The ecology of the Philippines, its island topography, its tropical climate, and its resulting complex of peoples and languages cause it to have the difficulties of Indonesia in integration, in resource development, and in morale. Perhaps the most significant advantage has been the policies of the American colonialists which, like those of Japan in Taiwan and Korea, provided a modern base of entrepreneurship, transport, education, and bureaucracy, making the Philippines more modern than most other Asian states. The system of government encourages pluralism and has enabled the society to adapt to modernity at a relatively rapid pace.

The time since independence has not been sufficient to bridge the gaps in culture that still prevent the Philippines from being a unified nation, but its vital and critical intellectual community, its press, cinema, literature, and television combine to create a capacity for integration missing in its giant neighbor, Indonesia, which shares so many of its problems. This same core of creative and professional people provide the country with a richer administrative capability, both in domestic and foreign affairs, than is available in all but the Group A states.

A key inhibitor to viability is the much larger group of alienated, ill-trained and poorly motivated "educated" high school and college graduates who are more a barrier to development than a contribution in terms of human resources. A second critical factor is the alienation of the many minorities from the Tagalog-dominated Manila regime. The political system, which has made a ritual of elections and logrolling in the legislature with far greater burdens placed upon parties for the financing of campaigns than they can bear, is certainly the most democratic of all the states under consideration, but its emphasis on the rites of democracy rather than on the development of the populace seriously undermines its political system. The social distance between the masses of peasants and white-collar workers on the one hand and the affluent businessmen and politicians on the other has widened year by year, a trend which further dissolves the earlier faith in the political system. National morale in the Philippines, as in Thailand where the same problem exists, deteriorates as a consequence and encourages insurgent movements. Consequently, although the Philippines has many of the attributes of a viable state, these key inhibitors may well prevent its power from being appropriate to its population size, which is second only to Indonesia within our grouping.

North Korea

This Communist government enjoys most of the advantages that South Korea inherited in terms of an integrated culture, a politicized society, and a significant core of managers and technicians—some trained by the Japanese, others returnees from Russia and China. It had a further advantage of industrialization and political organization denied to the South in its first years. Its population size and economic performance have been similar to Taiwan's, but most recent trends suggest that North Korea may be reaching a stage of development that demands a more competitive economy and open political process if the rate of development is to continue. The earlier advantage of a command economy and monistic political system will probably become an inhibitor to normal growth as the society and economy become more complex and the educated demand less constrained behavior than a directed political and economic system can permit. As demonstrated in other Communist states, this liberalizing transition is a time-consuming process, and several decades may pass before the North Koreans will be free to take full advantage of the human and material resources currently being developed.

North Vietnam

Although subject to devastation because of the war, no other Southeast Asian state but Singapore has as integrated a political system as North Vietnam. Because the system has a Communist ideology with powerful nationalist connotations in terms of its leadership and practices, it is highly revolutionary and therefore capable of changing traditional social and economic behavior patterns within a short period. Most of the elements of power cannot be rated highly; yet the profound importance of an integrated domestic political system is clearly illustrated in this case. The capacity of the system to maintain a high national morale throughout the period being considered has already been demonstrated. The data suggest that North Vietnam will have difficulty developing as rapidly as the other Group B states because of shortages of skilled workers, low agricultural productivity, poor transportation and communication, and resentments of tribal minorities; yet all these inhibitors are not likely to prevent the single factor of high political motivation from being the most influential power element. As in the case of the Koreas and Taiwan, North Vietnam continues to risk being a pawn of the great powers, either as a field of battle or as an isolated state prevented from developing normally. This risk is low, however, as demonstrated by the aforementioned cases.

Indonesia

No Southeast Asian state has experienced such major changes in its political system as has Indonesia since independence. This phenomenon is a function of the elemental cultural diversity that will be a determinant in its politics for decades to come. It is a critical inhibitor to any long-range planning. The material and human resources are sufficient to accommodate Indonesia's deserved position as a major world power, but the barriers to integration—cultural, political, economic, and military—are not likely to be broken by rational planning in Jakarta. In none of the other thirteen states is the need so great for national organizations which function equitably throughout the politically critical population centers. Transportation is gravely underdeveloped and unlikely to improve rapidly because of the terrain, which is a second contributing inhibitor to viability. Education ministers, as in the other large Asian states where a majority are functionally illiterate and the central governments are so distant, are simply unable to field a sufficiently large bureaucracy to cope with the problem. The problem of secondary and primary education may well be insoluble until smaller intermediary centers finance and construct their own systems. The quality of central leadership is exceedingly important to Indonesia's future, where national social and economic functions are so critically underdeveloped. The range of achievement is most dependent upon *fortuna* and political genius. The material resources and the economic potential have existed since independence, as have the inhibitors, and the state has yet to prove itself viable.

Burma

Burma shares with Indonesia and the Philippines the inhibitor of diverse cultural communities with little loyalty to the central government. Time has not reduced the problem, and the insurgencies that commenced at independence continue two decades later. No political leader or central organization has bridged the barriers to trust. A second challenge to the state comes from the political system itself. As in Thailand, Indonesia, and the Philippines, a legislature and elections have been tried as a method of resolving the succession crisis and, as in all but the latter, this democratic method has failed. Coercion and the efficient use of violence, except in Indonesia where violence was terribly inefficient, have been critical to the survival of the state. Like Indonesia, Burma has considerable potential power in its agrarian sector and in its energy available for industrial production, but the prospects for efficient exploitation of these sectors are dim because of chronic political problems. Efforts by the government to use foreign-born residents as scapegoats for the lack of progress and to create an indigenous socialist ideology that will motivate the populace to work for the state have only been moderately effective. The challenge to Burma's viability is severe; yet its value as a buffer state between India and China will contribute to its survival.

Cambodia

The development indicators deflate the general optimism that many held about Cambodia's future in the 1950s. Neither the economy nor the political system has sustained the early high rate of growth and expansion of political participation. Dominance by Sihanouk throughout this period prevented internal violence through coups or competitive elections, but it also caused the political process to atrophy. Key interest groups—the military, the civil service, the mass movement party, the landholders, and the business community—necessarily had been circumspect as the premier readily resorted to coercion when brooked by opposition. Elimination of American aid in 1963 and curtailment of Chinese support further delayed economic expansion, albeit buying time for continued stability. Recent warfare and renewed U.S. assistance have only divided the country. The shortage of manpower will become increasingly critical, exacerbating the problems already evident in rural development. Finally, insurgency support from China and North Vietnam is sufficiently debilitating to almost guarantee chronic political instability as long as the Vietnamese minority is present in Cambodia.

Laos

The need for a buffer state on the China and Vietnamese border is Laos's strongest claim to viability. Such an international status will continue to earn foreign aid from the superpowers. Internally, for many decades there is not likely to be a political process that adequately encompasses the hill tribes so as to earn their loyalty and thereby create political viability. New transportation is critical if the Lao themselves are to be integrated from their village communities. Those states involved on Laos's borders—Burma, China, Thailand, Cambodia, and Vietnam—must anticipate decades of concern for their border provinces because of the weakness of the Laotian central government.

Singapore

As a free trading port and manufacturing center, Singapore can survive indefinitely if the commercial patterns of Southeast Asia generally are not disrupted. Its internal political process is sophisticated, and its economy is more in equilibrium than any other state of the region. Its utter defenselessness is a strength if used wisely in diplomacy, as Singapore is a threat to none of its neighbors. Like Switzerland, it can apparently operate as a genuine neutral to the advantage of all. Yet, in the event of a major shift of power in Southeast Asia, either a heavy American, Soviet, Japanese, or Chinese presence with permanent bases, its status would change and its viability would be seriously affected. The prospects of reunification or war with Malaysia, or of dissolution of Indonesia, are destabilizing possibilities in the future. Either step *might* advance Singapore's economy, but probably would deter its rate of growth.

South Vietnam

Most unpredictable of all these states, South Vietnam's viability depends upon two unquantifiable variables—internal political trends in the United States and in South Vietnam. Both politically and economically the state has suffered gravely from the war, more so than the North, and although agricultural potential is greater than in the North, the industrial and political development prospects are questionable. Whatever the outcome of the war, it will take a full decade for the country to recover the impetus commenced in the mid-fifties in terms of economic growth. Political integration will be a very difficult problem for any government controlling Saigon.

Summation of these already abbreviated evaluations would not be fruitful; however, the reader who has come this far only to be exasperated by judgments with which he disagrees should take heart. Subjective sentiment influences my analysis as surely as sharks swim in the South China sea; thus, I recognize that the foregoing conclusions are not scientific despite the initial effort to aggregate data and utilize objective analysis. In this chapter, I crossed over into an artistic venture whereby portrayal of general conditions is largely an exercise in judgment and imagination; others with expert knowledge may well disagree, with ample justification, in specific cases. Nonetheless, the future changes envisaged are based upon each state's environment, a situation inherited and not culpable, and now described before moving on to the concluding prescriptions.

chapter three

The Incomplete State

The foregoing chapter has analyzed the elements of viability with the purpose of evaluating the relative strengths and weaknesses of the ten states in Southeast Asia and three comparable East Asian countries. Now our concern is to examine the condition of Asian states, with emphasis on Southeast Asia, in terms of their institutional heritage. The first issue of preeminent import is the vocabulary we use to discuss politics. Consider, for example, the notion of citizen, or political participant.

In Southeast Asia most people live in villages, and we observe that villagers do not act like their urban brethren. Villagers do not conceive of themselves as political men, as citizens. Rather than Malaysians, Burmese, Vietnamese, or Indonesians, their primary self-image is usually formed by the environment, language, and institutions of their locale. Such minorities as the Meo, Karens, Atchenese, Naga, or Bugis have little identification with their respective states; and the villagers among major ethnic groups—the Javanese, Burmans, Thai, Vietnamese, or Khmer—are only remotely related to the authority of the state. When discussing Asian politics, therefore, because of this communal characteristic, such richly meaningful terms as popular representation or public interest must be used with caution.

Westerners and modern Asians often assume that the philosophic bases for the state are readily transferred into Asian cultures, that if the state exists as a legal and geographic entity, then somehow these other concepts will penetrate the thought processes and philosophies of the people cohabiting within the state. The assumption is unwarranted. What we observe about change in Southeast Asia, it seems,

(Notes for this chapter begin on p. 202.)

is not often what we call it, and the difficulty rests not alone with our vocabulary but also with the questions we raise. They have become so specialized that we miss the relevance of historical experience in collecting current data.

A synoptic approach to political change accentuates the importance of institutions alien to traditional Asia, which apparently were vital to rapid change in modern Japan and the West. This interpretation is not meant as a denigration of classic cultures but as an analytic tool for getting at the problem of impotence which characterizes most states in contemporary Asia. Although colonial powers introduced the state as a contractual concept as well as a political institution, they left in their wake, after World War II, governments unable to direct change in the fashion new leaders desired. Western administrators from the colonial era did not endow their Asian wards with sufficient capacity to carry out self-imposed constitutional obligations.

In addition to the administration dilemma posed by rising human expectations and needs, the agrarian states of Asia commenced with nearly inoperable political systems because of the very disparate communities. People hostile by tradition were thrown together within superimposed boundaries which were often meaningless to villagers. Policies of the Americans, British, Dutch, and French colonial powers differed in their emphasis, but none took serious action to alleviate the destructive tensions which the diverse communities would bring to bear upon the new sovereign governments. Indeed, the colonialists generally accentuated the problem of communalism during their rule by isolating hill peoples from the lowlanders through separate administrations.

The problem we find in Southeast Asia is not unique. For example, in China, where colonial influence was considerable but never commanding, an early effort to mobilize the population created a different situation. The long civil war, coupled with the Japanese invasion, threw hundreds of millions of cultivators into a common political experience. Ancient language and territorial barriers were temporarily bridged as warfare drew the Chinese together. Communist cadre exploitation of this opportunity to revolutionize traditional communities succeeded for a time, at least, and perhaps permanently, in creating widespread awareness of the need for central power in the face of incursions from a more modern West, Soviet Union, and

Japan. Still, China is a land predominantly peopled by illiterate villagers who possess an inadequate technology and who witness continuing struggle to establish control over their environment. A few million at the most, more probably a few hundred thousand leaders, exercise what power the political system possesses. The countervailing pressures by military, party, and bureaucratic factions within that system retard effective planning or implementation. Finally, China faces the same formidable barriers to systemic political change as do the agrarian Southeast Asian states: population pressures, illiteracy, low energy resources, discontinuous communication and transportation systems, and resurgent parochial loyalties.

The Chinese case illustrates how the state, to succeed, needs to command a measure of loyalty from its inhabitants, from villagers and townsmen alike. Since World War II loyalty has been sought throughout Asia by leaders espousing egalitarianism, yet traditional inequities are breeding communal and ideological violence. The lack of trust in the state as the authoritative institution, the recurrent violence and political instability, the absence of what Hobbes defined as love for civility, for the law of the commonwealth, account for much of the slow rural change and the squalor in most cities. The essential problem is that most villagers distrust the state as a source of change; yet they lack the training or incentive to use the manifold forms of new technology that will permit them to modernize. But for a very few of the smaller states, our indicators point to a bleak foreseeable future.

THE ESSENTIAL CAUSE [1]

Southeast Asian cultures are magnificently endowed with institutions; yet few of the strong institutions in which villagers believe are related to the state. Most are provincial in character, such as the spirit cults, subcaste divisions, religious leadership, cultivation practices, and a host of other important local institutions. Seriously lacking are institutionalized methods of organizing politics, education, taxation, law enforcement, and an equitable justice under the aegis of the state. Despite the state's ancient heritage in the West, Southeast Asian governments lack the authority to command reorganization of the lives of some 250 million people upon the basis of the state. That authority is seriously contested, despite a century of effort by colonial administrators to engender respect for the law and justice derived from statehood.

The burden of our interpretation does not rest upon the truth of Marxist theory that capitalist colonial powers did not encourage justice but sought profits, and thereby created a basic contradiction by promoting economic growth while opposing social change. Nor does our interpretation of the essential cause for weak states rest upon the popular Asian view that the colonial administrators' cultural and racial prejudice prevented them from preparing natives for self-government. Both truths characterize early and even nineteenth-century colonialism, but in their last decades of sovereign rule, another truth appeared in colonial practices. That was the motive stimulated by belief in progress. Progress, as development was then called, was not seen as a process towards some other goal; it was itself the goal.

Colonial administrators had no *theory* of development. Their assumption was that progress itself would serve the noble end of uplifting their wards. It helped to legitimize their rule in the eyes of Americans, Europeans, and even Japanese late in the game. Although some still fail to make the distinction, it would seem clear to most thoughtful leaders and observers today that development is not an ultimate value, but a process of planned change through new forms of economy and education, which interact with rising income and status. We can theorize about development because it is a means to gain the higher goal that motivates Asian leaders as well as most statesmen to increase their country's power in order to protect their way of life and secure dignity for their people. The colonial administrators, who often interpreted progress to mean simply economic change, erred by ignoring the necessity of interweaving the new economic systems within the fabric of indigenous culture and local politics.

The state emerged apart from the local community structure and village people. Although some administrators learned local languages and studied Islam, Buddhism, and the pervasive animistic cults the better to understand indigenous cultures, such efforts did not lead to the happy marriage of local cultures with the state. Indeed, those who actually did marry local women and thereby bound themselves to the native culture were ostracized from the higher levels of colonial service. How weighty even now is the damning judgment of a Westerner who has taken too much to Asia and "gone native." Consequently, there were only weak connections between village folk, or most Asians, and the colonial regimes. The political architecture Europeans and Americans created was poorly designed to serve the cause of statehood. Once independent, the governments, in fact, were nearly as alien to villagers as were the colonial regimes.

Poorly designed political architecture is a fundamental barrier to development, yet little can be done by foreign powers or even indigenous bureaucrats to resolve the problem. The blending of this Western institution, the state, into indigenous cultures may never transpire, or if it does it will certainly function differently from its Western counterpart. Consider that indigenous political institutions—councils of elders, headmen, monarchs, and aristocracy—are directly linked to precolonial social organization. The differences between Europe and Asia in the fourteenth and fifteenth centuries, despite the European heritage of Roman law, were not so great politically, for the nation state was not yet conceived. Most people lived in village communities remote from the king's justice. The contemporary differences in social organization are enormous. The Asian counterpart to Europe's three centuries of rationalism and concomitant growth of political power through the union of industrialization and the nation–state was colonialism.

Whereas the beliefs and institutions of Western man were profoundly changed by the enlightenment—he became modern—most Asians retained their premodern isolation under colonial rule. With few exceptions colonialism, compounding the problem, swept from influence the monarch and the creative spokesmen for high standards in local culture. Villagers fell back on the normative sanction of their community institutions, or followed chiliastic reformers like Burma's Saya San or Java's Surontiko Samin. In music, religious writing, language, architecture, drama—the range of expression that binds the civilization of societies to local communities—standards generally deteriorated. Although primarily responsible, colonialism was not the only cause of the erosion in cultural standards among Asian polities. Political violence was endemic in Southeast Asia because common standards of authority could not be imposed or accepted. The terrain, the climate, and the state of technology discouraged the consolidation of cultures and power that characterized Europe during its modernization.

Because of this hiatus, during colonial domination, in the growth of indigenous civilization, some commentators on Southeast Asian history envisage a period of cultural consolidation, a return to the riverbed of precolonial authority during the next few decades. That authority was based on normative principles which legitimized rulers, not states. The position of the stars at the time of a monarch's birth, the prophecies of astrologers, the importance of regalia, the tribute of neighboring rulers to acknowledge his status: these institutions related to the moral suasion of the ruler, to his capacity to enforce standards of performance and conduct. They legitimized *his* power and position, not that of the state. The right of the state and a civil code to be distinct from the relationship between a monarch or emperor and the cosmological system of sanction was not considered in precolonial Asia.[2] An anthropomorphic concept of authority prevailed in that the person of the monarch was conceived as the source of power. His personal relationship with cosmic forces would determine the ultimate course of events. The notion that the state and the law should be institutions separate from and beyond the ruler, questions raised by Marsilius of Padua and later by Jean Bodin, and now a common assumption in the West, was not even considered a political question by Asian philosophers.

Speaking generally, in Southeast Asia a political dialogue was missing, perhaps because no body of men were educated outside the court or the religious bureaucracies; nearly all people retained their identity with the village. In medieval Europe, urban populations spawned secular universities in Paris, Geneva, Bologna, London, and Padua, and students studied jurisprudence as well as science. From these scholars came jurist philosophers and civil lawyers who propagated the secular norms for statehood so familiar to Westerners today. Not only church and state but ruler and state as well were separated by intellectuals and the monarchs and aristocrats whom they influenced. These were utopian thoughts by writers striking out against the authority of clerics, but they were more than the rantings of isolated heretics for they gave secular legitimacy to the state. Their counsel was sought by men of means. The rise of mercantile city–states, with organized guilds, banks, and commerce created rulers who demanded new forms of normative rebuttals to the traditional demands of Rome and its civil representatives for taxes and levies. It was a profound political and economic necessity that caused them to seek a new kind of legitimacy. The civil codes which made order possible within the secular states were created by jurists hostile to a world dominated by religion. They leaped back to pre-Christian Roman jurisprudence for the law's form and integrated the customs drawn from local communities for the law's content. And so the state and its secular base of legitimacy evolved, first in the debates at universities, then within the autonomous cities, and finally stretching out to encompass language and ethnic communities.

The development of the nation–state, commencing in Machiavelli's time, permitted a concurrent growth of political thought that attempted to explain man's relation to ultimate authority in terms of positive as well as natural law. Community customs and political culture were fused by the nineteenth century, enabling European states to acquire ascendant power in the world. Never before could such masses of men be mobilized for secular political purposes. This process created the colonial era which crested in Asia early in the twentieth century. In Europe, America, and Japan, "the nation" had become coterminous with "the state" and generally within single-language communities. Where there were well-defined ethnic or language minorities within the state, politics was usually a strained affair. Paradoxically, the very Western powers that were experiencing this process of fusion throughout the nation, between village community and state, set about creating multiethnic and linguistically heterogeneous colonies with little heed to the problem they were creating.

The political significance of this vast political difference between Asia and the West often escapes those who speak of the "nation-building" and development process. There is no precolonial basis for secular legitimacy. There is no traditional concept of the state as a territory with demarcated boundaries. There is no precolonial institution that functioned like the metropolitan universities, creating the jurists and the itinerant judges who integrated diverse customs into a common legal system. Nor, of course, is there precedent for councils of legislators trained in the law. There are, to be sure, old metropolitan centers, as in Malacca, Pegu, and Manila; in many of the medieval kingdoms sophisticated literary and mathematical education flourished. But the purpose of knowledge was not to create procedures for a normative standard, intertwined with political architecture. Insofar as students studied man, they sought to understand him, not to mobilize him through political institutions. Scholars memorized, in

Southeast Asia, Sanskrit, Pali, or Arabic texts of the Hindu, Buddhist, or Islamic scriptures, and their worldly derivatives, the dhammathats, rajianitis, and lokanitis derived from the Manu code; or, in Indochina and other Sinic-influenced lands, they studied and memorized the Confucian-derived code in order to attain the understanding of established norms, not to create new codes of behavior.

In Southeast Asia no countervailing method of legitimacy was devised, apart from that relating to the monarch. For most people, social conflict was resolved within the village; thus, the normative codes, like the Le or Gia Long codes in Vietnam, the Koran in Indonesia, the Manu Kye in Burma, or the Dharmashastras in ancient Mon kingdoms, were not properly legal systems, but served more as admonishments. The codes were ethical, not juridical, for their purpose was to provide rulers and mendicants with authority for their judgments. There was no institution of secular law apart from the ruler's representative. In Indonesia, Malaya, and the Philippines we have no record of even this kind of normative thought, outside the writings of the syncretic Moslem aristocrats, the *prijayi,* originating in Java and Sumatra. No bureaucracies existed to carry out the policies of courts except in the Chinese empire. That China did have a secure bureaucratic tradition when the Western colonialists appeared helps account for her resistance and early innovation of a Western party system of governance.

Heine-Geldren properly characterized the conception of kingship in Southeast Asia as being cosmological, with the polity being a microcosmos dependent for harmony upon extraterrestrial powers. Because harmony within the community was commonly believed to derive from forces outside man's control (as in ancient Greece), there was no conception of the bureaucratic function that derives from the opposite assumption that order is man-made. Villagers paid taxes not to anonymous functionaries to satisfy the law, but gave gifts to the king's local governor (as they would propitiate the spirits) to keep a stronger power from interfering and disrupting harmony in the local community. And finally, that most critical task of government, the raising of armies and police to keep a monopoly of violence, was carried out on the basis of a king's righteousness. Villagers obeyed the monarch, or refused his request for men to fight or labor, depending upon their perception of his righteousness.

Philosophic assumptions were not the only factor that caused

Southeast Asian politics to be so unlike the state system that evolved in the West. Probably the region's debilitating environment and its many geographic divisions inhibited evolution of larger political units such as did evolve in the broad plains of China. The environment caused more primitive people to adapt their family structures to fit in the tiny villages among mountains and hills on the mainland and in the Sunda archipelago where shifting agriculture sustained tribal civilization. Larger polities developed along riverine plains and by the sea where rice agriculture and fishing produced more wealth. The wealth, in turn, supported the elaborate cosmological polities just described, polities that were inherently unstable owing to the style of personal governance and the continuing warfare between rulers.

To summarize, Southeast Asia lacked key institutions which developed within the state system as we know it. Legal codes, secular organizations in metropolitan centers, bureaucracies and universities, and professional military and local police were absent and unnecessary to leaders and intellectuals when the Europeans appeared on the scene. States could not have existed for neither the concepts nor the institutions affecting political life were suited to such a political system. The human resources to administer a secular, noncommunal society were absent. The village communities and monarchic empires in Southeast Asia had developed their own cultures on similar political assumptions for hundreds of years and were as certain as were the Europeans that their way of life was superior to any other. Clearly, the European powers faced a great challenge when they set about creating states in the region.

The political dilemma that eventually faced the colonial powers arose only when they elected to assume administrative responsibility for a people. During the early centuries the problem never arose, for Westerners were not motivated to establish strategic outposts to protect investments. But commencing with English–French wars in the mid-eighteenth century, the sense of possession seized the minds of politicians and bankers alike. The consequence, of course, was the obligation to establish order and eventually to administer the affairs of the East Indies and most of mainland Southeast Asia. The treaty port system in China offered another solution, but in the end extraterritoriality proved no more acceptable than outright governance for nationalists. The problem of rule for the French in Indochina, the British in Burma and Malaysia, the Dutch in the East Indies, and the Americans in the Philippines was approached with different policies, but no solutions were adequate. To illustrate the nature of the problem, consider three of the colonies—Burma, Malaya, and the Philippines—in terms of the institutional architecture devised by their governors. With the benefit of hindsight, and with a lesson to be learned, the critical want of a political foundation for the state clearly emerges.

The Philippines

The Philippine case is most familiar to Americans. The need for human resources was recognized by the Spanish in the final years of their rule under the influence of liberal thought then sweeping through Europe. General education was the first step. By 1880 the Spanish had established over 1,600 boys' and girls' primary schools with 175,000 students enrolled. Later, the Americans emphasized education for democracy and leadership as well with primary, intermediate, and secondary systems, and the University of the Philippines, created by 1908. By 1940 nearly 4,000 students were in the several universities, 90,000 in secondary schools, and nearly 2 million at the primary level.

Unfortunately, the kind of education introduced was not suited to the economic system. The urban American standard of living was the model for the educated in a rural society where most people lived at a subsistence level. The great education effort created Philippine white-collar workers seeking jobs from the government, the foreign-owned businesses, or a career in politics, rather than creating indigenous entrepreneurs who could compete with American managers in the sugar and pineapple plantations or in mining, the large Chinese family groups dealing in rice and foreign trade, or the Japanese businessmen in shipping, textiles, and light industry. Almost no Philippine executive talent was available at independence. The education system failed to produce managers and entrepreneurs; it merely reinforced the traditional status function of education familiar throughout Spanish colonies.

What of the legal system? Ralston Hayden, one of the more eminent and judicious governors, noted in 1943 that there had been a unique development of common and civil law, the former with strong roots in the precolonial period when Malay culture was dominant, the latter under Spanish juridical influence. Several powerful American jurists served out their careers in the Philippines and through their thousands of opinions established precedents for a modern legal system. Law as a career or as a preparation for politics came to be highly valued throughout the Islands. But the law as an ethic to live by was not so popular. Flagrant violation of the civil and criminal codes remained commonplace among the educated and wealthy through tax evasion, pressure on officials to prevent land surveys of their vast, tenant-operated holdings, and through widespread smuggling.

The attitude toward law was closely related to the kind of political process that developed. Americans took pride in the political system and self-government. The first political party appeared within a year of the American occupation and the first national elections were held in 1907. But politics ran aground of the economic arrangements whereby a few families in each province, through their wealth, controlled the nomination of candidates for the municipal elections and the province representatives. The first National Assembly, a single-house legislature, set the style for elite government and although the Jones Act of 1916 changed the system to two houses with a view to broadening the base of representation, the socioeconomic structure prevented any fundamental change in the working of Philippine democracy. Two leaders, Sergio Osmena and Manuel Quezon, dominated the party process throughout the colonial period, each representing factions of the elite Nacionalista party. Opposition parties formed—the most successful being the Democrata in the 1920s, but it was dissolved in 1933 and the trend toward radical opposition began in the tenant farming areas of central Luzon. The rural-based Sakdalista party, forerunner to the Hukbalahap revolutionary movement, galvanized the farmers' frustrations.

Commonwealth status in 1935 and the promise of independence within ten years answered the demands of the established Nacionalistas but did not respond to the challenge of the large unrepresented rural population who, through mass education, were becoming politically aware. The political parties institutionalized a style of politics that preserved an oligarchical government in the face of a rapidly changing society. The Japanese invasion temporarily obscured the challenge of the radical opposition, but endemic distrust for the urban party politician by the small farmer led to civil violence shortly after the war. Cynicism born out of that distrust remains the Philippine's gravest political problem.

Professional police and military institutions were also initiated in the Philippines earlier than in the rest of Asia. The Spanish established an artillery school in the eighteenth century and the ill-fated Aguinaldo government created a military academy in 1898. But these early efforts collapsed and no significant Philippine military force appeared until the Americans created constabulary and scout units in the 1920s. By 1935 the constabulary force was sufficiently professional to handle a mass training program as well as normal internal security. General MacArthur predicted that the Philippines could field a million men by 1946 and therefore was capable of meeting any military threat. Yet, there appeared the same tragic flaw as in civil education and business. Filipinos had no experience in the planning and management of their own forces.

Finally, what of the impact of colonial policy upon the cities? Only four urban centers could be considered as cities in the sense of providing urban services and central commercial organizations for themselves and the satellite villages, those being Manila, Baguio, Cebu, and Iloilo. Davao, for example, listed a population in excess of 130,000 in 1952, but less than 50,000 lived in the town—the remainder being villagers in nearby barrios and family hamlets. Like most other Asian states, the capital has a huge population and dominates politics as well as life styles, deepening the division between government and villagers.

Burma

British policy in Burma was founded on different premises than was American colonial policy which emphasized democracy and self-rule as quickly as possible. The British faced a more thoroughly integrated traditional polity, for Burmans, who constituted three-fourths of the population, and Shans identified the monarchy as theirs. The Burmans had vivid memories of their king, their aristocracy, and their style of rule, as did the minority communities who had suffered repeated conquest from Burman regimes.

The minorities welcomed British intervention against the Burmans and their elites supported British efforts to preserve their cultural and political autonomy. Thus, ruling Arakanese families viewed Western education as an opportunity to maintain their high status and were the first "Burmese" to gain admission to the law courts. Other minorities joined the standing military; the Chins, Kachins, and Karens fought for the British against the Burmans and also served in Europe during World War I as the "Burma Rifles." After destroying the central political institutions, the British faced Burman communal insurgency and used Indians or minority troops to police the Burmans.

Law enforcement was equally troublesome, the effect of commercial agriculture and direct rule upon social organization. Crime rose dramatically—the homicide rate, for example, became the world's highest. Substantial effort finally was made in the 1920s to bring educated Burmans into the court and police systems. Several Burman lawyers were on the High Court by 1930, others were advanced to the superintendent of police grade by 1940; nonetheless, both the courts and police were controlled by the central government in Rangoon, where British officers retained major influence to the end. Compared to the Philippines, where the corruption of local politics undermined the judicial process, the centralized system in Burma tended to be more judicious and efficient. Yet, even the Burman judges and police were often viewed as traitors by the villagers who saw them as servants of alien governors.

The civil and criminal codes devised for Burma were a unique mixture of positive law developed in India over the previous century and of customary law extracted from the Burmese ethical codes, the dhammathats and lokanitis. Like other Theravada Buddhist kingdoms, the Burmans had their own code that allowed considerable interpretation by provincial governors, monks, or village headmen appointed to serve as judges by the king. Justice was determined largely by community norms. British policy created the skeleton for the state by encoding a country-wide legal system and establishing relatively rigid enforcement but failed to connect it to the dynamic culture of community life, thanks to administration by foreigners until the last decade of rule.

Development of industry and entrepreneurial capability suffered from the same kind of difficulty. British policy, like American policy, favored the experienced businessman who could make efficient use of credit. The Indian moneylender and the Chinese merchant moved in after the opening of rice lands in the delta to serve as entrepreneurs between the great European firms and the hundreds of thousands of

Burman and Karen cultivators. Corporate organization was alien to Burma, except among the Arakanese who had an early flair for business, and the depression of the 1930s threw the small holders back into the hands of Indian creditors. Burma's was clearly a dual economy, with most Burmans subsisting on a preindustrial level while the Europeans, Chinese, and Indians operated the commercial organizations.

Urbanization patterns reflected the dual economy condition. Rangoon, Burma's only city, was as modern as any in Southeast Asia, yet few Burmans lived there. Mandalay had under a hundred thousand people at independence and, being the site of the monarchy, it retained a predominantly Burman population; yet even there the small manufacturing sector was foreign-dominated. Moulmein, Prome, and Bassein, the next largest towns, were also commercially developed by British, Chinese, and Indian investors. Akyab, the capital of Arakan, was the only indigenous town that developed commercial corporations locally, and these were limited to family enterprises.

Education policy reflected the British philosophy of elite government just as the American philosophy of mass education was reflected in the Philippines. Prior to colonization, monastery education was nearly universal; thus, literacy was unusually high in Burma. With the uprooting of several million people in the migration to cultivate land in Lower Burma, the monastery education system declined and was gradually replaced by secular village schools. Also, the apprentice arrangement, whereby village craftsmen served as guildmasters for the youth, disintegrated under the commercialization of agriculture. Functional literacy was probably limited to a half of the adult population by the turn of the century, although for the few with wealth a superior education was available in mission boarding schools and in a few public high schools, which were opened in the larger towns. Rangoon University, founded in 1920, produced several dozen excellent Burmese scholars and civil servants. But the graduates were mainly of Indian or Chinese extraction, or from the Christian minorities, for most Burmans failed the entrance exams because of the English problem. Finally, the number of graduates was far too low—less than 3,000 by 1940—to meet the government's needs.

Politics in Burma reflected the bifurcated economic and socialization pattern. No political parties were formed until after World War I and, until the Japanese invasion, all of them were based in Rangoon and controlled by the elite educated Burmans. The Legislative Council, formed in 1921, employed a few dozen lawyers who developed great talent in parliamentary practices, but little rapport was established with the villagers. The urban educated politician participated in a cultural milieu foreign to most Burmans. Many elections were held after 1921, but rarely did more than 10 percent of the population vote and, not until after the nationalistic Saya San rebellion in 1930–32, were there candidates who attempted to represent villagers. U Nu, a graduate and schoolteacher in the delta, returned to join Aung San and a dozen others in a university strike in 1936, attempting to create a mass movement; subsequently, a few older politicians with rural identification encouraged them to join their weak political party, the Dobama Asi-ayone. By 1940 the students had become such a thorn in the British flesh that most of the leaders were jailed. The Japanese responded to the opportunity for an indigenous political base and covertly transported a small cadre of ex-students to Japan for military training. The group later provided a nucleus for Burma's first district-based political party, the Anti-Fascist People's League, and the first modern Burman military, the Burma Independence Army. Organized politics, like the army, had a much later start in Burma than in the Philippines and subsequently suffered from severe disruptions, for they were institutional aspects of an urban culture, like the legal system, law enforcement agencies, commerce, and government. To most Burmans, this infrastructure of the state was foreign.

Malaysia

Development in Malaysia was akin to the process in Burma because both were British colonies, yet there was a significant difference, partially due to the Islamic heritage. The local sultan's position was preserved in the Advisory system which allowed British civil servants to "suggest" policy to the sultans in the Unfederated Malay States. The Residency arrangement within the Federated Malay States permitted the British official to administer policy. Through trial and error, and with considerable pressure from London to keep administrative costs at a minimum, a political process evolved that allowed local elites, in the Unfederated States especially, to retain their prestige and much influence over Malayan matters.

After the 1880s a stronger obligation to rule prevailed among the civil servants, but never to the point that a common economic, educational, or political policy could be worked out for Singapore and all the states. Essentially three types of government prevailed up to the Japanese invasion: One, the most Western, for the predominantly Chinese Straits Settlements; another for the four Federated States of Negri Sembilan, Selangor, Perak, and Pahang; and a third, the least concerned about social change, for the Unfederated States. Centralization of power was forestalled until after independence by British and Chinese entrepreneurs who feared the heavier taxes that would come when the poorer but politically more potent Malay states gained control of the central government.

Meanwhile, among the Malays themselves, heavy migration continued from Sumatra throughout the period under consideration. This kept them vitally conscious of their culture and religious heritage, as well as of the rising nationalist movement in the Dutch East Indies. Generally, the migrant Malays sought land in the Federated States and Johore for rice farming, while the migrant Chinese wanted credit for business, and the Indians saved to return to India. The three races coexisted with a minimum of social friction and considerable isolation from one another. All but a few Malays remained in the villages, removed from the modernization of their country.

Education was the only real avenue for advance among those Malays who did leave the village, and it was the preserve of the aristocracy. Although residents and advisors had established English schools before the turn of the century—Selangor's State Council had even made education compulsory for boys seven to fourteen in 1891 —generally, Malay parents were reluctant to send children where the Koran and Arabic were not taught. Also, most British officials opposed widespread education. Mr. Frank Swettenham, who served much of his career in Malaya and was one of the most influential residents, commented that:

> . . . it is a question (of) how far we are justified in giving to our native population an education which unfits them for manual labour and gives them a smattering of knowledge that may only make them discontented with their lot in life, while it fails to supply them with new careers or even to qualify them to compete successfully for subordinate Government posts.[3]

In 1904 only 11,000 students were enrolled in the Federated States and the much heavier Malay population in the Unfederated

States had a far lower figure. The first modern teachers' college was established in 1922, compared to 1908 in the Philippines and 1920 in Burma, and salaries for teachers remained so low in the districts that few would venture outside of the larger towns, where they could have additional employment. Yet, and perhaps this is the most critical issue, in the more advanced Federated States, a few hundred students from the Malay elite graduated from the seventh standard English schools every year. The quality of education was comparable to the most prestigious of preparatory schools in England. The best-educated Malays found themselves the equal of the best-educated Englishmen, for they competed successfully in the matriculation examinations and later in Oxford and Cambridge. After the founding of Raffles College in 1928, it was possible for Malays to gain a degree in their own country. But, as in Rangoon University, most students were Chinese, Indians, or Eurasians.

Whereas education was the avenue for Malay secularization, business was the key to modernization for the Chinese. Prior to 1870 the infamous Chinese societies were drawn into wars between petty sultans in Perak and Selangor and did little to develop the community; but the violence died down as the British forward policy brought these areas under their control. Work and experience in the tin mines permitted the Chinese to earn profits when the first British investors failed, so the colonial administration encouraged immigration of hundreds of thousands of Chinese to be employed by an earlier generation of Chinese laborers who had become mine managers. This huge influx gave several Malay states and the Straits Settlements of Penang, Malacca, and Singapore a Chinese plurality. British policy left internal workings of these Chinese communities—taxation, social welfare, education, law enforcement, even public utilities—to the Chinese businessmen to develop.

Because of their common, humble beginnings and the laissez-faire British policy, the Chinese system of mobility was responsive to the ambitions of the migrants. Through their own banks and liberal use of British capital, the course of opportunity extended from the mines, where a laborer of two- or three-year residence could obtain a loan for a small business, to Singapore or Penang, where with luck and diligence he could establish a position. Manual labor, the trades, merchandising, corporate business, and the professions were all open to the Chinese and the pattern to success became well-established.

The civil service, police, and judicial system, as in Burma, was controlled by British officials at the top and a mixture of Eurasians, Indians, Chinese, Singhalese, and Malays in the lower ranks. In the least-developed states—Perlis, Kelantan, and Trengganu—law was administered largely in accord with Islamic tenets and enforcement was left to the village headmen. In the urban centers—Penang and Singapore—English civil and criminal codes were the basis of a strictly enforced legal system.

Political parties were not even permitted in Malaya before the Japanese invasion, despite the underground operation of the Malayan Communist party in the late 1930s. Armed forces stationed in Malaya were drawn entirely from other colonies with internal security maintained by companies of Gurkhas and Indians. Some Malays eventually were recruited by the police, a trend begun during the occupation when the Japanese were hunting Chinese Communists, and increased with the British return. Nonetheless, as with the political parties, the military and police were an alien institution to the villagers.

Development of cities in Malaya, as in Burma, was a result of the dual economy. The Straits Settlements and Singapore became the center of commerce and higher education. The University of Malaya transformed Raffles College into a university with excellent standards. Singapore grew to become the most urbane of Southeast Asian cities because of its function as an international trading center; however, well-educated Malays tended to identify with London as their metropole, rather than Singapore which had a less prestigious status. Penang and Malacca also became multiracial cities with a marked English character. Over 300,000 Malays were living in the Straits Settlements by 1940, showing that they were not completely Chinese or English cities, and much of the urbanity that came to typify the Malaysia known to Westerners evolved in these three cities.

Comparison of colonial policies in the Philippines, Burma, and Malaysia reveals several surprising trends. Students of colonial policy generally rate American programs in the Philippines as the most enlightened in Southeast Asia. Our study confirms that by most of the standards, the Philippines were best endowed with human resources to develop itself as an independent state. Of the three we have analyzed, Burma would probably have ranked second and Malaya third around 1950, although both seemed far behind the Philippines in the areas we have considered. Such a view could scarcely be sustained twenty years later. Malaya enjoys the highest economic growth and, until the 1969 riots, had greater political stability than either Burma or the Philippines. Recent communal tensions, and inept governance, could destroy the accomplishments of the previous two decades.

Inadvertently the British in Malaya hit upon a proper balance of institutional change which allowed for optimum development. That balance emphasized a pluralist political structure, cautiously constructed within the traditional cultures of the several communities. Both the conservatives and liberals were proved to be correct in that superior education for Malays was essential, but it was properly limited to a few until such time as the economy could sustain more general education and provide jobs for the increased numbers with higher expectations. Thus there were enclaves of development, the Straits Settlements and the towns of the Federation, while the bulk of the population was left alone, untouched by modern values and the state.

If we reverse the proposition, as was the case in the Philippines, we find rapid social change due to mass education and high politicization, without a concomitant development of economic resources so that urban centers could economically absorb the modernized Filipino and provide for him dignity and faith in his own society. By failing to develop a corporate economy with domestic managers (while at the same time inculcating through education expectations that could only be fulfilled by such an advanced economy), the Americans left a dismal situation.

Burma experienced an immediate crisis of statehood. As in Malaya, the bulk of the population had been isolated from educational and political change, but a significant percentage were recruited to assist in economic development by opening commercial rice agriculture in the delta. This disrupted their traditional institutions, as did also happen to the educated Filipinos, yet offered them no modern institutional identification. Unlike the Chinese, who created their own corporate enterprise, the Burmans were unable to compete. Like the Malays, they still identified with their land as small holders and placed low value on commercial or manufacturing investment which yielded no apparent real property. Secondly, the Burmese shared with the Malays and Filipinos a distrust of their urban centers, which were filled with Chinese and Indians. Once independent, the Burmans were politically strong enough to act upon their sentiment by repressing the alien races. The critical role of the Indians and Chinese in capital formation and entrepreneurship was considered less important than their potential political danger as foreign agents, or simply as reminders of the colonial experience. Karens, Kachins, and Shan minorities also were considered hostile by chauvinists who recommenced the repressive policies of Burman dominance characteristic of precolonial rule.

The Burmese case illustrates the chronic disability faced by a unitary system that attempts to govern multiple ethnic communities. No doubt the insurgency was encouraged by a British policy that divided minorities from the Burmans, essentially freezing the communal animosities prevalent under the monarchy. The state they left was divided by traditional distrust, yet controlled by the majority of Burmans who were suppressed throughout the colonial period. Education, the police and military, business corporations, the urban leaders, and even the political parties were distrusted by most village Burmans.

The genius of the Malay situation was to be found in the neat balance of forces that prevented any group from having the capability of eliminating or politically oppressing the other, and the obvious advantage for the elite groups to be gained through cooperation. We can see in retrospect that failure to develop political parties, mass education, a common civil code, even a strong army, was less significant than the positive benefit gained through recognition by each important elite that they could take advantage of the weakness in the state only at the risk of destroying the state. Now, new chauvinistic Malay and Chinese elites may ignore that risk and the earlier success by the Alliance Party.

This carries us back to the proposition set forth at the outset, that development in all its forms is jeopardized if it is not sustained by all the politically significant communities. Once independence was gained, until May, 1969, every important group in Malaya believed itself to have ties with the state. Cooperation and trust was possible between Malays and Chinese even in the face of an insurgency by a faction of radical Chinese. In Burma, to the contrary, and in the Philippines as well, the small landholders, tenant cultivators, and the minorities have not had sufficient returns from the center to trust it. And now, unfortunately, even in Malaysia the communal distrust is not resolved, and the state is constantly threatened by violence or succession. Without common acceptance of its authority, no state can endure.

Hobbes lived in an era torn by communal wars as well as by class and religious bigotry and made an apt comment for this era.

> The final cause, end, or design of men, who naturally love liberty and dominion over others, in the introduction of that restraint upon themselves, in which we see them live in commonwealths, is the foresight of their own preservation, and of a more contented life thereby; that is to say, of getting themselves out from that miserable condition of war, which is necessarily consequent . . . to the natural passions of men when there is no visible power to keep them in awe. . . .

And again:

> If the sovereign of one commonwealth subdue a people that have lived under other written laws, and afterwards govern them by the same laws, by which they were governed before; yet those laws are the civil laws of the victor, and not of the vanquished commonwealth. For the legislator is he, not by whose authority the laws were first made, but by whose authority they now continue to be laws.[4]

Colonial policy in Malaysia introduced both these ideas with moderate success, while the policies in Burma and the Philippines failed. These three cases illustrate the problem common to the region. The communal issue and the alien quality of modern institutions which divide urban leaders from village folk is commonplace there as well.

In a political sense these problems converge during the crisis of authority that accompanies succession. The direction of political change among Southeast Asian states, in their efforts to compensate for their inherent institutional weakness, becomes quite clear in the analysis of succession throughout Asia in the postwar period!

AUTHORITY AND SUCCESSION [5]

To cope with the problem of diverse political communities and superficial identification with the state, most Southeast Asian governments have gradually limited decision making to fewer leaders at the center. Outside the region, in India, presidential rule is sometimes practiced, and all but a few remaining contemporary governments are frankly authoritarian. Various factors account for this trend. Governance by an administrative elite is a pragmatic solution to the need for a system of decision making during a time of political stress. The early postindependence development of opposition parties diffused power and further confused the planning process. With the death or imprisonment of first-generation nationalist leaders, a syncretic style of governance appeared. That style reflects the transmutation of authority from a Western-style democratic representation to an authoritarian, quasi-traditional rule.

Political succession is a way of transferring authority. The process is intriguing if only because of its classic quality, for procedures of changing leaders have always interested political philosophers. Its current significance arises throughout Asia where leaders in new states struggle to institutionalize political authority. Achievement of widely recognized legitimacy for the state follows only from the integration of values, the creation of consensus. Therefore, one measure of political development can be taken by studying the mode of succession, for to the degree that a procedure is tested and found acceptable, then to that degree the state probably has gained acceptance among the populace.

Succession, of course, is fugue-like, constantly reoccurring at every link in the political process. New leaders replace old not only at the sovereign level but in villages and towns as well. However, the mode of acquiring and relinquishing community leader positions is difficult to study in any society (although mark it as a critical kind of field research for students of comparative politics), and this comment is necessarily focused on the top of the process because of limited data. In the two decades since most Asian states gained sovereignty, patterns of political change have appeared which suggest principles about succession itself.

The first characteristic that clearly emerges is the crisis posed by succession of the chief executive. A routine mode of changing executives thus far has appeared in only five states, notably Afghanistan, Ceylon, India, Japan, and the Philippines. And in three of these countries the routines are so recently established or are so seriously challenged as to call into question their efficacy. In several other states succession procedures have yet to be tested, for the principal leaders who designed new systems still retain power, specifically China (Mao

Tse-tung), North Korea (Kim Il-sung), Taiwan (Chiang Kai-shek), and Singapore (Lee Kuan Yew).

In the majority of Asian states the process of succession has been catalyzed by coups, assassination, or struggles between military factions which manipulate or combine with civil groups seeking greater power. This style of struggle is uncomfortably familiar in the United States these days as well as throughout the Third World, but its inefficient execution in Asia is disturbing. The mass violence or threat of coercion accompanying succession in recent decades demonstrates that the political architecture in many states is fragile. The sanguine expectation of some that constitutional procedures (or conversely, that monolithic military control) would develop concurrently with rapid modernization has not been in either instance a clear trend. Only at the affluent end of the scale, within Asia's most urban state, Japan, are constitutional procedures generally uncontested. Serious disturbances arise during succession or when it is perceived as imminent even there, but they are truly threatening among Asia's predominantly agrarian states except where two mitigating factors are present: a powerful constitutional legacy from the colonial period, or an authoritative monarchy sustained by an oligarchic legacy.

Despite this dreary observation, there is some countervailing evidence to hearten those whose faith in development rests on elections. In addition to the five states where there is institutionalized succession, in eight other states intermittent constitutional succession has obtained, notably in South Korea, Thailand, Cambodia, Indonesia, Malaysia, Burma, Nepal, and Pakistan. Some would contend that South Vietnam should be added to this category. Much more surprising is the fact that within this century, nineteen of the twenty-one Asian states have experienced one or more competitive elections for legislative or lower levels of political office. Considering the alien nature of the electoral process, this represents rapid cultural penetration. One is hard put to locate any other Western institution that has enjoyed, or suffered, depending on one's values, such widespread experimentation, if not acceptance.

To summarize then, these two incontestable conclusions establish guidelines for our subject: procedures for political succession are usually ill-defined and, if defined, only occasionally followed in contemporary Asia; nonetheless, one method, the practice of competitive elections, has been generally attempted and in Japan has become a deeply rooted tradition.

Several salient relationships suggest themselves as propositions about political succession in Asia.

(1) *That political parties play a vital role in succession during the early years of statehood, but as the society begins to suffer displacement from modernization, strong pressures for order tend to place military leaders in dominant positions over parties.* Of course the real role of political parties is controversial because of the argument surrounding their definition. Frequently parties are mere cliques within an oligarchic elite, or they are ideological movements with neither membership nor policies defined. These truths notwithstanding, rhetoric is not difficult to separate from accomplishment. For example, in Japan, from the mid-twenties to the mid-forties, political parties existed but had diminished influence over succession while military and civil, bureaucratic, and business factions competed for power, occasionally by means of assassination. Highly disturbed social and economic conditions consequent to the depression, rapid modernization, and the war policy undoubtedly contributed to the declining efficacy of constitutional procedures. Comparable declines in the significance of parties were observable in China and Indonesia since 1965, and in Burma and Pakistan since 1958, when military factions seized control over provinces or at the center concurrently as their respective societies suffered severe social or political disturbances. Stress from rapid urbanization in Thailand's primate city, Bangkok, paralleled the rise of the generals' control over succession since the early 1950s.

(2) *That a previous colonial presence has a significant but not a determinant influence upon constitutional practices and, thus, upon succession.* There are two important types of exceptions to this general condition of declining constitutionalism and, as a consequence, lessening party influence. One occurs in states experiencing severe social or political stress but where powerful institutional legacies of the colonial period sustain the political system, i.e., India, Ceylon, Malaysia, and the Philippines. Competitive parties have sustaining institutions that endure from British and American colonial days, and here recall the resources discussed above: free universities, autonomous transportation and communication systems, independent courts,

elites integrated through English language education, and administrative policy officials relatively secure from military manipulation. The private sector, especially business and private education, functions as an alternative arena for the ambitions of the newly mobilized migrants from villages. These various institutions restrain the pressures for martial rule that arise under the duress of modernization. Politicians retain commanding positions in government.

The other kind of exception is where the colonial institutional legacy was weak but where individuals act as both party and military leaders, creating an autarkic system that preserves party dominance, as in Mongolia, North Vietnam, North Korea, and Taiwan. Within the three smaller Communist states, party chairmen have dominated the military, keeping alive a myth, at least, of civil government and democracy. Taiwan, also a single-party state, likewise has a close connection between military and party leaders, with the Kuomintang being the dominant political force.

In other states, however, the push of military commanders into top executive positions is a definite trend, reflecting the general condition whereby only the last recourse of order, the military, stands against the whirlwind of social disruption created by modernization. China, Indonesia, Burma, Pakistan, North and South Korea, Laos, and North and South Vietnam have already taken this turn, albeit with differing levels of military involvement.

(3) *That a predominantly urban population is a sufficient, but not a necessary cause for competitive elections.* Competing parties and pressure groups dominate the selection of premiers and legislators in Asia's two urban states. In Singapore the People's Action party under Lee Kuan Yew, and in Japan since 1952, the Liberal Democrats, under a series of moderate conservatives cast in the pragmatic mold of Premier Yoshida, have successfully conducted elections with almost no violence and a minimum of repression. The high rates of literacy, political consciousness, sensitivity to mass media, high income, and cultural homogeneity in these two urban states help explain the success of competitive party politics. However, as noted in proposition (2), urbanization is not an essential social condition to sustain party competition in succession.

(4) *That a predominantly agrarian population tends to accept succession of sovereign authority without elections or with single-slate elections, except as noted in proposition (2), where electoral legitimacy is sustained by other strong modern institutions.* Here the conditions are reversed from the urban setting. Agrarian states have low rates of literacy, little political consciousness, an embryonic mass media, subsistence income, and ethnic or linguistic heterogeneity in lands inhabited by cultivators, with only a small elite which struggles within itself for supreme power. Examples include most of the states under consideration at some point in the past two decades. States somewhat advanced in the shift to urbanization all have active party systems although the bulk of the population is politically malleable. Here the war-torn states of North and South Korea, North and South Vietnam, and Taiwan serve as illustrations. From one view, China could also be included in this category as it has the largest urban population in Asia—over one hundred million—although its aggregate ratio is about 85% rural which is similar to most of Asia's agrarian states. In any case, somewhat over a billion people in three of the big four agrarian states, and over 100 million in the remaining smaller states, live under oligarchic or autarkic rule in which supreme authority is assumed in no prescribed fashion.

(5) *That culturally heterogeneous states suffer from fissiparous pressures that severely impinge upon and disturb the transfer of authority.* States with dissimilar ethnic cultures have experienced increasing friction with the passage of time, and particularly during the period of succession. The most recent example is Pakistan, while earlier cases include India, Indonesia, Burma, Laos, and Ceylon.

(6) *That antiregime ideology as well as communal distrust is sufficiently strong in most Asian states to make any government's legitimacy unacceptable to some groups.* Such groups often feel compelled to use terror in their opposition effort to change regimes and reform political systems; conversely, governments facing extremist opponents tend to suppress them.

Obvious examples arise from the Communist states as well as South Korea, South Vietnam, and Taiwan, with various levels of terror and government suppression in all of the other states except postwar Japan. Of course the idea of a loyal opposition enjoys considerable currency in all of the "competitive politics" states; yet even in India, Ceylon, Singapore, and Malaysia, political incarceration of opponents to the regime is occasionally practiced. Despite the pressures that appear to be built into the process of rapid change, these states have a remarkable record of maintaining free speech and a free press.

The six propositions just offered tend to be mutually reinforcing —that is, many states serve to illustrate several propositions. What they suggest to me are likely probabilities, or relationships arising from social conditions that will sooner or later appear. In other words, these factors should be accounted for if one is speculating about any critical political act. Succession clearly is such an act. Just how each of these propositions relates to the initial two conclusions is not entirely clear, although several connections are apparent as one considers the events that have transpired in Southeast Asia. Let us now turn to that area in this concluding section.

Few would deny the fragile nature of states in Asia. The dangers consequent to that fragility are certainly ever-present in the minds of premiers, presidents, and chairmen. The action of abdication or sudden loss of supreme authority not only appears threatening; it really is. There may very well be assassins lurking on a golf course, or insurgents penetrating the defense communications system and war office. The real worlds for Generals Ne Win, Lon Nol, Praphas, Suharto, and Thieu, as well as the civilians, Marcos, Razak and Souvanna Phouma, are not markedly different in terms of the security with which they hold office. Some would argue that their particular policies created their respective insecurities. This is a specious assertion as demonstrated by the evidence sustaining the foregoing propositions. The style of succession, like the style of governance, varies greatly between the states of Asia, but the establishment of an authoritative procedure is generally in doubt, for political authority itself is vague.

This means that if routine political succession is a valid indication, then the notion of "developing states" as applied to Asia is misleading; developing economies or communications systems, perhaps, but the majority of these states seem as pressed now as ever before by disorderly forces bent on seizing supreme power. Therefore, orderly assumption of authority must be viewed as a considerable achievement.

Nonviolent succession is probably more relevant to Asian states as a mark of authoritative transfer of power than is constitutionalism. Sihanouk's transformation in the 1950s from monarch to premier, U Nu's "delegation" of power to Ne Win in 1958, Shastri's sanction by the Congress party, and Souvanna Phouma's assumption of pre-miership in 1962 represent substantial achievements. There were no deaths and a minimum of public unrest.

If my premise is correct, that the act of succession poses a threat to the continuity of states in Southeast Asia, then clearly political succession is a real problem in development. Yet, men will grow old and chief executives must eventually release power. All the states have survived one or more such changes. Perhaps we should wonder that they have and be less surprised when the architecture shakes, or even collapses, as a new tenant moves into office. The marvel is the sheer ingenuity with which leaders manage to assume the mantle, invisible though its legitimacy may be. Perhaps the most important lesson to be learned from this analysis is a reconfirmation of the political prin-ciple advanced by Aristotle—that people, most of the time, prefer order to chaos and will usually accept, without critical evaluation, assertion of power that successfully gains the ascendant position.

Only two states in Asia, Japan and the Philippines, have "tested and found adequate" their modes of executive succession. In the Philippines, since 1946, six men have gained the presidency, all through constitutional means despite some violence during each cam-paign. In Japan, despite the failure of any opposition party to gain power, some ten national elections have successfully transferred power within the Liberal Democratic party. Of the other states, India, Ceylon, Malaysia, Thailand, Indonesia, and Singapore *may* be capable of adhering to their constitutional systems, thanks to their earlier suc-cessful experience in competitive elections. But for the remaining states, we have an empirical measure of the tenuousness of their authority, for political succession is a critical problem in each (see Table 3-1). More fundamentally, the authority of the state is often questioned or meaningless, making state disintegration a general pos-sibility throughout Asia. The state itself is often a barrier to political development in Asia.

Table 3-1. Political Succession in Asia
1946–1969

	1945	1950	1955	1960	1965	1970
Afghanistan	T	------------	--------I/T---	------------	---------I/T---	----	------
Burma	ML	----·EC -----	---- EC -------	- EC -- ML---	- EC --MR---	-----------	?
Cambodia		x/T·EC·EC(2x)	x·· x··EC ·ML·x	·EC-(9x)·ES·/T	--ES-- x -----	---- x --- x--
Ceylon		x·--EC -------	---·EC --------	- EC·--·I – EC -	-- ML-- x ----	-EC-----·EC
China		x-------·MR------	---- x ---ES --	------------	---x ----	-- x -----------	----- ML--· x
India		x·---------	----EC·---------	------EC -------	----EC·--·I -----	--I--EC ---·el
Indonesia		x---x---· x	--x-x-x---EC -	--x-x--ML-· M-	----------x ------	--ML--·· x ---
Japan		EC/T·EC·x·EC	-- EC--EC-----	--EC---EC----	-EC---------EC	-----EC/T --
Korea, North		ES----	·x---x ------	--x-ES-- x ---	--ES------------	-x --- x----
		x ---				
Korea, South		EC·----	---x – ML---·EC	--ML – EC-·ML-	ES·M·EC·ML·EC	---EC------
Laos		EC/T-- x-	·x-----	-- x--x -	-EC·x--x·EC·ML ·EC··M· x----	-EC· EC/T·-
Malaysia		x----x ---	----el--el----	-el--EC-------	---EC--	-----EC ---	----EC--
Mongolia		-----------	-	---- x ----	---------	---x··x -	- x-- x---x --·x	------------
Nepal		x/T··-------	·	·x/T- x··x·x·	--x--/T-x--EC -	·/T-------- el -	------------
Pakistan		x----	-	-	------EL· x-	-·x··x··xM·L ·E·S	-ES-----------	-EC-x--·l··?
Philippines		EC-----	--EC	-----------	--EC·	----·I--EC·-----	---EC---------	-EC-----EC
Singapore				EC·-x--el--EC-	-·el --x--· EC--	-----ES-----
Taiwan		el--ES–·ML--	-	·el--el-·x--el--	--el-------	---el ---	--el------· el --	--· el ---el--·
Thailand		EC/T·M·EC -ML(3x)-M------	------EC-M-M··x	---------- I ---	------EC/T
Vietnam, North			ML	-----x-------	--ES------------	------------
		EC/T-ML··x/T	------------			
Vietnam, South			ML	--x---·el ------	---------M··M–M·	-·xel–EC--x -

---

EC = competitive elections
el = local elections
ES = single party elections
I = incapacity due to resignation, illness or death
M = military law

ML = martial law
MR = revolutionary militant government
/T = traditional head of state
x = major cabinet change
? = succession imminent

part two
Development
and Security
Policy

chapter four

Future Asian Conflict Situations

Although political prescriptions are hazardous, for policy makers they are the most germane dimension of political science. Conceptualization of both conflict and development problems must precede such advice and is the task faced in the next two chapters of Part Two.

Identification of existing and potential conflict situations in Asia is an essential step toward minimizing the scope of future wars. Errors in policy would be certain if the great powers were to ride on the flow of contemporary political relations and ignore trends that might lead to large-scale war, or to seek political influence and leadership without a deep understanding of existing and latent conflicts. This chapter, therefore, aims at further illumination of the several Asian political problems that may develop into overt conflict. My object is to identify general causes, to isolate specific grievances, and to suggest some methods of redress short of war.

A crucial assumption underlying this analysis is that the evolving Asian interstate system is unstable owing to conflicting tendencies toward fusion and toward fission. By tendency toward fusion I mean that several processes contribute toward persistence of the existing system of sovereign states, but not necessarily toward the continuance of their current policies. "The position of the ideal . . . equilibrium is in the . . . system, never attained, continually 'striven after' . . . (but) changing because the data change." [1]

Three processes account for whatever equilibrium exists. The governments themselves are persistent stabilizing forces as leaders and administrative–military elites struggle, often through coercive measures, against disintegrative pressures from the various revolutions

(Notes for this chapter begin on p. 202.)

(political, economic, and social) within each state. These revolutions cause the "data change" that in turn accounts for the changing ideal state of equilibrium. Furthermore, indigenous cultures provide people with a world view and meaningful institutions that leaders conserve, both to maintain their power base and to preserve their own identity. Another factor contributing to the equilibrium is the presence in Asia of the two superpowers, the United States and the Soviet Union. Both tend to restrain the major Asian powers from violent measures aimed at enhancing their great power prestige. Moreover, in pursuit of their own interests, both superpowers, and particularly the United States, apparently view the existing state system as worthy of preservation, fearing that its destruction would increase the threat of a nuclear exchange. Generally, the forces for equilibrium are still being defined or constructed.

The fissiparous pressures build up as the postcolonial era recedes and traditional communal political associations re-form. The postcolonial state system is challenged by new forms of embryonic polities. Somewhat resembling the "nations" so familiar to the West, with their common territory, language, culture, and historical memory, these embryonic polities are not congruent with current state boundaries. Their leaders question the sovereignty of existing regimes because of their alien ways, and they often envisage utopias far different from the equilibrium I have just described. In some instances this compulsion to construct a new polity, if free to evolve, would swallow existing states and subject them to larger federal control, but most frequently the primordial desire to associate with like people creates pressures to fracture the state into smaller polities. Universalist ideologies like democracy or communism may or may not affect these ventures in radical politics while the result in any instance is the creation of fissiparous pressures that destabilize the political process and the interstate system.

These countervailing tendencies—both the equilibrium and the fissiparous—suggest analytically distinct but interacting causes of future conflict in Asia. These include: (1) disputes arising from unsettled or ill-defined boundaries; (2) ethnic communities with territorial identity in more than one state; (3) linguistic, ethnic or religious minority communities with an unsatisfactory status; (4) traditional or ideological enemy neighbors; (5) territory over which great powers have competed for strategic control; (6) new great power competitions (as between China and Japan) caused by modern technological capabilities developed in communications, education, industrial and agricultural production, and military security; and finally, (7) the exacerbation of any of the above causes by a leader bent on aggrandizement.

It will become apparent in our study of these several types of problems that motives for conflict should be isolated. Some are inclined to chalk up war and insurgency to "territorial appetite" or "leader lust" for more power. The personalities of key leaders may indeed contribute to specific conflict, as was the case in Sukarno's *confrontasi,* but popular support for war or any prolonged violence in Asia in the future will necessarily rest upon one or more of the "structural" causes outlined above. For that reason, it is beneficial to consider the fundamental sources of these problems.

Disputes Arising from Unsettled or Ill-defined Boundaries

The political questions raised by the problem of unsettled borders is directly related to the problem of sovereignty and legitimate control over a people and their territory. Although ostensibly a legal matter to be settled by survey teams and foreign ministry negotiators, this is often a basic political problem of extreme complexity because of historical antecedents. Demarcated borders were not significant to Asian regimes as they were to the European states. Not until forced by the colonial powers through treaty demands did rulers accept exact definition of their territory. Asians viewed the whole issue as a queer legalistic bent of Europeans.

Europeans entered Asia in force *after* their feudal period and considered a specific territory, marked and defended, as a key factor in establishing sovereignty, whereas throughout Asia suzerainty rather than sovereignty was important, and its measure was taken through tribute. The Great Wall of China, which may come to mind as an exception to this generalization, was not conceived as a territorial marker but, like the Gobi Desert to the west, as a physical barrier to contain barbarians. The tribute system served well to delineate political relations, and, to accommodate such a radical innovation in political relations as suggested by the West's legally based system of sovereign states, forced the Chinese to modify their diplomacy,[2] and more fundamentally their world view. In pre-Muslim India "a king might render homage to his conqueror and retain his throne. Thus vassals usually became so by conquest rather than by contract . . . conquest did not involve the absorption of the conquered kingdom, but merely its reduction to vassal status"; thus, borders were unnecessary.[3] And in Southeast Asia the Buddhist and Muslim polities, which suffered frequent violence between ethnic groups, depended primarily upon personal alliances through marriage and occasional military forays across their natural territorial divisions, mountain ranges, and rivers, to create their numerous short-lived empires.[4] These polities were not conceived of as contractually defined entities with demarcated borders. Only the Japanese developed a comprehension of territorial sovereignty in the Western sense, and they earlier experienced an extended feudal period as did the Europeans, which probably accounts for their mutual respect for the polity as a legally delimited entity.[5]

One looks in vain through the precolonial literature of Asia outside of Japan, particularly in the dynastic and monarchic chronologies where such statements ought to be, for description of delineated boundaries. Maps indicated general areas controlled by rulers, but they were notoriously vague without reference to scientific topography.

The colonial experience, of course, modified attitudes among Asian elites and in so doing we find, after the European withdrawal, a widespread acceptance among governments of boundaries as a key to identifying the limits of state sovereignty. Thousands of miles of boundaries have been marked since World War II, the greatest proportion along the China border. But the vast bulk of the Asian populace is in the villages and has little if any comprehension of the political meaning to such boundaries. Thus, for several decades it will be an easy task for indigenous insurgents working with villagers to ignore legal borders if it suits their purpose.

The meaningful boundaries to most people will remain the natural divisions imposed by culture and terrain until such time as the propagandists for the states or regional federations have established new identities in the minds of villagers. This does not mean that national armies, composed of mobilized levies from the villages and new urban slums, will not fight to protect borders. Such conflict has already broken out in the Rann of Kutch, Kashmir, Ladakh, the Northeast Frontier Area, Cambodia, the Ili Valley, the Amur Valley, and in Northern Kalamantan. These particular boundary wars will probably recur until political settlements obtain. Other borders are latent sources of conflict derivative of the second type of problem in our analysis.

Disputes Arising from Ethnic Groups with Cross-boundary Territorial Claims

Asian governments today are making a great effort to develop popular loyalty to the state. But to have loyalty to a state means to identify with it through some cultural institution, a function performed so admirably in the West by national cultures. For the time span of this study, however, the nation is not likely to provide a widely shared identification for most Asians. Even with rapid urbanization over the next two decades, three quarters of Asia's people will still be living in villages. Without a true communications revolution, villagers will retain only a casual identification with national institutions from outside their world. This means a considerable gap remains between leaders espousing the national cause and villagers with only a provincial community identity. The problem is particularly acute at the outer edges of governmental control and, for a different reason, among overseas minorities.

Consider first the issue of the frontier minorities, who are often hill peoples or, if along desert or prairie areas, nomadic clans. Traditionally lesser monarchs, chieftains, or family heads controlled territory that was difficult to traverse and distant from the capital. Mountains, rivers, and the hostile climate protected the people of such areas from the more powerful societies. The frontier areas may have been inhospitable, but they were relatively secure except against the strongest armies of the dominant polities. The political relationship, if any, that existed between the larger polities and the frontier peoples was not based on alliance but on trade, tribute, and blood ties of marriage or concubinage between the elites. Numerous illustrations occur in the arid regions of northwestern China, around the Himalayas, the hill areas of Burma and the Indochina peninsula, and the outer islands of Indonesia and the Philippines. The situation still persists in varying degrees and therefore remains a key political factor.

These cases illustrate the principle that "Differences in environment (including behavior patterns) . . . are the chief if not the only reason why historical changes have proceded at different rates in different places, and why more complicated systems have not diffused more rapidly from the centers of development." [6] Although overstated, this opinion suggests that in the coming decades various technological advances will hasten the breakdown of this traditional isolation, but it is unlikely that sufficient change will occur in the foreseeable future to completely revoke traditional behavior and attitudes. In political terms, this means that frontier peoples are likely to retain such distrust of the majority ethnic communities who control the state that they will not develop a primary loyalty for the state until well into the twenty-first century. More specifically, such self-identified frontier peoples as the Shans, the Nagas, the Free Thai, the Mongols, and the Uighurs are certain to remain thorns in the side of any government in Rangoon, Delhi, Bangkok, and Peking until they are physically or culturally absorbed, or left alone in autonomous polities.

The problem of overseas minorities—the Chinese, Indians, Koreans, and Pakistani—likewise poses a political threat to governments although the dimension of the problem is different. In this instance the people are migrants who often retain cultural loyalties to their native lands, loyalties that potentially may undermine their political identification with the state to which they have migrated. Since few Asian societies are today assimilative, the process is likely to remain chronic. In the twentieth century only the Thai, and to a lesser degree the Burmans, of all the Asian societies have been able to integrate significant numbers of an overseas minority, in these cases the Chinese. Chinese throughout the remainder of South and Southeast Asia, Indians and Pakistani in Burma and Malaysia, and Koreans in Japan all live with various forms of social ostracism and political disenfranchisement.

As with the frontier minorities, the overseas minorities pose a latent political threat to any government in these nonassimilative societies. Unfortunately, the problem is exacerbated as nationalism gains in strength, for these states maintain a "national" ethic which largely reflects the values of the majority ethnic community. Such communities, particularly outside the urban areas, are highly charged with that pattern of values we commonly associate with Gemeinschaft, the associative, ascriptive, nonsecular behavior pattern of the traditional community. "Outsiders" are viewed with hostility and frequently become scapegoats for deeper socioeconomic problems, as was the case with the Jews in Hitler's Germany. The situation is tragic in that many of the skills needed for development are held by the overseas minorities who often have craft or entrepreneurial talents; nevertheless, the political dimension of the problem is likely to continually overwhelm the economic advantage which would be gained by conserving the skilled manpower of the Chinese, Indians, and Pakistani.

Disputes Arising from Regional Linguistic, Ethnic, or Religious Communities [7]

In Asia, only Japan, and the Koreas are completely free of ethnic minorities who pose a serious political problem. Also, Singapore, Hongkong, and Mongolia are sufficiently homogeneous to avoid the political issue inherent in large minority communal groups.

Afghanistan, China, India, Indonesia, Pakistan, Burma, Thailand, Ceylon, Cambodia, Malaysia, Laos, the Vietnams and the Philippines each have a significant political problem stemming from communal identities. The importance of the issue was clearly revealed in the February 1967 election in India, which found a majority of the states with strong communal and linguistic-based political parties formed in the wake of a declining Congress party. Likewise, in China Maoist factionalism has again unveiled the hostility felt by Tibetans, Chaungs, Mongols, and other indigenous minorities toward the Han. In Burma the Shan, Karen, and Kachin insurgencies continue twenty years after independence; and the Malay–Chinese antagonism crystallized in the Singapore–Malaysia split and in the 1969 race riots.

These examples illustrate conflict situations within states which could spill over into interstate warfare if the antagonisms are encouraged or, more important, believed to be encouraged by other powers. Such fears have fueled the fires of the Sino–Soviet debacle as Soviet agents are accused of provoking Chinese minority factionalism in the late sixties. Similarly, the 1965 Kashmir war threatened to create long-feared communal violence between Hindus and Muslims in India; thus, Pakistan was accused of fomenting civil war. And again, the 1953 KMT crisis in Burma's Shan states was widely believed by Burmans to indicate American machination of Shan insurgents working with the Chinese Nationalists.

The gravest threat, however, to the equilibrium of Asia is posed by the possibility of state disintegration due to communal conflict. The heterologous condition is especially acute in India and only relatively less so between East and West Pakistan, between Indonesia's Inner Islands and Outer Islands, and within Burma.

The data in Table 4-1 offer a rough indication of the problem in those states where it is most severe. The territorial and communal

Table 4-1 *—Territorial Communal Groups Based on Primary Identity

Estimated Number and Percent by 1985

India (*Total Population Estimated 750,000,000*)

Major Non-Hindi Language Groups	Millions	%
Telegu	68	9.0
Marathi	55	7.3
Tamil	53	7.1
Bengali	51	6.8
Gujerati	33	4.4
Kannada	30	4.0
Malayalam	28	3.7
Oriya	27	3.6
Rajastani	26	3.5
Punjabi	25	3.3
Assamese	10	1.3

Indonesia (*Total Population Estimated 180,000,000*)

Major Ethnic Groups	Millions	%
Javanese	81	45.0
Sundanese	21	14.2
Madurese	14	7.5
Coastal Malays	14	7.5
Makasarese-Buginese	8	4.2
Minangkabau	6	3.3
Balinese	3	1.7
Chinese	3	1.7

Pakistan (*Total Population Estimated 215,000,000*)

Major Language Groups	Millions	%
Bengali	117	54
Urdu	72	33

Remaining 13% divided between Punjabi, Pushtu, and Sindhi

* Estimates based on Indian Census, 1961; Pakistan Census, 1960; and the U.N. Statistical Yearbook. Projections assume a 2.5% annual increase from 1965 to 1985. The figures should be considered as only rough estimates for purposes of proportions and size.

Burma (*Total Population Estimated 38,000,000*)

Major Ethnic Groups	Millions	%
Burman	27.0	71.0
Karen	4.5	11.8
Shan	2.3	6.1
Arakanese	1.5	4.0
Kachin	.6	1.6
Indian	1.2 †	3.2
Chinese	.8	2.1

Ceylon (*Total Population Estimated 21,000,000*)

Major Language Groups	Millions	%
Sinhalese	14.5	70
Tamil †	4.5	22

† Best estimates based on the 1953 urban census assuming Indian (Tamil) emigration of 180,000 in the 1963–65 period.

identity of these people is generally more meaningful than the vague sense of being Indian, Indonesian, or Pakistani. Evidence of this condition is found in the parties, political movements, and insurgent separatist organizations formed after independence. Provincial separatism has torn the fabric of Burma since 1948 when the Karen National Defense Organization became an insurgent movement with extensive rural support. Shans, Kachins, and even Mons, a tiny residual minority of the once dominant Mon Khmers, have since formed their own militant associations that refuse to accept union with the Burmans. These several insurgent movements sputter intermittently, and such deeply rooted organizations are likely to be dislodged only with a substantial inducement from the center. Possibly, long-range economic growth will resolve the issue, but the time span during which payoff from the center in benefits such as education, employment, and aid to town growth will be longer than most observers expect.

The problem in India is not yet so acute, but the trend is emerging. Under Nehru the Indian political process functioned deceptively well. Three successive democratic elections, an annual 2–4% rise in the GNP, and acknowledged leadership of the neutrals in world politics combined to lend legitimacy to India's central administration. But domestic politics overwhelmed the Congress party after Nehru's death and even before, in 1956, when the communal groups succeeded in restructuring state boundaries along linguistic lines. A decade later, in the state and national election campaigns, the Congress party was nearly eased out by the plethora of communal and provincial-based parties, and by 1970 the President's rule was briefly imposed over several states to preserve the center's dominance. Although most parties sloganeered under ideological banners, each secured funds, workers, and ultimately votes—largely through its provincial base. The future for any India-wide party is indeed dim. Bengalis support the Communist party (Marxist) or the Bangla Congress; Orissa supports the Gantantra party, as do several other states; and the Samyukta Socialist party has Hindu support in Bihar and Uttar Pradesh. The Jana Sangh and Swatantra, parties of the right, have developed a multistate base, but their long-run appeal will probably remain urban.

The potential for disintegration is great in India with its huge minority populations, four of which will soon exceed fifty million. Assam already has support for an independence movement, and, of course, Kashmir is regularly threatened by "liberation" from Pakistan. Should famine come while the central government is weak, it will raise such questions about the capacity of the political system that India may collapse, leaving the smaller but possibly more politically viable communal states to pursue their own foreign policies and attempt to master their own fates. The scramble for allies and outside assistance accompanying this devolution of power would clearly upset the entire Asian equilibrium condition. The strong civil and military bureaucracies, the judicial system, and the India-wide interests of planners and businessmen provide a frame for the current polity, but the stress on the frame will be severe in the next decades.

Traditional or Ideological Enemy States

Memory of past wars has been a basis for enmity in the West and is no less so in Asia. One feature that is distinctive in Southern Asia, however, was the long colonial occupation which reduced the frequency of local wars, thus creating an extended gap between the heroic epic wars of precolonial days and the resurgence of nationalist heroics in the postindependence period. For example, the classic conflict pattern in India that Kautilya memorialized persisted up to the arrival of the Europeans (and contributed to the ease with which the British absorbed the small princely states). The long warfare between Thai and Burmans preceding the colonial period was totally quelled after 1825. The Thai attrition of Malay and Khmer peoples on their borders ended in 1896 as French and British diplomatic pressures, and the recurrent battles between Javanese, Sumatran, and Malay polities, were terminated by the Dutch and British. Thus, the European colonial presence, extending in Southern Asia for periods of 60 to 250 years, stifled popular warfare against enemy neighbor states. This impact may result in less influence by the "traditional enemy factor," since three to ten generations have lived without the violence that was normal prior to the colonial period. It is conceivable, therefore, that suspicion of neighbor states may not have the significance in this region for another generation, until governments are formed with a wide popular base, which will reintroduce popular traditional prejudices harbored within the villages throughout the colonial period.

In Eastern Asia, however, the situation during the imperial era was decidedly different. Japan and China retained their sovereignty though Korea and portions of China were occupied by Japan, and the China treaty ports were developed under European sponsorship. Here Japan earned the enmity of neighbors. Only when a new generation of leaders evolved in Korea and China long after World War II did ordinary trade and diplomatic ties develop. The Normalization Treaty with Korea came two decades after the occupation terminated and in the same year (1965) that Japan's trade with mainland China rose sharply. Although other reasons account for twenty years of hostility, the long period before resumption of economic relations between Japan and her former East Asian conquests was in part the psychological consequence of debasement suffered because of colonization and defeat in battle—an important factor in the interstate politics of East Asia. The situation is particularly interesting when Eastern and Southern Asia are compared. In the latter area, traditional antagonisms have played only a minor role in recent years. The newly formed states sought their own identity and minimized regional international conflict, indeed, the states tended to ignore one another until after 1965 and the decision to terminate *confrontasi*. In the case of Eastern Asia, however, Japan is still viewed with suspicion and occasional hostility by her nearest neighbors—Formosa, Korea, and China.

The phenomenon of traditional enmity has emerged in peculiarly diverse areas. The Korean and Vietnamese wars were instigated partly as a consequence of Chinese resurgence as a great power. South

Koreans and Vietnamese have been reminded of China's traditional hegemony and arrogance toward their "lesser" cultures and since the Maoist Cultural Revolution the Communist North Korean and North Vietnamese governments have exhibited considerable caution toward their ally of the previous decade. And North Vietnamese (Tonkinese) are again facing Thai in an extension of the precolonial conflict over the Mekong basin. The antagonism between these peoples is in their classic tradition, only Communist ideology and the anti-Communist American military presence introduces a really new factor of unknown significance over the long run. Cambodian–Thai hostility, latent since 1896, broke out afresh over the Viharn Temple issue in the late fifties, and in the mid-sixties Vietnamese armies again began to flow into the sparsely populated eastern region as they did prior to the French colonization. Likewise, Pathet Lao insurgency is in part a reaction to renewed Viet involvement in Laotian politics after the French withdrawal, an involvement with roots back to the fourteenth century.

Another sturdy variable in this category has been Russian expansion against regions to the south in Central and Eastern Asia. The traditional Sino–Russian enmity again emerges in the Ili and Amur River tensions as well as through the Tashkent Agreement by which Soviet influence rose to a new high in the subcontinent. Soviet wooing of both Pakistan and India, as well as North Korea, and the search for security agreements in the early 1970s can largely be interpreted as a reassertion of traditional contest between Russia and China, the strongest Asian states, even though both are governed by communist elites.

The ideological question as a factor creating enemy states cannot be ignored in Asia for it has played a role in conflict since World War II. Conflicting belief systems (nationalism, communism, capitalism, and socialism) explain not only the Korean and Vietnam wars but Kashmir, the Sino–Indian struggles, West Irian and the Indonesian–Malaysia confrontation. In domestic politics, ideology probably will become more significant as a political factor, suggesting that it will exert even more influence on external relations. Nationalism and communalism as a messianic commitment is almost certain to emerge among unstable urban peoples and politically mobilized youth who must face the frustrations eagerly exploited by opposition groups struggling to gain power. These frustrations are accentuated by the population explosion which further slows economic growth in peasant societies. The political arousal of the masses, characteristic of modern politics, raises the probability of internal violence to a near certainty over the next several decades. It will promote a resurgence of enmity towards neighbors, who may be used as scapegoats by elites or who may be actual manipulators of violence in the competition for national aggrandizement. The form of the ideology will continue to vary, and mixes of nationalism-capitalism-communism-socialism policies will remain difficult to differentiate and unpredictable in development. What must be emphasized is that usually ideology will be the wrapping, the package for the expression of political feelings caused by more elemental motives. The desire to preserve power by elites, be they communist, military, or socialist in definition, will frequently be the motive for this category of conflict, as will the preservation of central power and defense of state interests against other states.

New Great–Power Conflict Due to Technological Advances

The progress of technology is unmistakable and its capacity to influence international politics is certain. Technology in our time has enabled two powers to wage war anywhere in the world and has extended to a multitude of states the capacity to become part of a world economic system with an influence commensurate to the importance of their exports. Technological advances have made virtually all forms of minerals and energy resources progressively more significant for economic development and all techniques of communication of crucial importance for political development. Leaders of Asia are no less aware of these facts than are we in the West and many envisage advanced technology fulfilling the vision of progress by providing them with capability to maintain political sovereignty, secure economic development, and advance social welfare. Security from outside attack or insurgency is a *sine qua non* to these other goals; therefore, we can anticipate pressures from the major Asian powers to create their own defense and, conversely, efforts by the middle and small powers to gain the protection of the superpowers against great power aggrandizement, partially as a consequence of the improving capability of Asian states to wage warfare. Social cohesion and other psychological, economic, and cultural aspects of power provide the milieu within which technology must operate.

Table 4-2.—The Balance of Power in East Asia, 1970

Region and Country			Pop (mn's)	GNP (bn's)	Military Power				Defense Expendi- ture: 1969 ($'s, mn's)	Defense Expenditure as Percent of GNP	
					Army 000's	Navy 000's	Air 000's	Combat Air- craft		1965	1968
Southeast Asia:											
N. Vietnam	North		18.7	2.2	450	3	5	133	500	13.8	12.5
S. Vietnam			17.5	2.5	421	31	21	125	444	7.5	9.5
Laos (govt)	Center		2.7	0.2	65a	—	2	50	20	6.4	6.3
Cambodia			6.5	1.0	35	2	2	45	64	2.5	2.3
Thailand			34.2	5.4	85	21	20	115	154		
Singapore	South	ASEAN	2.0	1.2	10	*	*	(b)	109d	(e)	(f)
Malaysia			10.3	3.3	39	3	3	30	132	2.7	3.9
Indonesia	Center		116.0	9.1	275	40	50	550c	229	9.6	2.1
Philippines			36.7	7.1	19	6	9	60	123	1.5	1.6
Burma			27.0	2.2	130	6	7	21	111	6.3	5.1
Australasia											
Australia			12.3	26.8	48	18	23	230	1225	3.7	4.8
New Zealand			2.8	5.0	6	3	5	33	98	2.2	1.9

Table 4-2.—The Balance of Power in East Asia, 1970

Northeast Asia									
China (mainland)	800.0	78.0	2500	141	180	2800	7250	8.5	9.0
China (Taiwan)	13.8	4.0	400	34	85	375	302	9.0	7.6
Japan	102.0	142.0	169	39	42	518	1344	1.3	0.8
South Korea	31.0	5.2	550	47	23	215	290	3.4	4.5
North Korea	13.3	2.8	350	10	25	590	692		
South Asia									
India	537.0	40.5	848	20	57	625	1491	3.8	3.6
Pakistan	112.0	13.8	300	9	15	250	542	5.3	3.7

General Note: Source for this table is The Institute for Strategic Studies, *The Military Balance, 1969–1970* (London, 1969), pp. 39–52, 58. GNP and Defense expenditure figures are computed in US dollars, converted at market rates of exchange.

* means less than 1,000 men.

— means nonexistent

a Pathet Lao force put at 30,000 men.

b 20 Hunters on order; at least 24 pilots being trained.

c Of which no more than 200 may be available for squadron service.

d For January 1969–April 1970.

e For most of 1965 Singapore was part of Malaysia.

f About 4%. No annual figures (see note d).

Table 4-3.—Rating of Asian–Pacific Powers * 1970–1980

Super Powers	Great Powers	Large Powers	Medium Powers	Small Powers	Insignificant Powers
USSR	China	Indonesia	Australia	Afghanistan	Ceylon
USA	Japan	Pakistan	North Korea	Burma	Laos
	India	United Kingdom **	North Vietnam	Cambodia	Maldives
			South Korea	Malaysia	Nepal
			South Vietnam	New Zealand	Pacific Island States
			Taiwan	Philippines	Singapore
				Thailand	

* The criteria for power include military, industrial, communication, and energy capacity, as well as relative population sizes, homogeneity, political consensus, and public consciousness. The ratings are arbitrary and tentative due to the instability of many states. Alliance reinforcement is not weighed.

** Dependent upon continued defense arrangements with India, Malaysia, and Singapore.

Bases for communications and military deployment will be in demand for most of the period contemplated. The United States and the Soviet Union now have need of tracking stations for satellites. In the reasonable future other missile producers in Europe, as well as Japan, India, and China, will be similarly affected. The competition for islands and offshore bases throughout the Pacific and Indian oceans will increase with this rising demand and could create serious tensions. Certainly there will be courting of receptive governments in an effort to secure installations, as the United States has done in Thailand, and it is probable that the medium and small powers will seek superpower arrangements for security against nationalist aggrandizement by great Asian powers. The pattern of nonalignment, so popular in the fifties and sixties, probably will not disappear, for some countries (Burma, Nepal, Afghanistan) will persist in avoiding any alliances. Such a course will have a cost, however, for all Asian states need capital and technical assistance from those with an industrial endowment, an endowment which will be shared more copiously with allies than with hostile or neutral states. Certainly, hostile Asian governments cannot expect aid from their perceived enemy as the Sino–American case so well illustrates. Conversely, some countries (South Korea, Taiwan, Thailand, and Malaysia) have advanced economically more rapidly through their alliances with industrially advanced powers than has Burma which has accepted less aid so as to protect its neutrality and sovereignty.

The trend toward a world economic system will likely continue, as with GATT and the development banks, and through rising trade. To meet their technological needs, a scramble for alliance with one or the other of the superpowers or major aid givers could develop, thereby increasing the potential supply of bases for the aid givers. The Asian great powers, except for Japan, would be restricted to their own territory in the development of advanced military technology. Their only alternative then would be alliance with one another, as, in fact, Pakistan and China have done. Peking probably had a triple entente in mind in its courting of Indonesia but, as that case demonstrates, these states primarily share only poverty and will have little to offer one another other than the joint denial of superpower presence, and diplomatic support. The same, of course, is true for India. Therefore, in the remaining third of this century it seems most likely that the extent of the conflicts arising from superpower military competition will really be determined by the U.S. and the U.S.S.R.; if they continue to have a *modus vivendi,* the lesser powers are unlikely to provoke conflict over the issue.

Economic development requires advanced technology which in turn creates stress upon scarce resources and weak market systems. The quest for increased productivity and larger external markets is creating tensions among Asian states. Today China, Japan, and India compete in Southeast Asia with textiles, light consumer goods, and machine products. Japan generally has the upper hand in production where intensive capital investment and quality control is essential, but China and India clearly feel the need to compete, as do several of the smaller industrial producers—Korea, Hongkong, Singapore, and the Philippines—which are displacing Japan in a few labor-intensive sectors. On the one hand, these several Asian markets may eventually serve one another following the comparative advantage principle; on the other, until natural advantages are sorted out, there is bound to be uneconomic competition between powers utilizing trade for political purposes. Although wars in the future are not likely to be fought primarily because of competition for markets, such tension will be a contributory factor to conflict in the Asian region.

A less general problem, but one of crucial interest to the industrial states, is the matter of primary imports from or through the
Asian–Pacific region. Japan, for example, was vitally concerned about
oil supplies in 1940 when she decided to invade Southeast Asia. The
situation is no less critical today or throughout the period under consideration. The flow of oil from the Middle East through the Indian
and Pacific Oceans could not be interdicted without threatening
Japan's vital interests. As China, India, Pakistan, and Indonesia
develop greater need for energy and food imports, as standards of
living rise, and as the urban sectors increase (Asia's urban population
will exceed 650 million by 1985), demands for both external primary
and industrial imports will rise precipitously, probably in excess of
10% annually. The capacity to deny such trade, through military
interdiction or boycott, will continue to rest with the superpowers
but may also be developed by a great power that chooses to invest
in a submarine fleet. Such a threat would clearly exist for the other
Asian powers if Japan, China, or India were to develop an attack
submarine fleet. Should the Soviet Union or the United States aid
in the development of this naval capability, it would represent a clear
threat to the others with a vital economic interest in trade through
and within Asia, and probably require all the great powers to construct a counterbalancing force.

Modern communication, of course, is a third area where new
technology is critical. Powerful radio transmitters and equally powerful jamming devices have been a vital feature to the cold war and
appear to be essential features to the state-building process. Elites
seek to project their ideas and visions to their rural population and to
defend against subversive propaganda from hostile powers through
radio and, in the future, television media. Elaboration of media
capability is a certain trend among all less-developed states as they
seek mass support for public policies. Furthermore, intranational communication, from village to province capital or to central army head-
quarters, is a critical need for any Asian government seeking to
stabilize itself. Accurate intelligence and fast reaction to insurgent
movements depend heavily upon secure radio communication. Consequently, one can anticipate that disruption of such networks would
be the goal of belligerent internal groups or enemy powers. The electronic feature of warfare in Asia will come into its own. Paper and
newsprint is another aspect of mass-media technology that has stra-

tegic significance. Governments bent on mass-literacy programs need millions of books and much larger quantities of newsprint than in the past. As with trade, one can anticipate greater influence for the powers that have the capacity to provide, or deny, the mass media to the Asian states.

Conflict over Strategic Territory

Historically, wars were often fought to gain control of strategic territory. There is no reason to assume that the efforts to dominate key approaches to a country's vital regions will not cause violence in Asia as states seek security. This problem has already contributed to three significant Asian wars since World War II: China's entry into Korea following the American advance to the Yalu, the Sino–Indian struggles over the Himalayan passes, and the Indonesian drive to eliminate the British base in Singapore.

If it is correct to assume that responsible military leaders will be concerned about their state's security, it should follow that they will attempt to deploy their armies accordingly. Only neighboring states with the closest interests will allow this concern to lapse. Therefore, an increasing buildup of armed forces along critical invasion routes is to be expected as states develop greater power. China, Taiwan, India, Pakistan, the Koreas, the Vietnams, and Indonesia have already set this goal; some other states may eventually follow suit.

But a number of states are too small ever to hope for a capability of defense. SEATO, of course, was devised as an alliance system to service such smaller states, and the idea of regional security will persist no matter what happens to the current organization. A shifting pattern of alliances, particularly with the superpowers, is quite possible for the lesser states with their weak resource base. The Lowland Countries' relationship with Great Britain in the nineteenth century is analogous. Neutrality, as in the Swedish and Burmese case, is also a possible choice, but one that requires considerable expenditure for a self-sufficient defense.

One peculiar aspect to this problem is that we, as yet, do not know what territory is perceived as strategic by many governments. Frequently, in the past, wars have broken out because states did not realize what neighbors considered to be their key land. For example, the Chinese had operated road-building equipment and had run patrols over Ladakh for several years without encountering Indian resistance, suggesting that Delhi did not view the formidably high plateau as strategically important. And on several occasions since Burma's independence the Chinese have sent patrols across the border into defenseless areas and removed their military only under diplomatic pressure from Rangoon. The question of credibility is of tremendous importance in preventing such actions, as is obvious from the above examples where transgressed states were militarily weak and seemed disinterested in the territory concerned. Conceivably, high defense budgets and mobile striking forces will be essential to a state that wishes to avoid loss of territory or conflict caused by miscalculation.

When to anticipate violence caused by strategic confrontations is a crucial consideration. Any hypothesis attempting to cope with the time factor is inadequate, since it is usually the unique mix of related factors that sets off warfare. Therefore, the best we can do is to point out indicators that suggest trends toward confrontation. Commonplace indicators, which remain valid, are mobilization and movement of troops. Importing new offensive weapons, missiles, and jets, for example, has obvious meaning, as does a sharp increase of domestic propaganda evoking a warlike sentiment. Long-run indicators are to be found in war-office contingency plans, defense allocations, level of weapons manufacturing, and content of training in military schools—all evidence that a good intelligence network should acquire. For a number of years the Thai exchanged such information with the Burmans and Malaysians, which allowed all three to reduce defensive measures on their borders.

Undoubtedly, the gravest threat of this sort to the Asian equilibrium comes from the convictions of the Chinese leaders as to what, along their borders, is strategic. Obviously, there are priorities that change under different circumstances; thus, the Yalu was viewed as critical in 1950, Quemoy and Matsu in 1958, the Himalayas in 1962, and the Amur since 1967. Until now the Vietnam approach does not seem as vital to China, despite the intensive American war effort there, although a new Chinese leadership or a modified international environment could change that perception. Changing perception requires a constant reevaluation of strategy on the part of China's neighbors and the other great powers, except for the obvious certainty that any industrial complex or atomic facilities are of highest constant strategic value. Given the steadily advancing range of missiles and the developing capacity of Asian powers other than the Soviet Union and the United States to target these industrial complexes and facilities, we can anticipate a fundamental concern on the part of Peking if Japan, India, Indonesia, or any of the lesser states were to seek IRBM (intermediate range ballistic missile) capability. Naturally, the concern is mutual as Peking develops its own capacity to strike at strategic territory in the interior of its neighbors.

A time of grave tension is certain to come when this missile capability is developed. The mid-1970s is likely to be the beginning of this period, which will then persist unless political relations become amicable among these giant Asian neighbors.

Leader Aggrandizement

Two types of conflict could evolve from the development of a militant movement by a charismatic leader. One would be the kind of *revanchist* conflict so familiar to nineteenth-century Europe, caused by German leaders creating a German state contiguous with German-speaking peoples, or among Italians who followed Mazzini in the futile struggles of the 1840s and '50s. Such a grand strategy as conceived by Bismarck could enable some future Indonesian leader to succeed where Sukarno failed in uniting the Malay peoples of Southeast Asia into one grand coalition dominated by the Javanese. Similarly, an ambitious Thai general might drive to confederate with Shan and Thai minorities in Burma and China. More immediately, current Japanese policy has succeeded in restoring the million Japanese-speaking Ryukyuans to Japan. Such reassertion of political control over common-language groups is a certain pressure throughout Asia.

The other kind of conflict that could evolve from the same phenomenon, a charismatic leader and an aroused populace, could set off the disintegration of several states. For example, the decline of a responsible Indian central government and a loss of authority by Indian civil servants and police would encourage such a movement among Bengalis, which in turn would clearly threaten the present state of Pakistan. East and West Bengal share a language and ecology, if not a religion, and the Bengali-speaking population will exceed a hundred fifty million by 1975. Such a sizable body of people, sharing the same ecological pressures and united by a significant national literature, traditional heroes, and ancient folklore is quite susceptible to nationalism as it developed in Europe among German-, French-, and Italian-speaking peoples. To a lesser degree, a comparable situation exists among the Dravidian language groups in South India. The same type of pressure could pull Sumatrans out of Indonesia and Shans or Karens out of Burma. Even China, despite its powerful party, civil, and military bureaucracies, is susceptible to this fracturing process as suggested by the Cultural Revolution crisis and the purge of Kao Kang in 1954, which was in part a reaction to Manchurian separatist pressures.

A severe weakening of the state system as it now exists in Asia through a Third World War or a major inter-Asian conflict would very probably lead to disintegration of large states into more homogenous small polities. Great internal stress, such as rapid inflation or widespread famine triggers the same ethnocentric militancy. A series of bad crop years resulting from drought or unseasonable rains creates enough stress to cause crime waves (dacoity) and even insurgency. This human reaction already has reappeared in India, Burma, Thailand, Indonesia, and the Philippines where provincial or communal leaders with ideologies and strong ambitions exploited frustrations arising from bad conditions, which are perceived to be worsening, and then attacked the central governments.

It is clear from these two versions of "leader aggrandizement" that the dynamics of politics in Asia pulls states with both centrifugal and centripetal forces. Leaders looking for a cause and a following will not be disappointed, and violence will persist; but the critical question for outside powers is: Does conflict caused by "leader aggrandizement" have international significance? In most instances it should not, assuming that the centrifugal (communal) conflicts will not normally be supported by outside powers. It is the centripetal force whereby a leader looks across state boundaries that poses the real threat to the system.

Potential Modes of Conflict Settlement

With any mechanical or organic system, the surest method of preserving its equilibrium state is to prevent disequilibrium through regular maintenance or homeopathic remedies. Similarly, Schumpeter and Keynes pointed to remedial fiscal and monetary measures that central governments might take to stabilize economic systems and prevent the wild fluctuations that characterized early capitalism. So with a political system that undergoes severe stress from endogenous and exogenous pressures, the key to equilibrium is strong reaction by the authorities responsible for the operation of the system. The actors with power to influence the political systems of Asia and the Pacific regions are primarily the central governments within the region and the superpowers. Clearly all have something to gain through self-preservation, and most run grave risks if the system is seriously disturbed.

This chapter has attempted to isolate the fundamental causes of conflict or disequilibrium over the coming few decades. Others might rephrase the causes for disturbance, but the differences are likely semantic, and the essential causes are probably exhausted by this taxonomy. The set of prescriptive measures that follow from this analysis of conflict should be useful in curtailing and possibly preventing major violence. If one accepts the assumption made in the preceding paragraph, namely, that in most cases state survival is a gain, then it follows that the Soviet Union, the United States, and most of the existing Asian governments will seek to strengthen the system itself in order to prevent threats to their own national interests; for the state system clearly serves the interests of current authorities.

The most critical step is to establish a credible commitment to the interstate system by the various governments. At this point the United States, Japan, China, and India, by different audiences, are thought to challenge the basic pattern. The United States is seen as a challenger in Asia because of its military presence since World War II and its vast array of capabilities, the Japanese because of their economic power, the Communist Chinese because of their huge population and potential as a revolutionary regime, and India because of its enmity with Pakistan. The Soviet Union is not generally seen by Asian (but for Maoists) or neutral actors as threatening the equilibrium nor are any of the other Asian actors, by themselves, perceived as capable of elemental disruptions without outside aid. For the period under consideration, Pakistan, and Indonesia, the most unstable large powers, will lack the self-sufficiency required to wage major war alone. Therefore, the United States, Japan, India, and China, for different reasons, hold keys to creating belief in the survival of the Asian state system.

Insofar as these four powers appear to exacerbate the causes of conflict, they will erode belief in the current interstate system. Conversely, action sustaining institutions that resolve conflict will encourage commitment to it. Thus, support for Panch Sila won much acclaim for China in the 1950s, whereas their overt propaganda for the various Liberation Front movements in the 1960s not only destabilized Asia but, in the end, cost the Chinese considerably in political losses. Revolution, suggesting a new set of governments and a different interstate political arrangement, is not a comfortable prospect for those in power or for the establishments that sustain the leaders. Therefore, the United States, given its tremendous political and economic investment in the Asian equilibrium, is in a position to introduce policies that may reduce causes of conflict or prevent their spread. America's capabilities are considerable, and its reasons for seeking to influence the direction of change in Asia are quite compelling. The critical question remains, however, what modes of conflict settlement are effective for what type of conflict? Japan seeks to ameliorate difficulties via economic assistance, yet increasingly other governments view the aid as a camel's nose under the tent, a step to economic hegemony.

The various causes of political violence, as suggested at the outset, are interrelated but clearly some are more potent than others. Taken in the order of priority, I judge the frustrated minority community problem to be the most deeply rooted and insoluble. A successful historic solution to this problem has been federation of autonomous regions or polities, federation until such time as central governments and economies are sufficiently strong to sustain rapid and steady economic growth. In the past, political federation has usually been a transition stage preceding disintegration into smaller sovereign states or unification into some form of larger republic, á la Italy. If this is the pattern that evolves from the explosive forces of famine and communal distrust, then the most prudent policy of the other actors would be negotiation and aid aimed at re-creation of a modified federal system that would accommodate provincial demands. The superpowers and a consort of other international and national actors would assist in performing the most critical functions of the central government—allocating resources—while a modified and more acceptable political system is developed. In a sense, the Aid India Consortium has done just this. In some situations, e.g., where new sovereignties can be created with small risk of major violence, the feasibility of federation may not be so great, as in the Singapore–Malaysia case.

Such parallel policies are generally impossible to devise except under intensive pressure, as during the Kashmir war of 1964–65. Therefore, it seems advisable for superpowers to prepare contingency plans for cooperation when the crises break out. Such plans do not require prior agreement, an unlikely goal given the U.S.–U.S.S.R. rivalry, but they would suggest a style of thought and a mode of action that represents an intelligent and reasonable response. Knowledge of such plans would make the prospect of complementary action more credible. The Tashkent Agreement was such a credible response as was the American firm caution against Indonesia during the *confrontasi* crisis. Actions to internationalize the food-aid program to India and China, and pollution control in urban areas, are other examples of joint programs bolstering peaceful solutions to conflicts.

Of course, outside interests will not often be complementary; therefore, the modes of settlement will usually be unique and dependent upon diplomacy. A flexible negotiating position is the most critical factor, with a credible and complex military capability on the part of both superpowers as an essential backdrop to every diplomatic intervention. The most positive outcome of the Vietnam conflict may be the long-range relevance of such military power to upcoming Asian leaders. Perhaps the gravest error on both sides in the earlier stages was the failure by the Vietnamese to reckon with the relevance of Soviet and American military capability. The tragic war should encourage other Asian leaders to accept compromise at an earlier stage in conflict situations. Certainly the United States and the Soviet Union should urge prospective Asian allies to reflect on the costs of future wars.

The possibility of political disruption in Asia will be particularly acute if territorial communities break away from weakening central regimes and seek international recognition. The type of government seeking recognition may largely determine the response and degree of disturbance. For example, had Singapore been dominated by Barisan Socialists when it broke from Malaysia, it might have struck a defense pact with Communist China. Biafra in Nigeria posed just this dilemma at the outset. If a new government in Kerala or West Bengal were to break from Delhi and invite a major Soviet or American presence, what policies should these powers follow so as to minimize disruption of the equilibrium? Or if Communist China were to suffer further dislocations and the southern maritime provinces (or powerful Szechwan, or the three Manchurian provinces) form themselves into autonomous states, then what action by the major powers would most effectively sustain the equilibrium? Such events seem unlikely but not impossible, and the policy designed to cope with them should be thought through before the event.

The most immediate and recurrent cause of conflict throughout the period, it seems to me, will be ethnic minorities and traditional enmities. For the reasons noted above, this motive for violence will be frequently impossible to influence; however, policies by outside powers can greatly affect the scope of violence once it breaks out. United Nations' Observation Teams may sometimes be effective in preventing violence due to misunderstanding, but a balance of military force, sustained by the major powers and with a clear understanding of superpower interests in the region, will be more generally useful.

The closely related issue of conflict over strategic territory is scarcely responsive to control by a UN presence, and the risk of escalation increases if great powers attempt to guarantee support in the event of war between neighbor states. There frequently may be no solution to this problem until the local hostile powers change their perception of one another. Historically, there is ample evidence for this sort of solution in Europe but little evidence of any other lasting mode of settlement. Outside powers may encourage a change in perception by urging an elaboration of the points of contact between the contending states and the international community. A deepening involvement in external affairs, when combined with internal development, sometimes contributes to a modified perception of "enemies and friends," an example being the United States and the Soviet Union during the Khrushchev era and again in the SALT discussions. Of course, one need only look to the Arab world and to Israel to find evidence to the contrary; yet, more frequently the trend is in the other direction.

Another mode of settlement has proved effective in the cases of clear-cut leader aggrandizement, and that is firm military opposition. Unfortunately, the situation is not usually "clear-cut" and always leaders rationalize other causes as reasons for war. The more effectively leaders interlard their sense of personal mission with causes that touch the hearts of the populace, the more difficulty encountered with a military response to their aggrandizement. The Vietnam conflict is illustrative whereas Sukarno's policy failure demonstrates the efficacy of a firm military response when a leader has stepped beyond his political support. Outside powers can act effectively upon this type of violence only if their intelligence of the domestic political process is excellent and if they can act with the authority of military strength. Additionally, the range of monetary, economic, and political pressures that can be marshalled in opposition to an expansionist Asian power is considerable and can prove effective over time. The critical issue is agreement or, at least, acquiescence to the response on the part of the major powers.

The increase in great power competition due to technology is, in my mind, the most difficult problem to forecast. Space research, for example, originally a source of conflict between the Soviet Union and the United States, has tended to bring the two states together in their space policies. Some argue that proliferation of nuclear weapons would have the same impact on Asian governments, whereas most experts take the opposite position that nuclear proliferation in Asia would increase the risk of violence. Several trends are emerging, however, which may suggest insight into the wider problem. Technological knowledge and skill are exceedingly important and, insofar as advanced states share their experience and commit themselves to research on problems peculiar to Asian societies and economies, they may gain influence over the direction of change in those societies. Research on methods to improve productivity, communication, education, public health, to control urbanization, water pollution, and flooding, and to leapfrog innovations so as to create hope when the population problem seems to defeat most development efforts—such research may threaten to create new kinds of competition, but they will be the tensions of success rather than failure.

CONCLUSIONS

One of our gravest problems in the past has been simple ignorance of Asia—ignorance by Asians concerning one another and ignorance of Asia by the remainder of the world. A number of the old shibboleths still remain, but in the past twenty years three of the most powerful actors in Asia—the United States, the Soviet Union,

and Japan—have, in their own ways, made great efforts to comprehend the complexity of Asian peoples. There is still more image than
reality in most of our minds, but the cultural and social science research undertaken has vastly increased our ability to understand the
underlying causes of conflict, if we but take advantage of what we
know and not mistake inaccurate images of the past for accurate
knowledge recently discovered by area specialists.

Utilization of this knowledge in the application of a policy aimed
at development without major violence will make for a more effective
policy. Finesse and sensitivity to local aspirations will avoid blunders
caused by acting for an audience that is a shallow minority or one
that lives elsewhere. Too frequently there has been no political dialogue between Asians and Westerners—only reactions to actions that
demand a reply. Comprehension of motives and self-interest is a key
to successful political interaction and cooperation anywhere; without
knowledge of the causes of conflict, the sources of settlement are not
likely to be found.

This study points to general conflict causes that will persist. The
effort to define the causes is crude, but the problem is crudely stated
and the phenomena are even more crudely perceived. We can rarely
predict politics accurately and seldom diagnose them correctly; rather
we define the principles on a time-sequential basis and then learn
from experience which principle to apply at what moment. The principle of conflict is a constant in politics; the variables defined above
are all influential, but if we can affect the variables, it in no way diminishes the importance of conflict. Conflict will remain; our concern
has been to expose as many significant causes as possible so as to suggest how the course of events might be guided.

Violence is sometimes necessary before conflict can be resolved;
but violence, or war, is not sufficient to resolve issues unless either
mass assimilation or genocide is acceptable. The latter alternative
must be avoided if politics and civilization are to have human meaning. Yet, there will be strong pressures to practice genocide in Asia
in the future. The number of people we are considering is immense,
the political solution to their many problems impossible to attain in
a few short decades, if at all, and the risks involved in any major decision considerable. The scope of violence could range beyond our
comprehension given the numbers of people and the variety of methods
that can be employed to eliminate them, unless those with power

search for modes of settlement that deal with the basic causes of conflict.

Of course, with the prudent allocation of force, violence need not "range beyond our comprehension." Past policies by the super-powers (Korea, Vietnam) suggest their understanding of the need for some limitations on use of violence. But we have no assurance that future governments, with unstable political systems, will be either prudent or reasonable. Should irresponsible leaders gain power, only the clearest understanding by the other major powers of the need to preserve the equilibrium will prevent a large-scale debacle. As the preponderant outside power disposed to use its influence in Asia, the United States has a particularly difficult role to perform. The primal issue is the definition of its goal, our next consideration.

chapter five

The Conceptual Problem in Southeast Asian Development

The notion of political development is general in nature and impossible to conceptualize unless one constrains the meaning excessively. The meaning connotes a positive good in ordinary usage. And when particular denotations are applied, such as integration,[1] interest aggregation,[2] system maintenance,[3] or communications expansion,[4] conceptualizations which are operational, therefore measurable, the implicit connotation persists that something worthy is happening. While it is contestable that what we seek to measure is worthwhile, it is certain that the proponents of political development have yet to state its ultimate value. We simply do not know what we are talking about when we use the term, or advise and teach others, often with considerable passion, to engage in the act. The goodness that men seek in fostering the process of political development remains obscure.

What most writers assume about political development is that it eventually will have a peaceful consequence, the creation of a world order based on nation states.[5] Furthermore, the avenue for realizing this noble goal is expected to be found through national growth, the eventual fulfilment of the United Nations model. Surely the family of nations idea carries a majestic rhetorical appeal. If all nations could but recognize the right of others to have a place in the sun, then the foundation of world peace would rest secure.[6] But there is a deceptive logic in transferring the *legal* conception of the state, as a family of sovereign equals, to a *political* concept of the nation–state. The political meaning of one state–one vote, as in the General Assembly, is blatant nonsense when it infers equal power, or the right to equal power, on the part of all states.

Because the nation–state has concrete significance as the source

(Notes for this chapter begin on p. 203.)

of the enormous power acquired by the West, it is an appealing model for political scientists and leaders of the new states as well. Unfortunately, nation–states are conceived as both the end and means of modernization. The model evokes an image of power and control over the environment, despite the fact that most Western countries are not strong today and are dominated by a few great powers or by multi-national corporations. Such countries as Norway, Denmark, Austria, Belgium, or the Eastern European states enjoy legal sovereignty, but only the naive would contend that in the political and economic spheres they can act without first considering larger interests with which their economies and security interact and upon which they are dependent.

The central difficulty with the nation–state model is that the contemporary world is undergoing vast and fundamental change in its modern arena. Although the process of change afoot in the non-modern, more traditional arena is slower, it still is affected by the modern world. Several transformations are occurring in this century,[7] so that the spatial isolation characteristic of earlier centuries, when nation–states flourished, is gone. The multiple effects of modernity encapsulate mankind, pulling men in contrary directions, but with more intensive cross-cultural contact.

It could be tragic if the notion of political development, meaning nation-building, is seriously subscribed to by those responsible for affairs of state. There has been, and there will be, no peaceful consequence to the universalization of the nation–state system. In another age, when change was not so accelerated by science, and technology was not so rampantly applied to affect the environment, it was feasible for leaders to guide people out of their communal identities and into the realm of nationhood. But in the latter third of the twentieth century we will witness a doubling of the human population without a commensurate increase in governmental or social capacity to cope with these multitudes and their expectations.

The problem is not merely one of providing enough food and subsistence, a historic situation familiar to statesmen; rather, a disaster that threatens us all obtains through our insistence upon transforming men into participants within new national societies. Leaders of new states, with our intellectual encouragement, make village and urban slum youth aware of their prospects as affluent citizens long before the institutions exist that will create their affluence. Those advocating political development have assumed that the nationalization of human-kind within the state system would lead to the creation of sufficient power to permit politicians to cope with the awful population crush. The error is in the timing. New institutions simply cannot be created in one generation. The new national identities will take many decades to formulate; meanwhile the result of rising expectations is increasing frustration.

It is, of course, too late to turn the clock back, for the phenomenon of nationalism has spread throughout the world, from Mauritius to Quebec. What is called for now is an antidote. The prescription to alleviate the excesses of nationalism is well-tested by theorists and practitioners—it is the cultivation of indigenous pluralism,[8] to create organization for diversity. Planners should not lose sight of the strengths already within their own cultural fabric. The power of traditional community institutions is considerable. Indeed, the Rudolphs have coined the apt phrase "the modernity of tradition" to suggest the strength for change that rests within extant social and cultural communal institutions.[9]

Upon turning to Southeast Asia, the unreasonableness of the several assumptions underlying the concept of political development-cum-nation-building becomes particularly revealing. We have described why few of these states can hope to avoid serious violence, if not dissolution, over the next four or five decades if they pursue nation-building as the highest political objective. To pin their aspirations on the nation, by inculcation of purely national values within the young, will only invite resentment from minorities and unrepresented rural folk. How much the better part of wisdom to construct the sense of commonality toward mankind within the context of the local community, the neighborhood of villages meaningful to old and young alike, than to transform youth into something unfamiliar, even alien. Southeast Asia's environment accounts for the considerable divisiveness that has affected its culture and political character historically; it continues to do so, and to compel integration is to get the cart before the horse.

Those newly initiated to Southeast Asia find ten states of apparent substance and stability. With somewhat greater attention to history one discovers that these states gained their current boundaries through the intervention of colonial powers. Through the preceding analyses of conflict situations and the origins of several contemporary

Southeast Asian states, the reader has gained some familiarity with the problems of planning change for villagers and townsfolk steeped in the richness of their own heritage, and suspicious of central governments. The instruments for implementing social and political change from the center are ill-suited to the task; for the undertaking is revolutionary, requiring the organization of agrarian folk into a movement that would cause them to desire basic reorientation of their lives. Such a movement requires the spark of a powerful will and the intervention of fortuitous events, as in Communist-controlled areas of Vietnam where mass mobilization may be sufficient to permit national mobilization. The Revolutionary Council of Burma also undertook such a transformation, thanks to the socialist commitment of Ne Win and his advisers; however, it is highly speculative as to whether his experiment succeeded. Official reports, as well as those few independent commentaries by visitors, indicate a village populace little changed from before.

Without massive military intervention, as in Vietnam or Korea, it is impossible to break, in a few decades, the life style that gives meaning to villagers. Was the horror of warfare worth the price of transforming these two societies? And even after all the bloodshed it remains to be demonstrated that the Vietnamese will, in due course, be able to create a modern state.

None of the other countries has experienced such a profound effort by central governments or political parties bent on rapid change. Nonetheless, one state, Singapore, has attained modernity with little of that grim application of central power associated with national revolution. The inducement of the free market, excellent education, and considerable freedom enabled Singaporeans to create a vigorous and productive society, relieved of most barriers to development that afflict their neighbors. We have seen why the urban character accounts for Singapore's rapid change. Were the government dogged by the demands of largely illiterate peasant communities it, also, would suffer the enormous drain upon its tax base that prevents its neighbors from achieving comparably rapid success in planned change.

Yet, the case of Singapore does offer a relevant lesson. The sort of planned change likely to succeed in this heterogenous region is one based on new urban centers to serve the large populations now remote from cities. It requires devolution of decision making, education, business activity, and cultural control away from the primate cities, that is, Rangoon, Bangkok, Djakarta, Manila, Pnom Phen, Saigon, and Hanoi. Irrespective of whether existing states remain intact, their present major cities will remain, for they already serve vital functions. But political change that will permit the creation of modern, civil societies is one in which ethnic and communal groups are free to create their own urban centers. For example, at the present time none but the Chinese, of the minorities in Southeast Asia, are able to influence their own destiny through control of an urban sector. Once their own cities exist, community leaders will promote change by their own volition. No one commanded the Chinese of Singapore, who are a majority in their state, to work vigorously throughout their lives. They elected to so that their children might gain a better education and also start their careers with more than a subsistence income. The social and economic systems were so structured as to invite their mobilization.

The case for devolution of power rests upon the assumption that, in this fashion, greater power can be gained to break the grip of disease and malnutrition. Sufficient control over the tropic environment will eventually permit hill tribes and rice cultivators alike to attain modernity. But it is a fundamental error to follow the political line now so popular among socialist and revolutionary regimes that envisages a unitary state with a population enculturated within the dominant communal culture. Such a total effort causes political life to be commanded by an elite in the center, and places such a burden upon the governmental institutions that this course cannot but *delay change.*

The inducement of human beings to want change rests within their own heritage; it needs but to be stimulated. Pride, dignity, and self-respect are the hallmarks of every community when viewed from inside; the tendency to denigrate aliens, parochialism, and suspicion are obverse characteristics seen by the outside observer. In Southeast Asia there is little basis for civility and mutual regard among groups.[10] A catalyst that will help to break this heritage of suspicion and distrust is the local city, the growth of a local urban complex which will permit nearby villagers to identify with, and gain the advantages of, modern technology so as to express their own heritage.

The economic value of town-centered change has already been demonstrated by several students of economic development.[11] The political value of local urban growth is even more compelling. The basic issue is one of providing the setting for expression or of creating the opportunity, through modern media and education, for local artists, craftsmen, and entrepreneurs, as well as politicians, to build upon their own institutions. A central government attempting to command the pace of change and life styles for ten, thirty, or one hundred million people is bound to be overextended and unresponsive to the perceived needs of local leaders. Conversely, expansion of education and employment opportunities in nearby towns permits ambitious youth to remain in a familiar environment. There is retention of the sense of community authority which is usually lost when villagers are forced to migrate to a distant and alien primate city.[12] Today, how familiar to the foreigner and well-to-do resident of any Southeast Asian city is the need for guards around his compound to protect against robbery. Yet in the traditional community, apart from the usual crimes of passion, there is little or no criminal behavior. However, the noticeable rise in political terror in rural regions suggests the logical end to rising frustration in the cities. Better educated youth turn to underground warfare as an apocalyptic solution for a bankrupt political system, built on the centrist beliefs of cautious independence leaders.

The problems of a unitary state system, constructed around the single nation theory of development, cannot be solved by simply encouraging local urbanization in towns and new cities. That is one measure; however, there are a host of finite steps that must be negotiated, with a basic political goal in mind, before each polity can hope to devise a system suitable to its people and traditions. For example, in Vietnam, thanks to the war, the classic hostility between the hill tribes and the Vietnamese is exposed and widely acknowledged, yet in Saigon few steps have been taken to create autonomous or separate regions for major Montagnard groups. Meanwhile, some students of North Vietnam found accommodation between Hanoi and the major tribal leaders in earlier, less onerous years. Even among the Vietnamese, the antipathy between religious factions, such as Hao Hoa, Catholics, and Buddhists, as well as the territorial suspicions among those from Hué, Saigon, and Hanoi, does not permit the sort of integration desired by centrists in either Hanoi or Saigon. No Saigon government has seriously sought accommodation among its elemental factions.

In Thailand the situation is not so strained, and students of the area find in Thai homogeneity a promise of success for the unitary state.[13] And the Thai government has made hesitant steps in the direction of dispersed development that suggests greater self-awareness of the political need for regional cities and cultural centers. Cultural divisions are less prominent than in Vietnam, and are probably less well-understood; yet anthropologists have ample evidence attesting to the depth of the problem that observers overlook when they call for a monistic government. Whether one speaks of Luë, Muslims, Chinese, Phu Thai, Lao, or Khmer and Vietnamese, they each represent substantial minorities whose resentments are clearly predictable if Thaization is pressed.

The problem of central chauvinism is more severe in Burma, Indonesia, and Malaysia, and only relatively less so in the Philippines. How, then, can the condition of ethnic, linguistic, and territorial divisiveness be attenuated? Apart from the common need for new communal cities, the issues which must be negotiated between current leaders and those now alienated from government will vary. Consider the Indonesian case, which illustrates some of the common difficulties. From the outset of independence, and before, the Djakarta leadership acknowledged the right of the outer islands to have local self-government. But economic planners saw little to be gained by investing in the remote regions, Sumatra excepted, inhabited by the minorities. Furthermore, the Javanese politicians and Sukarno, himself a Javanese, were anxious to reward their own constituencies. The combination of short-term political interests and expert economic advice was a combination of influence that far outweighed the political wisdom of long-term investment in economic growth of the outer islands. Consequently, the potentially large urban centers, such as Medan, Palembang, Amboina, Singaradja, or Makasari, were left outside the growth sector of the economy. Djakarta and a few other Javanese cities received much of the investment designed to help Indonesia prosper. Most Javanese towns were also by-passed, although twenty Javanese cities exceed a population of 100,000. Diversification of the higher-education system has encouraged some cultural growth in those cities where new colleges exist, but the direction comes from Djakarta and the pace of change is slow. There is little reward in terms of meaningful employment of many college graduates. The problem, fundamentally, is that no strategy for social change has been devised for Indonesia, despite its commitment to economic development.

The unrealized potential for regional growth in Indonesia would not be difficult to stimulate were the government to modify its view of how change comes about. Rather than depend upon the single model of human behavior that people must be commanded before they react and upon the hope that national values inculcated in the youth will motivate them to become efficient workers for the state, it would be entirely feasible to stimulate social, cultural, and economic innovation by creating financial credits and political rewards to town and village leaders who give evidence of innovative ability. The climate for change in Indonesia is real, thanks to several decades of influence from politicians, teachers, and the media, particularly radio and cinema.

Throughout Southeast Asia nothing is more real to community leaders than their identification with their territory, their families, their local authorities, and their religious shrines and traditions. Their concept of security is intimately tied to the symbols representing localism. Rather than attempt to crush local identity, as centrist governments have implicitly done in their nation-building planning, the strength of localism could be cultivated and encouraged by stimulating local and regional integration. Specifically, subsidies and technical aid should be provided to individuals or groups that demonstrate interest and talent in any aspect of the modern technology that is relevant to their locale. For example, freight and passenger transport; fabric, fertilizer, or machinery repair and rental cooperatives; private health clinics, technical and special education institutes; leisure facilities and entertainment companies; media such as a press or mobile cinema: these are all types of activities that town life needs and to which modern technology can be adapted to suit local environments. With suitable incentives, the creative talent needed to develop often appears within the town and surrounding villages.

The reason for confidence in the community responsiveness to the prospect of modernity is to be found in the evidence of numerous analyses by anthropologists and in the work of a few political scientists on intermediary level leadership.[14] The critical factor is the credibility, or the perception of credibility, with which the prospect for modernization is offered. For people to risk themselves in new ventures their government must be prepared to risk the devolution of decision making out to the communities. Risking local autonomy, or even secession from the state, is necessary, for without creating the means for villagers to relate to the larger society of their state, and mankind itself, villagers, as in the past, will be unable to break out of their customary patterns. The new life styles which modernity demands can develop only if the techniques are available within the community structure. Excellent examples are those towns located on new transport lines north of Bangkok, that is, Suraburi, Nakornsawan, Pitsanalok, Korat, Roièt, and Vientiane in Laos, which are all fed by the new Thai highway system. To the south, in the peninsula, Songkla has an even higher rate of urbanization. In these instances the Thai cities have profited from efforts by local citizens as well as by investment in new business and new university educational institutions from the center, and from investors outside Thailand. What better evidence of the community response to the prospect of modernization? The Thai case illustrates the proper goal of political development—that is, the creation of a civil polity founded on prospering local communities.

A civil polity is a goal for Southeast Asian states more suited to the environment of this century than is the notion of political systems or mass participation. The issue evolves from the very idea of politics. Without grasping its meaning in a Southeast Asian context, any idea of a political design for the future is groundless. Although the concept —civil—has its roots in Western jurisprudence, its function is familiar and prized in Asia. To an intellectual of Southeast Asia, civility connotes harmony among men and between man and the ethos. To relate peacefully, while pursuing self-interests within a commonweal, is a traditional art form highly prized and frequently portrayed in local drama. Conflict is assumed to be normal, but the nonviolent resolution of self-interests in competition is so commonplace in most village communities that it is not considered political; yet the process is the root of politics, the authoritative allocation of values within the community.

A civil polity is one in which the public interest is served by men accountable to their community. The perception of trust is real for those with political obligation—they are accountable, and those who suffer because of errors or injustice know precisely whom to blame. The traditional communities in the region are, of course, personal in nature; individuals are quite exposed to each other because their character is known. Enlarging the scope of the civil polity in order to include multiple local communities and still retain the sense of political obligation and accountability is the process by which political development, in fact, occurs.

To create a sense of political obligation among leaders, the worth of the endeavor must be clear; otherwise they will remain bound by their own community mores. To be obligated to observe the customs of all communities within the polity is to accept an accountability for justice in terms meaningful to those governed. The difficulty, then, in creating a polity that diverse peoples can accept is primarily one of resolving the problems of obligation and defining the public interest in a fashion that can be accepted.

The first decades of independence were spent by the founding leadership in designing ways of governance reflective of modern states; it was a form of self-reassurance that independence was real and that, in form at any rate, the state was equal to the most powerful. Parliaments, elections, political parties, civil bureaucracies, and the training grounds for the public sector, the universities, were all institutionalized. But in time the pathetic inability of these foreign styles of governance to work became obvious and new, simpler styles of military rule swept across the region. Only the most Westernized of the Southeast Asian states escaped this second generation of political fashion.

Now the hard issue of surviving succession crises, and of avoiding secession, faces most governments in the region; indeed, two regimes, in Hanoi and Kuala Lumpur, have already confronted the secession issue. Burma, Indonesia, Laos, the Philippines, and Thailand must live with substantial dissidence from peoples who do not believe their interests are being served by the government. In accepting responsibility for governance over peoples with different folkways, politicians ought to recognize the necessity of promoting their interests as their own. To ignore this trust is to invite insurgency.

Until now the potential for outside aid that might help resolve this intransigent problem has not been utilized. The problem is simply not defined, and, therefore, it is touched upon only at random. The final chapter addresses the issue of U.S. foreign policy, its goals in the region, and particularly the barriers to development that impede attainment of these goals.

chapter six

Regionalism and Nation-Building: Ends or Means?

That the United States has been a source of regional as well as local change is undeniable. Perhaps its most positive foreign policy objective in Asia since World War II has been its contribution to the growth of modern institutions, both local and supranational. From the formation of the Colombo Plan and the Economic Commission for Asia and the Far East (ECAFE), in the early postwar years, to the present, the United States has committed substantial funds to new industries, educational institutions, and transport. The American interest is understandable, for the task of getting on with economic growth, as well as maintaining influence, is easier to justify to Congress and the American public if several hundred million people are involved than if the effort is bilateral and catering to the interests of small populations at the local level. Both conceptually and by persuasion, justification is far easier when considered in regional terms, be it Africa, Latin America, or Southeast Asia. The difficulty with the regionalism rationale in Southeast Asia, however, is that it has been premature and often frustrated as a policy by the reality of the milieu.

Consider briefly the significant regional institutions which the United States has supported, either in policy declarations or by financing. The most elaborate, and perhaps least known to the American public, is the Colombo Plan which has created over $20 billion worth of aid throughout South and Southeast Asia since 1950. Originally a Commonwealth-sponsored group, the United States joined early to sustain the Colombo Plan as a channel for multilateral technical aid, primarily in the fields of education and vocational training. The benefits accrued by the participant societies are considerable and the U.S.

government is lauded for its assistance, but the oft-stated objective of regional development should be recognized for its rhetorical nature. Little of region-wide importance has resulted yet from Colombo Plan Aid.

The Economic Commission for Asia and the Far East is not to be compared to the Colombo Plan as an agency through which assistance from the developed world flows into the region. As one of several United Nations regional agencies (there are similar organizations in Africa, Latin America, and Europe), ECAFE has served primarily as a review organization for central government planners. Rotating annual conferences are held in the capitals of the participating countries, while a secretariat in Bangkok keeps communication flowing during the year between ministries, as well as administers training programs for officials. However, unlike the Colombo Plan, ECAFE has no funds to allocate for aid to its members. The U.S. government has helped to finance a significant portion of this operation also, approximately a third of ECAFE's budget, which has been half again more than any other country's support. Furthermore, the justification to Congress is the same as with the Colombo Plan—regional development.

Far more controversial than either of the two economic agencies just described is the Southeast Asia Treaty Organization, SEATO. Formed in 1954 as one of two chains of regional groupings patterned after NATO, the Eisenhower administration depended upon SEATO to contain communism in Southern Asia. Subsequently, after France and Pakistan dropped out, SEATO became primarily an organization in Southeast Asia bent on improving communications about security matters among U.S. allies in the region. Of the original participants, the United States, United Kingdom, Australia, the Philippines, Thailand, and New Zealand retain an active interest. Annual regional military exercises demonstrate their commitment to Southeast Asia security; however, since only two states in the area participate, the organization is a misnomer. SEATO also has a secretariat in Bangkok, and, as with ECAFE, sponsors various training and educational programs. The SEATO engineering college is the best example of its educational effort, and with its obvious merit its relationship to SEATO became unnecessary. It severed its relationship in 1965 to become an independent regional college, Asian Institute of Technology (AIT) but still with substantial U.S. aid. SEATO has been the most blatant

American effort to influence security considerations in South and Southeast Asia, and its failure to inspire military integration is one further evidence of it premature expectations.

The war in Vietnam, as it escalated after 1965, was justified by the U.S. government on grounds of the SEATO commitment, which was legally plausible, but which also demonstrated the peculiar wilfulness in U.S. policy. From its formation, SEATO was envisaged by U.S. officials as a security measure, for after the Geneva Agreements in 1954, Mr. Dulles perceived the region as especially vulnerable to Chinese or Vietnamese Communist subversion. Later, appeal to the SEATO commitment was justification for the Vietnam intervention, which lacked political logic, since SEATO was an American invention; our commitment was to our own perception of regional interdependence in Southeast Asia, not to the actual situation.

During the 1960s a number of indigenous regional organizations were formed, but these institutions were very fragile and often troubled by disputes. For example, MAPHILINDO, an acronym for a 1963 pact between Malaya, Indonesia, and the Philippines, did not survive its initial meeting. The Association of Southeast Asia (ASA) joined Thailand, Malaya, and the Philippines in 1961, but the dispute between the last two members over Sabah caused a prolonged hiatus from 1963 to 1966. In 1967 ASA was finally abandoned when its members joined Indonesia and Singapore in ASEAN, the Association of Southeast Asian Nations. Meanwhile, the three original ASA members and South Vietnam had joined in establishing in 1966 a larger regional group, the Asia and Pacific Council, ASPAC, that embraced Northeast Asia and Australia–New Zealand as well. Whereas ASEAN was largely the creation of Thanat Khoman, the Thai Foreign Minister, and Adam Malik, his Indonesian counterpart, ASPAC was initially sponsored by South Korea and subsequently dominated by Japan. In both cases Washington expressed delight at the formation of more regional organizations, commending the sponsors for their responsible and forward-looking policies.

After a decade of experience with SEATO the United States was careful to avoid any direct connection with either ASPAC or ASEAN; nonetheless, the armies of most participating countries were using U.S. weapons (Malaysia and Singapore purchased theirs on the commercial market), and many officers and skilled technicians were trained under the U.S. Military Assistance Program. The implications of a U.S. involvement, though indirect and denied by diplomats, was apparent. A multibillion dollar military assistance program, begun in 1946, had matured into a complex network of bilateral aid with a regional framework. Without U.S. weapons and technical cooperation it is doubtful that regional security associations would have been possible outside of communist Asia.

Further enhancement of the regionalism notion came through the Asian Development Bank, formed in 1966 with joint Japanese and American commitments. Patterned after the World Bank, ADB aimed to service the capital needs of Southeast Asia. Then in 1967 came SEAMEO, The Southeast Asia Ministers of Education Organization. As with the Colombo Plan, SEAMEO is primarily concerned with training and education, only its focus is on development of regional institutions that will service all the participating states. Again, U.S. funding provided the impetus for SEAMEO and a major AID allocation is set aside for it. A number of educational and research institutions, somewhat modeled on the SEATO engineering college idea were devised, including, for example, an English teacher-training institute and a tropical diseases laboratory. Local governments cooperate in providing staff and leadership. Although it is too early to judge the quality of SEAMEO programs, it is certain that each country seeks to serve its own interests in the organization, and since none of the participating states has educational systems that command much respect on the part of other states, it is unlikely that SEAMEO will flourish except as a national development scheme, and that only if the United States continues to underwrite it.

In addition to these several regional economic, security, and educational organizations, there are functional bodies concerned with law, higher education, publishing, communications, and parliamentary practices. None of these exercises influence over the indigenous affairs of each country; indeed, the general functional agencies of the United Nations, such as FAO, UNESCO, and the Development Fund probably carry greater weight with the region's governments. Nonetheless, the United States continues to encourage the proliferation of regional organizations, apparently because of its assumption that there is merit in size and scope of integrated multistate political systems of Southeast Asia. To paraphrase a persuasive advocate of regionalism, the United

States government still believes that, without the strength of numbers, the states of Southeast Asia will be coerced into subservience by their giant neighbors.

The nub of the problem with regional programs in Southeast Asia rests in their achievements. Do they advance the significant security interests of the participating states to work with these multiple bodies? Probably not. Although the experiment is interesting and may one day have a political payoff, in the next few decades the states themselves face so many traumas it is most unlikely that they can contribute to one another's survival. Insofar as the United States seeks to influence the course of events, these bodies do provide a conduit not otherwise available. However, Americans delude themselves in contending that regional political solutions are possible before the states themselves can generate the authority to govern their peoples.

Given the fragile condition of the states in the region, one builds castles of sand on a multistate foundation. However, it is another case to speak of technical development. Some local institutions are reasonably well-grounded, as is the case in the Rice Research Institute at Los Banos, or the AIT in Bangkok, or the harbor and trade facilities in Singapore. Such functional, nonpolitical projects can be valuable to economic development. Local leadership is quite aware of this fact, but also they recognize the American proclivity for regionalism and fit their plans accordingly. It is a game without any tragic loss thus far, unless one can consider the Vietnam war a function of regionalism myopia. It is perhaps arguable that three American presidents confused efficient economic development with regionalism and made the decision to intervene in Vietnam for that reason; however, that case is less compelling than the simpler explanation that the Vietnam commitment was merely an extention of the rationale underlying the Korean war, that is, containment of communism. Nonetheless, it could be tragic if at some future time the Americans were to use ASEAN or ASPAC, or some sequel organization, as a legitimizer for military intervention. We would again be intervening to secure our short-run interests, failing to consider the cost, no matter how we rationalized the action. Fortunately, the participating states have a clearer perception of their own interests and are unlikely to lapse into the state of mind that confuses the ideology of regionalism with the reality of functional cooperation.

POLICY TO WHAT PURPOSE

The purpose of any foreign policy is to achieve a goal, and the common intent is to advance the state's interests. However, prior to World War II the United States had no consistent objective in Asia, other than to maintain access to the trade markets that were opening as Asian countries slowly modernized. The primary products and extractive industries, which were so important to European colonizers, tended to weigh very little in the U.S. scale, thanks to its abundant natural resources and those of neighboring Latin America. Therefore, Asia seemed rather remote for most Americans, and that lack of interest was reflected in the government's policy.

U.S. policy changed radically after World War II, a war in which the United States found itself fighting on two fronts and suffering significant losses in the Pacific due to lack of preparedness. Thereafter, substantial military forces were stationed in the Far East. Technical and military assistance began to flow to those countries devastated by the war, initially including China as well as Japan and Korea; but after the Communist victory on the mainland, the focus of policy shifted to a buildup of those powers that could serve to counter the weight of China in Asian politics. Japan, South Korea, Taiwan, the Philippines, and after 1950, most of the Southern Asia states were accepting U.S. foreign aid, thereby forming a network designed to contain communism within China and the Soviet Union. The policy was tested and proved efficacious in Korea after the 1950 invasion from the north. Despite its unpopularity among the American public, the Korean war was a victory for the policy of containment. And despite China's enormous manpower, her proxy involvement of a half-million volunteers resulted in great losses and failure to dislodge the Americans from South Korea. Of course, China was successful in wresting influence from the Soviet Union over North Korea, but that gain was dissipated within the decade as those Korean party leaders sympathetic to Peking were stripped of their posts by Kim Il-sung.

Japan enjoyed rapid economic growth throughout the Korea war. The gains from war purchases were a stimulant to an economy that soon proved to be the most growth-oriented in the world. By

1965 Japan's national product was ten times its prewar level. The miracle is well-enough known to need no further comment, and Japan's future development has already been outlined in Chapter One, but its significance for U.S. aid policy deserves elaboration. By the mid-fifties the United States had had such success with its aid programs to Europe and Japan that the method of project investment for economic growth was transferred directly to the agrarian states of Southern Asia. Although there was no precedent for rapid economic growth in societies like those in the region, officials responsible for the program persisted in believing that it would succeed and thereby prevent the region from "going Communist." The domino thesis was widely subscribed to in Washington, and provided a rationale for aid to France in its Indo–China war, and then to the Republic of Vietnam after 1954. The same theory was applied to Vietnam as elsewhere in the region: by assisting in development of the economic infrastructure, the roads, communications, and education, as well as by introducing income-producing projects, the people would prosper and communism, perceived as an ideology of despair, would be eliminated. The model of Japan was proof of the development thesis—that economic growth would prevent communism.

Hopefully, the tragedy of the Vietnam war, both for France and the United States, is now sufficiently well-understood in the West, and particularly in the United States, to convince us that the first successes in economic assistance were due to the advanced state of technology and social organization in the developed countries. Europe and Japan knew how to use America's capital and absorb the technical assistance. Southern Asia did not because none of these countries was industrialized. The problem is not that Western efforts have been entirely misguided; the aid programs have contributed to economic growth. But none of the new states is prepared culturally or socially to modernize as the Western advisers expected. The question of timing has been generally overlooked by indigenous leaders as well as by aid administrators and Western intellectuals.

The thesis of this book by now should be clear, that development of technology and economic growth quite naturally is concomitant with changes in the culture and polity. Such change was under way in the West for three hundred years before the industrial revolution. These new states of Asia were expected to move ahead within a decade after their birth, on the assumption that colonial administrators had left sufficient institutional structure to cope with rapid change. Obviously, that assumption was wrong. Therefore, what time span should we think of in projecting development? The analysis in Part One provides partial answers. Certainly, it is not unreasonable to allow a half century from the time of independence for a traditionally agrarian people to commence rapid modernization. Such a period permits two or more generations to pass from the scene. The mistakes and successes of the first decades are learned, in time, and may be absorbed in the education system and the culture. Planned change may then become institutionalized. Of course, one need only consider the many Latin American states that failed to change for a century after independence to realize how tentative this estimate must be.

Our prognosis, therefore, is that the sort of states the United States thought it was aiding in the 1950s could exist by the 1990s. In the meantime, a decidedly different sort of assistance program should be devised, with different intentions than have prevailed in U.S. Asian policy since World War II.

The strategy that seems realistic for the next several decades calls for patience and considerable understanding of the human qualities involved in political change. What we have done, and will do, influences the future, and my thesis is not meant to denigrate the effects of past efforts. But the central political problem with our present goal is our single-minded emphasis upon nation-building and regionalism. The problems with that goal have already been discussed; what is called for is action related to community development, an emphasis upon new centers of urban growth, political organization, and employment opportunities. This calls for a shift from the present U.S. focus upon security and unitary state development. It means a number of new programs should be initiated, and several well-conceived but currently unpopular programs should be reinstituted. Before entering into these specific recommendations, however, greater consideration must be given to the shift in American policy priorities if the case is to be persuasive.

The solutions necessarily require long duration, for it means a new perception of American interests, as well as Asian interests, in the twenty-first century. The notion that there is security in development is to take the long view, but in the foreseeable future it is more realistic to assume that local conflict and violence will persist. The well-being and dignity promised in most constitutions as well as the

UN Charter will remain less a matter of fact and more a vision of the distant future. The tactic of planning a political design in the short run—that is, for the next two to three decades—at best will only firm up a foundation for more prosperity and greater human freedom in the next century.

Current U.S. policy toward Asia, and particularly Southeast Asia, calls for development of independent states with a capacity and interest in regional cooperation. Self-sufficiency and regional interdependence have been encouraged in the same breath, and, from the Dulles era onward, American Presidents and Secretaries of State have urged security upon the governments in the region. The rationale has been based on the assumption that Communist China threatens invasion or subversion. But now, with the U.S. disengagement process measured by the withdrawal of troops from Vietnam and the return of bases in Japan, Korea, Thailand, and the Philippines to follow, a reappraisal of U.S. assumptions is under way. The perception of immediate threat from China diminishes due to the Sino–Soviet conflict and as Chinese diplomatic belligerency diminishes elsewhere. It is conceivable, and certainly desirable, that the United States should seek to curtail its outstanding grievances with China. Measures taken in that direction affirm an eventual break in the log jam of hostility between the two countries. With that denouement in the future, it is in the U.S. interest to look further ahead than at any time in the past and to prepare for relations with Asian states on a decidedly different basis.

Since Southeast Asia has been the focus of major American intervention, it is in this area that the rapprochement with China should have its first impact. Even without detente, a shift in priorities is needed to prepare for future conflict situations. Since critical focus has been on a balance of power in Asia that would contain China, it follows that, with a decline in the perception of a Chinese threat, what is necessary is a reassessment of an Asian balance of power. Also, there is a need to reconsider the significance of regional security arrangements. Finally, the quest for regionalism and nation-building can then be reconsidered.

Taking these issues in order, it is reasonable to see a new balance of power, with China at odds with the Soviet Union, and with USSR policy bent on curtailing Chinese influence in other Asian states. It is likely that the current trend will continue toward interdependence of South Asian and Middle Eastern interests with those of the Soviet Union. Concurrently, with its increasing capability, Japan will engage diplomatically as well as economically in affairs of its Asian neighbors, to be followed by a growing interdependence of Southeast Asian states' interests with those of Japan. It seems prudent to assume a continued Japanese caution about reentering the region with military aid to troops because of its own constitutional restriction and because of both domestic and Southeast Asian opposition to such a step. Japanese activity, unlike that of the Soviet Union or the United States in the past, may not be viewed as so threatening to the interests of China. In short, Communist China probably will be able to live with a substantial Japanese economic presence in Southeast Asia, as well as in Korea and even Taiwan; however, the leaders in Peking are quite likely to feel threatened by the entente between the Soviet Union and India because of its military elements.

The position of the United States in this shifting relationship could conceivably be one of complete withdrawal, since the perceived threat of China was its original rationale for its Southeast Asian involvement; however, such a radical shift in policy would be imprudent. Several Asian states are heavily committed to an Amercian style of development, and it would be a severe shock to their societies and culture were the American presence completely eliminated. Also, there will be a strategic threat to American interests from other Asian powers if the United States is widely believed to be unconcerned about the future of this half of mankind.

As a country with enormous potential for assistance during the next half century of population crisis, when most Asian states are in dire need of advanced technology to counter the threat of domestic chaos, the United States merely would be inviting eventual intervention by one or more major Asian powers into its own internal affairs were it to ignore Asia. One could envisage Japan, India, or the Soviet Union leading a combination of lesser Asian powers in a successful effort to exploit world hostility to the United States' arrogance in such a circumstance. The potential for spread of nuclear delivery systems, as well as the development in Asia of less expensive but even more horrible systems of warfare made possible by advanced technology, would certainly be heightened. It would be folly for the United States to allow the current curtailment of military commitments to continue on into other spheres of activity.

To cope with the complex design of bilateral and multilateral relations that will develop over the remainder of this century, what is called for is greater willingness to engage in the nuance of diplomatic, political, and economic competition that will continue to increase between the superpowers and the great Asian powers. This will mean a declining intensity, but persistent range, of American activities in Southeast Asia, as well as Southern and East Asia, perhaps even to include technical and economic assistance to China in the future.

Of paramount importance is the timing in political change. Any misstep caused by offering credits or capital for only one form of development, or by restricting aid only to profit-making enterprises, would be to court political failure. The problems described before will not be resolved by applying such narrow criteria. Although I have emphasized the case for distributing urban centers as much as possible, even that principle is not irrevocable, for the art of political design is so complex as to escape definition by principle. What will work in "x" country may well not be applicable in "y" because of differences in culture or environment. Nonetheless, the signposts that aid us in allocating resources, or creating them, should not be ignored. The needs of each constituency, be it a communal group or a district of a million Javanese, must be evaluated in context. Where is the community of villages and their town or city, socially as well as economically, at the time a decision is made to create a new college, or to add a new curriculum to the secondary school, or to implement a textile project?

The United States is in a position to offer enormous assistance if it follows the signposts of experience over the past twenty years. For example, it is now clear that a credit from an international agency, be it the Asian Development Bank or the United Nations Development Fund, has less risk of being politically unacceptable than would a direct bilateral loan. However, for example, a private investment by Texaco may be more preferable for the development of Medan, Indonesia than a public credit because of the close human relationship and trust already established between the Texaco agents and local leaders. Or a consortium of universities may be a sounder political and educational agent through which to initiate a new educational development plan than would the United States government or UNESCO. The critical criterion is the feasibility of each project in terms of the particular needs of each country.

These needs must ultimately be considered political, for without political acceptance any effort will eventually be to no avail. And political acceptance must first be measured in terms of the locale. It is the last step that is most frequently ignored by planners who operate with a national rather than a community perspective. To perceive the "big" needs of a state is often to miss the political level within the community. Rather than build within the institutional structure of the population, it is too easy to cite economic criteria and then to proceed as though the political factor was secondary or irrelevant. That it is not secondary, indeed, that it is the first consideration, should be quite easy for an American who knows his own congressional system to understand. Unfortunately, those responsible for development abroad are usually quite ignorant of politics generally and their own politics in particular. Planners too frequently are technicians, not politicians, and they carry the baggage of economic or bureaucratic procedures around the world with them. Such baggage will cause the demise of us all if it continues to prevail.

Since politics is a changing kaleidoscope of reality, an art forever becoming but never achieved, planned change for Southeast Asia should recognize a radically different frame, or procrustean bed, than has been the case heretofore. This area will not be changing as rapidly as many forecast, but it will change year by year. Fine atunement to the whispers of new political breezes should be the prime criterion for Americans who would advise or direct aid programs. The breezes will be emanating from the extant political communities, more than from something artificially created by independence leaders and their colonial forebears. Ethnicity, language, religion, territory—these are the bases of political identity in most of Asia. To contend that it is wrong, or ignorant, or nonideological to pursue politics on such bases is to confess greater ignorance, to forget the reality of politics. People band together to protect their perceived interests. What is "their own" is defined in terms of trust and familiar human contact. In our rush to build nations and to create viable states, we have tended to ignore the very foundations of political reality.

Perhaps it is not too late to recoup the lost time before Asia's three, or five, or ten billion people—who knows when we will pass the line of no return from self-liquidation—will crush our last hope for harmony with nature and within ourselves. And be assured that until that harmony is established, the peace that we all desperately seek will elude us. Many Asian philosophers grasped that lesson centuries ago, a lesson we in the West once understood as well. But the conquests of science led Western man to follow a false god and to use the enormous power of technology to conquer other men rather than to master man's aggressive characteristics. It seems almost a revelation to many that in our own country we have gone too far. Our greed for consumption surrounds us and impinges upon our freedom to a greater degree than ever before. The solution of course is to be found not in forgetting the truths of science, but in applying them through new technology created to meet real human needs, not Madison Avenue ad creations. Techniques for educating the illiterate, for cultivating leached soil on tiny farms, for running simple machinery without the need for constant repairs, for organizing men to produce more efficiently without losing their individual dignity—these are the challenges that face us. They are not new, merely a continuance of the process of greater power and distribution understood by such diverse leaders as Lenin, Henry Ford, and J. P. Morgan. Creating more productive techniques, using them humanely, and distributing them to the best advantage is the secret of modernity. The future is at once bright and bleak in Asia, depending upon the choice of policy makers in the West, as well as in Asia. The "fiery pinions" of self-knowledge force that choice upon us all.

Notes

Notes for Introduction

[1] Johann Wolfgang von Goethe, *Faust* (New York: Appleton–Century–Crofts, Part I, Taylor translation, 1946), pp. 19–20.

[2] Fyodor Dostoyevsky, *The Possessed* (New York: Dell Publishing Company, Garnett translation, 1961), p. 727. Response of the monk Tikhon to Stavrogin's confession.

[3] From a flyer, YIPPEE, reprinted in Norman Mailer, *Miami and the Siege of Chicago* (New York: Signet Books, 1968), p. 137.

[4] A comment by Soedjatmoko in *SEADAG/Asia, A Special Report on Social Science Research in Southeast Asia* (New York: The Asia Society, 1968), pp. 85–86.

[5] Lucian Pye, *Aspects of Political Development* (Boston: Little, Brown, 1966), p. 63.

[6] *Op. cit.,* pp. 66–67.

[7] Karl Deutsch, *Nation-Building* (New York: Atherton, Atheling Edition, 1966), p. ix.

[8] Rupert Emerson, *From Empire to Nation* (Boston: Beacon Press, 1960), p. 299. [Italics mine.]

Notes for Chapter One

[1] In the case of Malaysia, consolidated figures are often not available as far back as 1958. The very low figure of exports in 1958 ($17 million) for South Korea made that year unsuitable for a base year.

[2] Department of Agriculture studies indicate that a $2 rise in per capita income generates an increase in annual per capita grain consumption of one pound. See Orville L. Freeman, "Malthus, Marx and the North American Breadbasket," *Foreign Affairs,* Vol. 45, No. 4 (July, 1967).

Notes for Chapter Two

[1] See: Alexander Peaslee, "The Optimum Educational Mix for Economic Growth" (Brookings, 1966).

[2] Russett and Alker, *World Handbook of Political and Social Indicators* (WHPSI) (New Haven: Yale, 1964). USIS, *Communications: Philippines*, 1966.

[3] *Statesmen's Yearbook, 1966–67.*

[4] *WHPSI*, p. 107.

[5] *Statesmen's Yearbook, 1966–67.*

[6] Peaslee, 1966.

[7] James Coleman, *Education and Political Development* (Princeton University Press, 1965), p. 530.

[8] *Statesmen's Yearbook, 1966–67.*

[9] Norton Ginsberg, *An Atlas of Economic Development* (University of Chicago Press, 1961).

[10] USIS, *op. cit.,* 1966.

[11] Peaslee, 1966.

[12] Ginsberg, 1961.

[13] Russett, 1965.

[14] Ginsberg, 1961; Russett, 1965.

[15] Peaslee, 1966.

[16] *Ibid.,* 1966.

[17] Russett, 1965.

[18] Grossholtz, *The Philippines*, 1964, p. 262.

Notes for Chapter Three

[1] This portion is a revision of a paper presented at the annual meeting of The American Historical Association, Toronto, 1967.

[2] The distinction in the West between state and government is still alive, particularly in France, but the idea of the state is profound and omnipresent in the writings of Western political philosophers and has long since ceased to be conceived in anthropomorphic terms.

[3] Frank Swettenham, *British Malaya* (London: Bodley Head, 1920) p. 258.

[4] Thomas Hobbes, *Leviathan,* Michael Oakeshott. ed. (Oxford: Blackwell, 1957), pp. 109, 175.

[5] The remaining portion of this chapter was originally presented to the annual meeting of the Association of Asian Studies as "The Problem of Succession in Asia," Boston, 1969.

Notes for Chapter Four

[1] Joseph Schumpeter, *The Theory of Economic Development* (New York: Oxford University Press, 1961), p. 62.

[2] C. Y. Hsü, *China's Entrance into the Family of Nations* (Cambridge: Harvard University Press, 1960), Chapter I.

[3] A. L. Basham, *The Wonder That Was India* (New York: Grove Press, 1954), p. 94.

[4] C. D. Cowan, "Continuity and Change in the International History of Maritime Southeast Asia," *Journal of Southeast Asian History* (Volume IX, No. 1), pp. 1–11.

[5] Edwin O. Reischauer and John K. Fairbank, *East Asia: The Great Tradition* (Boston: Houghton Mifflin Co., 1960), pp. 569–70.

[6] Carlton S. Coon, *A Reader in General Anthropology* (New York, Knopf, 1948), p. 614.

[7] See Walker Connor's two articles, "Ethnic Nationalism as a Political Force," *World Affairs* (Vol. 133, Sept. 1970) and "Ethnology and the Peace of South Asia," *World Politics* (Vol. XXII, October 1969); also Donald Horowitz, "Multiracial Politics in the New States," *Issues in Comparative Politics,* M. Stein and R. Jackson, ed. (Macmillan, 1970); Robert Solomon, "Boundary Concepts and Practices in Southeast Asia," *World Politics* (Vol. XXIII, No. 1), 1–23; and the author's *Politics Among Burmans* (Athens, Ohio: Ohio University Press, 1970).

Notes for Chapter Five

[1] Although Pye uses this concept frequently, he offers no simple, concise definition covering all aspects and usages of the term. The closest that he comes to this type of definition is when he says that "integration . . . deals with the extent to which the entire polity is organized as a system of interacting relationships, first among the offices and agencies of government, and then among the various groups and interests seeking to make demands upon the system, and finally in the relationships between officials and articulating citizens." See: Lucian W. Pye, *Aspects of Political Development* (Boston: Little, Brown and Company, 1966), p. 65.

[2] "The function of converting demands into general policy alternatives is called interest aggregation." Gabriel Almond and John Powell, *Comparative Politics: A Developmental Approach* (Boston: Little, Brown and Company, 1966), p. 98. "Interest aggregation may be performed within all the subsystems of the political system. Indeed, some degree of aggregation is almost inevitably carried out at all levels from individual interest articulation to the final decision-making. But the pertinent question for us is: what structures play the major role in aggregating the articulated interests into major policy alternatives? From these alternatives the authoritative policies for the political system are subsequently produced. . . . All the various types of structures performing interest articulation may also perform interest aggregation." (p. 100).

[3] Chalmers Johnson conceptualizes the system maintenance process in terms of "homeostatic equilibrium," which he says ultimately rests upon the "matrix-maintaining processes that take place within a social system—e.g., the control of deviancy, the avoidance and routinization of relations of conflict, coercive actions to maintain integration during a power deflation, normative definitions of social mobility, and many others." Johnson also says that "the homeostatic capacity of a system will be determined by value sharing *and* by the potency of these values with respect to a given environment." (p. 54)

For Johnson, changes in systems may "occur without disturbing a homeostatic equilibrium so long as the value structure and the environment change in synchronization with each other." Thus, "a social system can change its structure and still remain equilibrated." (p. 56)

See: Chalmers Johnson, *Revolutionary Change* (Boston: Little, Brown and Company, 1966).

David Easton sees a shift in systems analysis "away from systems maintenance as a central organizing theme." He sees the less ambitious concept of system "persistence" as being more valuable to the approach. According to Easton:

It is one matter to inquire into the conditions through which a system is able to maintain itself and quite another to seek to reveal the conditions of persistence. . . . Maintenance is weighted with the notion of salvaging the existing pattern of relationships and directs attention to their preservation. Persistence signalizes the importance of considering, not any particular structure or pattern, but rather the very life processes of a system themselves. . . . The idea of system persistence extends far beyond that of systems maintenance; it is oriented toward exploring change as well as stability, both of which may be interpreted as alternative avenues for coping with stress.

See: David Easton, *A Framework for Political Analysis* (Englewood Cliffs, N.J.: Prentice-Hall, Inc., 1965), p. 88.

[4] Daniel Lerner observes that "modern media systems have flourished only in societies that are modern by other tests. That is, the media spread psychic mobility most efficiently among peoples who have achieved in some measure the antecedent conditions of geographic and social mobility." See: D. Lerner, *The Passing of Traditional Society: Modernizing the Middle East* (New York: The Free Press, 1965), p. 55.

[5] A. F. K. Organski, *The Stages of Political Development* (New York: Knopf, 1965); also Lucian Pye, op. cit.; and William McCord, *The Springtime of Freedom: The Evolution of Developing Societies* (New York: Oxford University Press, 1965).

[6] The following references are made in the Preamble of the UN Charter. "We the peoples of the UN . . . reaffirm faith in fundamental human rights, in the dignity and worth of the human person, in the equal rights of men and women and of nations large and small . . . and for these ends . . . practice tolerance and live together in peace with one another as good neighbors, and to unite our strength to maintain international peace and security," etc. Also articles 1 and 2.

The following references are made in the Preamble of The Covenant of the League of Nations:

In order to promote international cooperation and to achieve international peace and security by acceptance of obligations not to resort to war, by the prescription of open, just, and honourable relations between nations, etc.

[7] Theodore Geiger, *The Conflicted Relationship: The West and the Transformation of Asia, Africa, and Latin America* (New York: McGraw-Hill, 1967).

[8] In the Federalist Paper 10, James Madison wrote: "By a faction, I understand a number of citizens, whether amounting to a majority or minority of the whole, who are united and actuated by some common impulse of passion, or of interest, adverse to the rights of other citizens, or to the permanent and aggregate interests of the community. . . . Liberty is to faction what air is to fire, an aliment without which it instantly expires. But it could not be less folly to abolish liberty, which is essential to political life, because it nourishes faction, than it would be to wish the annihilation of air, which is essential to animal life, because it imparts to fire its destructive agency. . . . As long as the reason of man continues fallible, and he is at liberty to exercise it, different opinions will be formed." Modern Library edition, pp. 54–55.

[9] Lloyd and Suzanne Rudolph, *The Modernity of Tradition* (Chicago: The University of Chicago Press, 1967).

[10] Walker Connor, "Ethnology and the Peace of South Asia," *World Politics* (Vol. XXII, No. 1, October 1969), pp. 51–86.

[11] John P. Lewis, *Quiet Crisis in India* (Washington: Brookings Institution, 1962), esp. Chapter 7. E. A. J. Johnson, *Organization of Economic Space in Developing Countries* (Cambridge, Mass.: Harvard University Press, 1970).

[12] J. S. Furnivall, *Colonial Policy and Practice* (Cambridge: Cambridge University Press, England, 1948).

[13] Fred Riggs, *Thailand: The Modernization of a Bureaucratic Polity* (Honolulu: East–West Center Press, 1966); David Wilson, *Politics in Thailand* (Ithaca: Cornell University Press, 1962); Donald E. Nuechterlein, *Thailand and the Struggle for Southeast Asia* (Ithaca: Cornell University Press, 1965).

[14] See G. William Skinner, "Marketing and Social Structure in Rural China, *Journal of Asian Studies* (Vols. XXIII 1964 and XXIV 1965), esp. pp. 195–228, 363–399; John Badgley, *Politics Among Burmans: A Study of Intermediary Leadership* (Athens, Ohio: Ohio University Press, 1970); John Powell, "Peasant Society and Clientist Politics," *The American Political Science Review* (Vol. LXIV, June, 1970), pp. 411–425.

Author Index

Subject Index